Where Did We Come From,

& Where Are We Going

GORDON CALAHAN

Where Did We Come From, and Where Are We Going?
Published by Hinode Press
Lakewood, CO

ISBN: 978-0-578-65302-0
BIOGRAPHY & AUTOBIOGRAPHY / Personal Memoirs
BODY, MIND & SPIRIT / Spiritualism

Cover design by Natasha Brown
Interior design by Victoria Wolf

QUANTITY PURCHASES: Schools, companies, professional groups, clubs, and other organizations may qualify for special terms when ordering quantities of this title. For information, email g.calahan@comcast.net.

HINODE PRESS

To all the people who are working on a path to recovery from addictions. I know how hard it is, I am working my own recovery path. May God help us all to find a happy, free and joyful life.

Ikebana, flower arranging, by Gordon Calahan

PROLOGUE

Every day in life is training, training for myself. Though failure is possible, I live each moment equal to everything, ready for anything. I am alive, for if I cannot endure today, when and where will I?

—SOEN OZEKI

I believe the mind, or maybe the subconscious, always wants to know about life and about the things we don't know about. Within human beings, there exists some type of innate draw to the unknown and a desire for discovery. We have wondered: Is the world round or flat? Does the Earth rotate around the sun, or is the sun rotating around the Earth? As scientific discovery has answered many of our questions, we are left with those that science does not yet explain. We may be inclined to wonder: Does God exist? Are there spirits? Is there reincarnation? There also exist seemingly unanswerable questions about the nature of humanity: What is the capability of the human mind?

Are we purely physical beings? Despite the ever-changing appearance of things, does there exist a constant reality, an underlying truth? We have asked thousands of questions and have postulated or presented even more answers. And the paths that we have taken to come to our answers are as varied as the answers themselves.

The Greek philosopher Aristotle (384–322 BCE) defined philosophy as the search for explanations of everyday events that inspire wonder. Yet, he suggested that a simple answer to a question wasn't enough; we require an understanding of the intricate parts leading up to that conclusion. Once we have gathered our evidence and think we have found a truth, we begin the journey down a path guided by that truth. We tend to take what enhances our hypothesis and discard what doesn't. At some period in time, and after exhaustive research, we will eventually convince ourselves that we think we know the answers to our questions, or we may create an answer that satisfies our curiosity, or a mixture of both. We may become bored and/or simply lose interest in finding the true answer, so we simply create an answer that satisfies us. However, our answers could be true, or false, or a mixture of both. Only with time, training, and experiencing our ideas in the world we live in will we find the truth. This is called wisdom. Is it possible to see beyond truth and falsity and see meaning only? The Greek philosopher Plato (427–347 BCE) would present lively arguments but detach himself from taking sides on either position. He would leave the student to make up his/her own mind and take a stance he/she agreed with. Plato believed that knowledge could only be arrived at through a person's own efforts, rather than simply listening to or reading the ideas of others. In order to exercise this type of free thinking and have an opinion uninhibited by others, a certain amount of expanded creativity is needed.

It is also this creativity that leads to our hopes, dreams, and fantasies. I heard about a teacher who was teaching five- and six-year-old children. She told the children that the Easter Bunny, the Tooth Fairy, Santa, the elves, and the North Pole did not exist and reindeer can't fly. Is it fair to expose a five- or six-year-old child to life's truths that they most likely won't understand? Does this deprive them of a happy childhood and diminish their creativity? Reality can be cold and devastating, but it never remains silent. As we become adults, we learn that life can be hard and unforgiving, but we learn to work through our problems. Should we give up our dreams, or fairy tales, or our belief in God, or in reincarnation just because someone says they do not exist? Or do these hopes, dreams, fairy tales, and beliefs provide us a way to smooth the rough highway of life?

The Greek philosopher Epicurus (341–270 BCE), eschewing mystical notions of gods and the supernatural, believed that body and soul ended at death. Fulfillment in life came from living a happy life while it lasted. He believed that gods don't punish or reward people and the universe is infinite. Epicurus believed that personal pleasure was the greatest good; his desire to minimize harm and maximize pleasure was dubbed the ethic of reciprocity. His idea of pleasure was modest living, study, seclusion, and keeping one's desires in check. This was, in his view, the path to tranquility: freedom from fear and pain were the ultimate goal. Of course, we don't know if he ruled out moderate use of drugs, alcohol, sex, and controlling everything he touched to satisfy his desire for tranquility. In today's world, is his perception of life possible? With all the influences in our lives today, can we rise above the fears, distrust, lack of discipline, and disloyalty to live in peace? In the short-term, maybe. In the long-term, we may need more to survive. I believe what we need is to love each other and to accept the feelings each person has. Feelings are not good or bad; they are just feelings and shouldn't be judged.

This book is a love story about three people: Gordon, Gordon's first wife, Sandy, and Nancy, his second wife. It is also about Gordon's belief that God and His spirits might have guided them on his life's journeys. I suggest that you contemplate and understand the beliefs and lives of Gordon, Sandy, and Nancy and then create your own beliefs and your own path. I will tell you my thoughts on life with the idea that something may connect in your life to make you a little more happy, joyous, and free. I have learned that there will always be certain ideas and beliefs that we cannot prove at a given time. I ask, should we discard a useful idea, or any idea, just because it cannot be proven? Could it serve us until we find the truth? Or can the truth actually alter and change as we grow and learn? When living life's adventures, we must remember one thing: we can always change our minds when we learn new ideas or discard old ideas that have been proven wrong or useless. With free will, we can live life the way we want to. We have the choice to believe whatever we want. My true story is about three people who traveled life, experiencing the joys and sorrows of what life can bring, and what I learned from the journey. It's a book about Gordon's faith, failure, accomplishments, and new horizons. It's also about motivation and inspiration.

I will present some ideas that are many years old and some that are new. From my experiences, studies, and travels, I have taken various ideas and made them my own. We are all affected by our unique environments and experiences and by our accumulation of information from these situations, whether conscious or subconscious. Yet, I believe that there are answers that exist beyond the influence of our experience.

In order to find these answers, we must venture into the Void. Miyamoto Musashi defined the Void in his book *The Book of Five Rings* as a place where "there is no obscurity and the clouds of confusion have cleared away." (Musashi 1989) The Void is the place where all forgotten ideas, thoughts, and beliefs end up, trapped until someone comes looking for them. It is a state of pure emptiness that allows one to access some type of greater truth. By modern definition, the Void is emptiness. But scientific investigation is finding that there can't be empty space and perceived empty space is actually filled with quantum field fluctuations. What we know of as empty space is actually probability and potentiality. If we start with a clear mind, no thoughts, beliefs, perceptions, or preconceived ideas, we can then collect all the information we need about a subject, belief, or idea and incorporate it into our daily lives—or reject it.

For thousands of years, we have searched for answers about God, reincarnation, the soul, and spirits and how they might relate to our everyday lives. My story is about how three people used these things to influence and enhance their lives. It is also a story about how paths can be chosen and about how certain ones may be avoided or overcome. My story is one of addiction and suicide—and also one of spirituality and love. So, do spirits and God exist? At this time, I don't know, but in the lives of Gordon, Sandy, and Nancy something happened that influenced their lives, which were mostly happy, free, joyous, and occasionally sad and disappointing. I believe that what was happening was an experience of how God works through spirits to enhance our lives and to provide the plans and paths to achieve our goals.

Come and join Gordon, Sandy, and Nancy in the Void; doing so may help find a loving, happy, joyful, and exciting plan for life. Sandy and Nancy lived two separate paths with Gordon, and I will tell you what we found. I realize that it takes a great deal of courage to look at the way we are living our lives. We may need to give up old ideas and look for new, unknown ideas and beliefs, which may be found in the Void. I know this because I have been there. So, I challenge you to join me and see what you can find.

PART 1

CHAPTER 1

No one saves us except ourselves. No one can and no one may.
We ourselves must walk the path.

—SIDDARTHA GAUTAMA, THE BUDDHA

September 26th, 1993

I remember September 26, 1993 as the day my life changed forever. It was Saturday, and my wife Sandy and I talked about going to an air show at the soon-to-be completed Denver International Airport. It was a beautiful day for an air show, and our friends Ben and Anne also wanted to go. Sandy was hesitant. She said she wanted to do some things around the house and do some shopping. She said she had seen several air shows so she would not be missing anything if she stayed home. I agreed. We also talked about dinner, and she said she had plans to meet her therapist and some friends for dinner. So I told her that I would have dinner with Ben and Ann and that I would be home around eight that evening. She was happy, we kissed, and off I went.

One of my hobbies was flying, and I loved airplanes. Sandy and I owned a Beach Bonanza named *Bonnie*. Together we flew *Bonnie* all over the United States for many years. Flying was also in Sandy's blood. She was always ready to fly anytime. *Bonnie* was like a member of the family. My father, who also was an avid flyer, had purchased *Bonnie* in the late 1950s. She was a beautiful airplane, all decked out in white and blue and always ready to whisk us away like a magic carpet.

I picked up Ben and Ann, and off we went to DIA. The show was a lot of fun, acrobatic teams, flybys, and a host of many different planes parked on the ramp, each showing off like they were in a beauty contest. I always believed that an airplane may have a heart and each is proud of who they are. Being a romantic, I like to believe that. When the show ended, the three of us decided to go to Ben and Ann's house to have dinner and hang out. Good friends always seem to be in short supply.

The time went fast; around seven thirty p.m., I departed for home. For some reason I missed Sandy. I felt lonely, and I thought that she would have enjoyed the show and dinner. I was looking forward to sharing my day and was looking forward to hearing about her day. Driving home, I thought about the things we had planned for the future. Our two boys, Rich and Don, were grown and on their own. I was looking forward to a life with just Sandy and myself. Life was going to be different, and we both agreed it was going to be an adventure.

I remember the evening was mild and the drive home was a bit tense, and I wondered why. Sandy and I lived on a neighborhood street in Lakewood, Colorado. We had bought our house new and had raised the family there. Generally, the neighborhood was quiet and peaceful. Tonight, the street was mostly dark, but the silhouettes of trees and other houses were still visible in the dim street lights.

I thought, "Everything is normal and so peaceful." I wondered, "Will Sandy be home?"

I hoped so because all of a sudden, a strange, cold feeling came over me. Had something changed? What was I feeling? Was I being told something? Was something wrong? My mind was confused and scattered. It is strange how fast the mind works, one moment peaceful, the next panicking. Had something happened to one of the animals? Or had someone been hurt, maybe an accident?

Suddenly, I realized the car was going faster. I felt I needed to get home fast. I felt cold, even though it was warm outside. Why was this happening to me? The day had been wonderful, so what could have happened to change that? I looked outside, and the world around me appeared to have changed. The street was darker, and the headlights on the car were not doing much to cut through the night and the darkness.

The advent of cell phones was still in the future; my wife was not able to call me, nor was I able to call her. My mind jumped back several years ago when I remembered arriving home only to see that there had been a fire at our house; our living room couch had caught fire and the remains of the couch were in the street. Looking back, I now wonder if only I had a phone to call ahead, would things have been different; but that was not to be. I would have to endure my confused feelings a little longer, until I got home. I accelerated faster. I felt confused and a bit panicked.

"Hold on, Gordon, things couldn't be that bad," I said. "Slow down," but I couldn't overcome my confusion. In all of my life, I had never experienced such fear and helplessness. I had flown hundreds of hours in our airplane, parachuted seventy-five times, served in the Air Force, and done many other dangerous things, but never had my mind panicked like this.

I turned the car the second to last turn before I would arrive home when something strange began to happen. The cold I had been experiencing was subsiding. I could feel the car warming a bit, and I began to experience a strange feeling. Calmness? Something was happening. A feeling of calmness came over me. I began to slow the car down, and the need to get home was less urgent. I did not understand why.

I began to feel that I was not alone anymore. I looked around the inside of the car, thinking I might see someone, but the car was empty. I told myself that it was impossible for someone to join me in the car. I had not stopped. Was I losing my connection to reality?

And then I thought I heard someone say, "Slow down, everything is OK." My mind couldn't accept what I had just heard, and I simply asked what was OK.

CHAPTER 2

I think a hero is an ordinary individual who finds strength to persevere and endure in spite of overwhelming obstacles.

—CHRISTOPHER REEVE

1940s–1960s

Sandy was a beautiful woman: five-foot-nine with brown hair and brown eyes. She had grown up in the town of Weston, Massachusetts, a town near Boston. Her younger years had been very traumatic. Her father was the owner of a successful paint manufacturing company and spent a great deal of time traveling and selling his paint products. Sandy was three years old when her father returned home one day to find that Sandy's mother was having an affair with another man. Enraged, he demanded that her mother leave the house and the marriage and never see Sandy and her older brother again. Sandy had to have been devastated. The questions she asked and would never know: Where had her mother gone? Was she coming back? No, she would never see her mother again.

Sandy grew up in a very large house. Her family was supported by a maid/cook, gardener and a nanny to take care of the children, when Sandy's Dad was out of town.

What is life like for a three-year-old girl who has just lost her mother and had a father who was away from home much of the time? Her father, because of his large income, was able to hire a nanny who would take care of Sandy and her brother, Jerry. There was also a full-time maid and gardener. Her house was big, surrounded by a large yard, where Sandy remembered playing much of the time. She loved animals and being with nature, where she could escape the chaos of her family. She was able to find solitude and order. She felt peaceful, and she saw nature as complete, existing on its own, able to survive without help from anyone. Nature is always forgiving and connects to us all through love and beauty. When she was five, her father remarried, and Sandy was confronted with a new stepmother and a new brother, John, slightly older, and a sister, Debbie, slightly younger. Sandy always said that her new stepmother married for convenience. The time was the mid-1940s, and World War II had just ended.

I can't imagine Sandy's childhood. The house contained several bedrooms and bathrooms with a large living room, dining room, and kitchen. There were also maids' quarters. I am sure she never lacked for physical things, but she said there was not any real love. Her stepmother was sick much of the time and not available to meet the family's needs. Her father continued to travel a lot. Sandy needed love, and that was in short supply. She had to compete with her brothers and sister for love.

During high school, Sandy loved playing sports. Her favorite sport was tennis. Playing tennis allowed her time to get away from the family and find happiness. She liked the workout, the companionship, the competition, and she had great love for the game. She practiced every day, and slowly she began to feel freedom from her family. Her confidence grew and, as time went on, her skill improved to the point that she was able to win a competition at her father's country club. This was a happy time for Sandy, for soon she would be going to nursing school, and she hoped for support from her stepmother and her part-time father. At about this time Sandy and her sister became debutantes, which made Sandy's future appear to be very promising. She felt life was going to be hard in nursing school. She feared going to school because she didn't want to fail and to lose what love she had from her parents. Yet, she was determined to be a nurse and fulfill her destiny and dream.

*Sandy had the advantage of growing up in a
wealthy family and one of the perks was
becoming a debutante, but could money buy love?*

There is a belief that we all come to Earth as a spirit or soul from Heaven with a specific mission or project to complete. In order for the soul to accomplish his or her mission, he or she must find a physical or material body to live in. When the soul has accomplished his or her mission, it returns to the spiritual world in Heaven. There is also another basic belief which Epicurus suggested: we create and live our lives for a short few years, we die, and life ends. I can accept either idea. The question I have though is: Which belief is more comforting? I believe the human psyche would want more than just to live and die. What is the point of living life? Why would I work so hard to accomplish something, only to find that my accomplishment had no meaning to others or myself? Is it possible that our soul, the nonphysical part of ourselves, is evolving by living many lives, each life building on the other? Was Sandy's life just a chapter on virtue through nursing? I don't know. What I do know is Sandy was determined to become a nurse and help those people who became sick and hurt through healing and love. She had no interest in becoming a doctor. For her whole life, Sandy always had a desire to help people, and her way of accomplishing this was through nursing.

Sandy received her nursing degree from Newton Wellesley School of Nursing in Boston. The graduation was large and typical of all graduations, with one exception. Sandy believed she saw or felt the presence of her birth mother in attendance. She was not able to make contact and would not ever see her again. Why would a mother abandon her child? What was in the mind of her birth mother? I believe there are moments in our lives that affect or leave lasting memories that we never forget. For Sandy, this had to be one of those moments. What had her birth mother been thinking? I don't know. I have often wondered why Sandy's mother never contacted Sandy at some point. From what I understand, her mother never remarried. Did her mother feel so ashamed that she felt contact would harm Sandy? Sandy's mother was caught in an embarrassing moment. Knowing her father to be a vengeful and angry man, he must have threatened her mother with dire consequences. He was a powerful man who would stop at nothing to have his way.

Thirty years later, Sandy's father would do the same thing again. He found out that Sandy's stepmother was having an affair and told her to leave with whatever she could carry. Fortunately, her lover was a wealthy man, and they got married. Maybe this was a time when Sandy saw who her father really was.

Something prevented contact. I know it left a lasting memory on Sandy, as we talked about it several times. After graduation, she made the decision to move to Denver. She wanted to spend time with her grandparents, who lived in Denver, and get to know them better. She also saw it as a chance to get away from her dysfunctional family and maybe find love in a new location.

Sandy came to Denver with the dream of beginning a new life as a registered nurse and spending time with her grandparents.

With the support of her grandparents and a nursing degree, she found work at one of Denver's leading hospitals. She made the decision not to live with her grandparents. She wanted to get to know her grandparents, but not that well. Right off, Sandy befriended another nurse at the hospital, Jo Ann, who by coincidence had room in her apartment for Sandy. The apartment was located on the corner of Seventh Avenue and Corona Street in Denver, a nice neighborhood with the mayor of Denver living across the street and the owners of Elitch Gardens Amusement Park next door. Sandy's life, as she knew it, was about to change in a way she never dreamed of.

CHAPTER 3

It is not as much about who you used to be as it is about who you choose to be.

—SANHITA BARUAH

1940s–1960s

In 1940, in a Denver hospital, a new baby named Gordon was born. His parents, Edgar and Esther, had lived in Denver for many years. Ed, as he was called, grew up in Trinidad, Colorado, and moved to Denver when he was a young man. He dropped out of school before graduating high school. He married Esther, who grew up in Denver and attended West High School. Ed's profession was construction, and he started his own business building and remodeling homes in 1935. About three years after Gordon was born, Sharon, Gordon's sister, joined the family. Life was typical of the early 1940s. Esther was the ruler of the house, and Edgar managed the construction company. The kids would awake in the morning to the smell of breakfast cooking, and Mom always sent them into the world with full stomachs. Ed and Esther's homes were always upscale—Ed had built them. The family would live in them for a year or two and then sell them and build another one.

Life in the 1940s was much different in many ways than it is today. Widowed women and retired people had a very hard time. A working woman was generally relegated to working in domestic jobs or office clerical work that paid low wages. Nearly all jobs were open to men only. During WWII, women worked in all kinds of professions and jobs and performed outstandingly, but after the war, when the men returned from the military, the women were replaced by the men. My grandfather worked for the railroad and had a management job. He was paid very well, but his wage only covered his daily expenses. He never owned a home or a car. When he retired, he was given a small retirement by the railroad that only covered his house, rent, and food for himself and his wife. My father's mother lived in a small one-room apartment by herself and worked odd jobs to survive. Her husband had died from alcoholism, I believe. Life was difficult for both parents. and they were barely able to survive. My father was a virtuous man and suggested bringing the family together under one roof. He made the decision to construct a home that would affordably bring the families together in one house with separate apartments. My mother thought it was a great idea and agreed. It also provided built-in babysitters. This was a decision that would someday change the lives of several people, one being me. So, my father selected an old three-story house. The house had been built for a very wealthy family around 1900. The first two floors were originally for the owner and his family, beautifully decorated with high ceilings with a lot of wood trim typical of turn-of-the-century homes. There was a large wraparound porch on the front and side of the house with manicured landscaping. A large entry hall with double doors led to the living room and a stairway to the upper level. The third floor was the maids' quarters.

Demolition began, and all the history of the house was removed. The ceilings of the house were lowered, new cabinets were installed, and a new kitchen with a top loading dishwasher was added. A new, modern home was created. The upstairs was remodeled and turned into three apartments. One was for my dad's mother, one for my mom's parents, and the third would be rented out.

From the age of seven, this is where I grew up. I attended Dora Moore Elementary School, Morey Junior High, and South High School in Denver. I was in the Boy Scouts, now called the Scouts, and was a *Denver Post Newspaper* boy during junior high. It was during my elementary school days that I remember connecting with my mother. I would come home from school, and there she would be. I sometimes remember sharing my experiences from school. She was understanding, and I felt trusted and accepted. She did not criticize me but offered helpful advice and guidance. Reading and spelling were always hard for me, so I would shy away from reading. It wasn't until several years later that I was diagnosed with dyslexia—a problem that even today I have to be aware of. It must have been very disheartening, frustrating, and sad for my mother, who worked so hard to teach me to read and spell, and I would let her down. I always loved my mother very much. She was always there for me. She would take care of me when I was sick or had hurt myself. She was there to guide me through my everyday problems, as only a mother can do.

My favorite pastime was listening to the radio. The radio featured stories about Superman, the Green Hornet, the Shadow, and many Westerns. There were also offers to buy Superman's decoder ring, a set of secret codes, and many other prizes relating to my favorite heroes. Remember, this was a time before television. As I grew older, I began building models of trains, planes, and cars. My father was interested in railroads and trains, so we worked together to build a train layout in the basement of our home. We would spend many after-dinner hours working on the train layout. He taught me many modeling skills that I would use throughout my entire life. One of my most memorable Christmases was when Dad gave me a model train of a Santa Fe diesel and passenger train. Christmas was always celebrated with my grandparents and friends with a big dinner, including turkey and all the trimmings. Mom would also cook my grandfather's favorite Swedish Christmas dinner, which was some kind of fish that smelled terrible and stained all the dishes black. I think it was Lutefisk, a Swedish fish.

I believe that for most of us, we learn our basic behaviors, our beliefs, our skills, and our leadership abilities from our parents. I spent a lot of time with my father, whom I also loved and respected very much, so I began to learn how he managed his business. When I started delivering newspapers, I soon became the assistant manager of the newspaper station, a simple job but a start in management and leadership. My father also taught me to be a man and the things a man of the 1950s should do, like chivalry (which is so needed today). When I was fifteen, he helped teach me to fly an airplane, and I soloed on my sixteenth birthday. This led to a life of flying.

Life for me was generally good, a lot of love as I remember. There were times when I made the wrong decision and was disciplined, sometimes with a spanking. Spankings were a good way of reminding me that being stupid had consequences.

There was a time when my parents would disagree, and there were violent arguments. For one thing, my mother never liked the airplane and wanted to sell it, and this would bring on angry arguments.

I remember our family attending the Methodist Church, where I was a member of the choir. While in high school, I joined DeMolay, an organization of young men who were too young to become Masons. When I could, I worked for my father part-time in the family business. My mother was the bookkeeper for the business and handled the company accounts payable and receivables. It was a lot of work for her and required a great deal of her time, but she never neglected my sister and me.

When I graduated from South High School, I applied to the University of Denver. I was told that I had very low reading and spelling skills, not something new. Their suggestion was that I should repeat one more year of high school. My parents were not highly educated; my father had an eighth-grade education, and my mother had taken one year of college. But thank goodness, they saw the need for my sister and me to go to college and get our degrees. My sister graduated from the University of Arizona. I was off for one more year of high school and then to DU with the full support of my parents.

As I said, struggles with reading and spelling would haunt me my entire life. I started DU in 1958 and attended class for four years. Near graduation there were two final tests. One was math, which I passed easily, and the other was for spelling and reading, which I couldn't pass even after several tries and tutoring. I resigned myself to the fact that I would never graduate. It was not until 1969 that I received a phone call from one of my college professors. It was the happiest day of my life. He told me that the faculty of DU had decided that, even though I hadn't passed the reading and spelling exam, they were going to let me graduate along with 129 other students. Think about that! How could something like that happen? This was seven years after I should have graduated. It has taken many years for me to understand how the universe might work and how that could have happened. Later in this book, I will explain my belief about how this happened, along with many more unbelievable stories.

In 1958 I joined the Colorado National Guard in Denver. There was a military draft at that time, and going in to the army was not appealing. My father, through his flying clubs, knew several of the officers in the Air Guard. This later would have a profound effect on my military career. I spent the summer of 1959 in basic training at Lackland Air Force Base in Texas. The best part of this experience was that I learned leadership, how to dress properly, how to become a member of a team, and discipline. The worst part was that it was hot, hard work with constant pushing by the drill instructors, and I had no time for myself. The payoff was the training I received that I would use for the rest of my life.

Upon returning to Denver, I was assigned to the flight line, where I would receive training on jet fighter planes. My sergeant had served in World War II and was relentless on my training. He also was an expert on jet aircraft. My long hours and hard work paid off, as I was promoted in rank every time I became eligible. This was important because in 1960 the Russians were causing trouble in Cuba, and our fighter wing was called to active duty. I was a sergeant by then and was in charge of my own airplane, an F-100 Century Fighter.

I was working for my father in the construction business when, at the age of twenty, I was called to active duty. Business was good, and my father said he wanted me to have fun on active duty, so he continued to pay my construction salary the whole year I served. He also gave me a new Ford Thunderbird to drive. This worked well, as I was able to help other people in my squadron have fun too. It was also a time of heavy drinking. After being released from active duty, I went back to once-a-month weekend duty with the Colorado Air Guard and returned to Denver, I became the crew chief on the commanding general's airplane. This came with a lot of responsibility and hard work. I had no idea that the general, George, and his wife, Kathy, would become very dear friends of Sandy's and mine later in life.

Chapter 4

Success isn't measured by money or power or social rank.
Success is measured by discipline and inner peace.

—Mike Ditka

April–June 1963

Sandy was so excited to move into her new apartment. With the help of her roommate, Jo Ann, she settled in and as you might have guessed it was my parents' home. Sandy and I had met shortly after I graduated from college and she had moved to Denver. The year was 1963. We were both twenty-three years old, and our birthdays were only seven days apart. I clearly remember the day we met. It was a warm day in early March, and I had been working in the yard and was taking a break. Sitting on the porch, I saw a white angel walking up the steps of the front porch. Or, at least, I thought it was an angel.

Sandy was dressed in a white nurse's uniform with white shoes and a white nurse's hat on her head. In the 1960s, all the nursing schools had a signature hat, and many nurses would wear them to work to designate where they went to school. Sandy was one of the last nurses in the hospital to give up her hat, a tradition I hated to see go.

Nursing schools had signature hats, worn by their graduates, that designated where the nurse went to school.

She looked so happy and walked with a little bounce in her step. At first, she did not see me, and when she finally did, there was a slight moment of hesitation.

"Hi, I'm Sandy," she said.

I knew at that moment that there was something magical about Sandy and that there was a connection between us. I think I hesitated a moment. With a little embarrassment, I finally replied.

"Hi, I'm Gordon."

The conversation was light. She told me where she was from and where she worked. I think I told her that I lived downstairs with my parents, and that I worked in my father's construction company, and that I was happy to meet her. I felt good all over, warm and excited. We exchanged a little more small talk, and finally she said she wanted to change clothes. I asked if we could meet sometime and get acquainted since we were living in the same house. She agreed, and I think my heart skipped several beats. I knew we were going to be good friends and at that moment there was an unseen connection, though I did not have any idea how connected we would soon be. We were two people from different parts of the world but with similar backgrounds coming together.

We met several more times, enjoyed coffee, and shared who we were. Our first date was dinner and a play at the old Elitch Gardens Theater, which still exists today, though unused. After the play, we danced in the Elitch Garden Ballroom. In the early 1960s, people attending the theater or symphony would always dress up. I wore a coat and tie, and Sandy wore a fancy dress. The ballroom was partially open to the outside, and the smell of flowers permeated the room. The room was crowded, and everyone was having an enjoyable time dancing to a full orchestra. Sandy was a good dancer. I left something to be desired, but Sandy seemed not to notice. We were both falling in love, and I could not have been happier. I am sure she was too. Our relationship became stronger, and one night in Sandy's apartment, we ended up in bed together while her roommate, JoAnn, was working. We dated a lot and spent a lot of time together. We were definitely in love.

Sometime later, she said she wanted to fly home and see her family and take care of some unfinished business. She would only be gone a few days, and I remember taking her to the airport. In the 1960s, you could walk to the planes. As she walked to her plane, I knew I would miss her very much. I knew I was falling in love with her and could see marriage on the horizon.

The few days passed slowly, and I was so excited driving to the airport to pick her up. Standing on the ramp, seeing her come off the plane, my mind flashed back to the day we met. She was so beautiful. When we got home, we went into the living room of my parents' house. My parents were not home, so we had the house to ourselves. We talked about her trip, and as we talked, I sensed anxiety in her voice. She was acting unsettled, and I thought she was just tired. There was still a sparkle in her eyes that I will always remember. Finally, she reached over and grasped my hands in her hands, which were warm and soft. I could feel a real closeness, a feeling of connection. My heart was beating faster, like something was going to happen. She said she had gone to Boston to talk to her stepmother about a problem she had and wanted her advice. My first thought was that she may have a health problem and wanted her stepmother's advice, as only a mother can give, to help solve the problem.

At that point, she held my hands tighter. I will never forget as she said, "Gordon, I'm pregnant."

Is it possible to think a hundred thoughts at the same time?

Yes, but the only words that came out of my mouth and heart were, "Let's get married."

I pulled her close and while holding her tightly, I said gently to her that I loved her very much.

With a slight sigh and just a slightly stronger grasp, she said, "I love you too."

We held each other for a very long time, not saying a word, just enjoying the moment. In my life, there has never been another moment like that. So much love, so much caring, so much giving to each other. When we finally let go of each other, there was a tremendous sense of relief. At that moment, there was a huge change in Sandy. She could see a life with a new baby in a home full of love. She later told me that the sole purpose for her going home was to talk to her stepmother about her options. Her stepmother suggested three options, probably out of many. One option was to marry Gordon, if he would have her. The second was to come to Boston and have the baby there. The third was to have an abortion. Sandy told her that an abortion was out of the question. A choice between the first two options would need Gordon's input.

Finally, recovering from the shock of soon becoming new parents, we spent the rest of the day talking about our wedding: when, where, and who would attend. That night, we shared our news with my parents. My parents were totally excited and, to our surprise, were extremely supportive. They offered to help in any way possible. So, as you might have guessed, we had to move fast. The wedding would be held in Denver.

CHAPTER 5

Two things are infinite: the universe and human stupidity;
and I'm not sure about the universe.

—ALBERT EINSTEIN

Where did we come from, and what did we believe? Gordon and Sandy are about to get married. They know very little about life, except what they learned from their parents and friends. They had education but very little wisdom. That would come later. Yes, they believed in God, but they learned about God from church teachings and not yet from their own experiences. At this point in their lives, God and how God works is of little interest. However, Gordon and Sandy both had a strong belief in God from growing up attending church regularly. Although the existence of God could not be proven, they both felt God played a big role in their lives. However, the question of spirituality was also of little interest. They had a life to live and a baby to raise. They had more pressing things occupying their thoughts. The existence of God has never been universally satisfactorily proven. So why spend time with an idea that was never proven scientifically to work? Yet, there is no proof that God does not exist. I believe that how God functions is solely up to an individual's unique perception.

The other day I asked my physical trainer, Britney, if she believed in God. She answered that no, she does not believe in all the Church dogma either. This made me wonder: do all people who believe in God connect Him or Her to a church? Personally, I have come to believe that God and the Church are separate entities. I strongly believe that God has but one objective, and that is to create Heaven on Earth. (I will go into more detail on this idea in later chapters.) The Church founders and leaders have created what they think God wants His flock to believe. These leaders, in many cases, have interjected their own personal beliefs in order to control their flock and have made suggestions on how the flock should act and respond. Many churches have taken God as the center of attention or basis for their existence. God, I believe, is not connected to any one church but supports all those who want to create Heaven on Earth. Therefore, I believe God can also work directly with individual people who also want goodwill, as they envision it.

Generally, there are two basic thoughts about the existence of God. One is that God *does not* exist and the control of my life is left up to me. The second thought is that God *does* exist and helps guide my life, making things happen that I could never make happen alone. Did Sandy and Gordon just happen to come together? To me, it seems like something more was at play. In between these two ideas, however, is the notion that there is indeed something else at work in my life outside of my control, but it is unnamed. Maybe there is a hesitation to label this outside force "God" because we don't all agree on the definition of this word. Let your mind wander and maybe question what you have been taught. Why do you believe or not believe in God? Are your beliefs what you have been taught, or are they determined by your own experience? Are they, perhaps, a mixture of both? And what influence do your thoughts and beliefs have on your everyday life? To this end, we also must consider the concepts of luck, fate, and the law of attraction.

Luck and fate are generally regarded as happenings outside of our direct control. If we believe in the common definition of these terms, a person is regarded as lucky or unlucky or with a good or bad fate sometimes from birth and sometimes it changes throughout one's life. However, there is also the idea that nothing is random and every event has a reason and/or meaning. Putting it in terms of Newton's third law of motion, "Every action has an equal and opposite reaction," or in terms of psychology, "Every cause has an effect, and every effect has a cause." Michael Beckwith, spiritual leader and founder of the Agape Church, says that LUCK is an acronym for "living under cosmic knowledge" and that when a person appears to have good luck, they are actually acting with a deeper understanding of how the world works. This idea infuses the law of attraction. The law of attraction brings the responsibility of one's life into one's direct control. This law states that the things that we focus on are the things that come into our lives. Yet, this focus can be performed on a subconscious level without our direct awareness. We may do things and have beliefs and behaviors that we don't understand. We are often caught in a belief and validation feedback loop based on things we learned as a child. Current thinking is that 95 percent of all we learned about life is learned before age five. Once we awaken to the things in our subconscious mind, we can acknowledge their existence and confront them in our conscious mind. This transition can arise in meditation practice. Be aware that what is trapped in our subconscious mind could be horrific. If you are going to meditate, find a practice where counselors are available. The law of attraction can be difficult to prove or believe in without direct experience of it.

The universe has many laws that we can all generally agree on. We generally can all agree on the laws of physics. Newton said that all objects fall at the same rate when in a vacuum and an object in motion will stay in motion unless acted upon by an outside force. There are also some things we know and can measure but we can't see. These include electricity, which travels in a wire or in the air. Some might say we can see electricity in a lighting flash, but are we seeing electricity or the light created by electricity? Electricity creates light and heat, but can we actually see this energy? What do we see when light is generated? We see the source of light and we can see the light on an object, but we can't see the light as it travels through the air. Does this mean electricity, energy, and light don't exist? Even though we can't see, feel, touch, smell, or hear something, it is possible, as we have been taught, to believe that it does indeed exist. There are some things that we can logically prove, but there are other things we cannot. Should an unproven idea be discarded? An unproven belief may improve our lives and attitude, and bring us happiness, joy, and harmony. Albert Einstein once said, "Logic will get you from A to B. Imagination will take you everywhere."

Albert Einstein developed the theory of relativity, one of the two pillars of modern physics, along with the second pillar, quantum mechanics. Einstein discovered the mass equivalence formula $E = MC2$. He also discovered the law of photoelectric effect, a pivotal step toward development of quantum theory. Quantum theory is a fundamental theory in physics that describes nature at the smallest scales of energy levels of atoms and subatomic particles. In regular physics, or macrophysics, we know that an object exists in a specific place and occupies space. This is how things move at everyday size and speed. In quantum physics, things exist in a haze of probability. The particles have a chance of being at Point A and another chance to be at Point B. How can this be possible? What kind of energy is this? What, how, or who controls it? Scientists are still trying to understand this. Could quantum physics or even the law of attraction be the way God communicates with us?

As my story unfolds, ask yourself, is this just good or bad luck? Or is there divine intervention at play? My second question is a lot more fun. With good or bad luck, I will live and do things my way and hope for the best. But with the possibility of divine intervention, I will share the responsibility with a higher power, maybe God. If I choose to share with God, how is this possible? Believe me, there is a way, but it is not simple. Soon, I will give you the plan and explain how God works for me through spirits and the Spirit World. What I believe is that I don't create plans alone, yet their implementation requires my free will as a necessary part of implementation.

CHAPTER 6

Optimism is the faith which leads to achievement.
Nothing can be done without hope and confidence.

—HELEN KELLER

July–August 1963

Sandy was so excited. All her fear and anxiety had faded away, and she became radiant. There was a beautiful white light surrounding her again. She was ready to go. I, on the other hand, was not so sure. One moment I was a young man with no cares. I could come and go as I pleased, but I had committed to marriage and raising a soon-to-be-born child. My father and mother had taught me to always take responsibility for my actions. Looking back on my life as a child, growing up, I realized that my father and mother had always been there for me. I never saw the sacrifices they made for my sister and me, but my sister and I always had what we needed, not always what we wanted, but what we needed. Sending us both through college had to have been a real challenge for them.

Sandy and I had created a baby, and I decided I was going to make both of them happy, joyful, and secure, no matter what it would take. I knew Sandy would make a great mother. However, in the short-term, planning a wedding on short notice would be a challenge. Sandy and I decided we could do it. A few calls to our parents, and we were on the way in short order. Sandy's stepmother and father would come to Denver just before the wedding. Sandy's father was a member of an athletic club in Boston. The Denver Athletic Club was a reciprocal club to the one in Boston, so Sandy's father suggested the reception be held there. Sandy wanted her wedding in Denver, as she had made several friends since moving here, and all my friends lived in Denver as well.

On August 2, 1963, Sandy and I had our church wedding. When Sandy came down the aisle with her father, she was the most beautiful and radiant woman in the world. She was wearing a gorgeous white wedding dress. I knew God had arranged this for me and for our families and friends in a way I could not have, even with all the time and money in the world. The wedding was a happy celebration, and the reception was also a joyous event. Our parents had worked so hard to make this all come together for Sandy and me.

Sometimes our parents could get a little carried away. Sandy and I had planned the first night of our honeymoon at the Broadmoor Hotel in Colorado Springs. Since the wedding and reception had been early in the day, we were quite hungry when we arrived at the hotel later that evening. Lo and behold, who should show up at the hotel? You may have guessed it, my mother and father. They wanted to spend a few private moments welcoming Sandy into my family. It was something I will never forget, and Sandy thought it was wonderful. And we got a free dinner.

*Sandy and Gordon were truly in love and
with the help of their parents had a happy
and joyous wedding.*

We said farewell to my parents, and Sandy and I headed to the lounge for one last drink. Alcohol was beginning to work its way into our lives. It was our first night of marriage, and the urge to be alone was overpowering. Emotions and animal instincts were off the scale, not to mention lust. Off to our room we went. I am sure most of you know what was on my mind and maybe Sandy's too. Back in our room, Sandy scampered into the bathroom, and in a few short moments, she returned. I had lowered the lights in the room, and for a moment, the light in the bathroom backlit the sexiest woman in the world, dressed in a black negligee. We hugged and kissed for a long time and finally made love. As we relaxed, I think we both knew there was going to be a lot going on in the near future. We talked a little and related to each other what our dreams were. We had a baby on the way, what should we name it?

Sandy said, "If it is a boy, I think we should name it Richard, your middle name."

Funny, I don't know what name we picked for a girl. Although we were dead tired, we talked on. Finally, we made love again, and while holding each other, we fell asleep. Sandy and I were now one, cemented together by commitment and the greatest love two people could create. What was our future going to bring? The last few months together had proven we could overcome the biggest obstacles, and we worked together complementing and supporting each other's ideas. This would be the foundation for our life in the future. It was that night that we both agreed, before we went to sleep, that we would always hold each other for a few moments. We kept to our promise most of our lives.

The morning came late for Sandy and me. We couldn't get enough of each other, so we made love again. It was interesting how sex turned to hunger, and we were ready for breakfast—or was it lunch? I don't remember. I do remember how happy we both were. It had been a grueling few weeks, and then it was time to plan for the future and enjoy the honeymoon. We were off to Durango, Colorado, to ride the narrow-gauge railroad train to Silverton, Colorado, the next day. I loved riding trains. It's a real adventure, and I hoped Sandy would find it fun too. Railroading had always been an important part of Colorado. The first trains arrived in Denver in the early 1870s. Over the next twenty years, they covered most of Colorado, serving the mining towns, farmers, and ranchers and making travel possible. The Durango and Silverton Railroads were the last remnants of what had been a vast railroad network in southwestern Colorado. Travel in the late nineteenth century in Colorado was extremely difficult. It would take a week or longer to get from Denver to Durango by wagon. The railroads shortened this to a day. Goods could be moved easily and in great quantities. Towns grew up, mining flourished, and agriculture was everywhere. Our honeymoon train trip would be an all-day ride back in history up to Silverton and back through the most beautiful mountains in Colorado. Being from the East, Sandy was excited to see the mountains that made Colorado legendary.

Our drive to Durango was leisurely; the weather was perfect, sunny, and clear. We talked about our families and friends. Sandy wanted to know more about my friend Brian. I told her that Brian and I had been friends for many years and that was why he was my best man at the wedding. Brian and I grew up together. Our parents were good friends. During high school, Brian and I cemented a friendship that would last a lifetime. Brian dated a girl from high school named Carol, whom he would marry. (They celebrated sixty-two years together in 2019.) Sandy was very interested in Brian and wanted to know all about him. I think she knew that the four of us would be spending a lot of time together. I told her how Brian and I had joined the Colorado Air National Guard and we went to basic training together. We later joined the Masonic Lodge, the Masons, and became Shriners together. We had a close bond, and soon Sandy would become a part of that.

We arrived in Durango in the late afternoon and checked into the Strater Hotel. The Strater is a part of Durango's living history. Furnished with Victorian antique walnut furniture, we felt like we were back in 1887 when the hotel was built. Sandy had never been around trains, and this would be her first train ride, a train with a coal-fired steam locomotive. The Strater was adjacent to the train station, so we decided to explore the station and train yard. On our exploration, we were confronted by a big black steam engine, smoke drifting from its smoke stack and steam coming from the electric generator.

Sandy said, "It looks alive and is welcoming us to Durango."

We could feel the power of Engine Number 478, and we knew it would pull our passenger train the next morning. Did I sense a little excitement in her voice—her interest, her desire to learn more about Engine Number 478? It had been built in the 1920s but was still a proud engine. I wonder if she was feeling a little connected to the trains like I was? Was she feeling a connection with the spirit that resided in the engine? I know she was very excited and was looking forward to the next day. I was excited for her. This would be the start of many more things Sandy and I would enjoy together.

As we walked back to the hotel, Sandy said, "There is something magical about trains, and I'd like to know more about them."

Her wish would come true, as there would be many train rides in the future.

I remember one train ride that was a bit unconventional, but so was our life. Sandy and I had been married about three years when out of the blue, while we were eating breakfast one morning, she said, "Let's try something different, a new adventure."

Sandy was always ready for adventure.

She asked, "What would it be like to ride a freight train like the hobos do?"

"That would be a real adventure," I said. "Let's do it."

"We can leave Rich with your mom and dad for the weekend in case we get delayed or have to stay overnight someplace," Sandy proposed.

We talked more, and the next weekend, we decided to ride a freight train from Denver into the mountains west of Denver. It was a sunny, warm Saturday morning when we headed to the railroad yard. There were several trains, and we choose a long freight train headed to the west. As we walked along looking at the black tank cars, several flat cars, and covered hopper cars, we finally came to an open door on a box car.

We looked in all directions to see if anyone was watching.

"All clear," I said.

We were about to jump aboard when an old, gruffly, wrinkled man looked out and asked what we were doing in the rail yard. I quickly told him that we wanted to ride the train. With a big smile, he said, "You two don't look like hobos."

"He should know," I thought.

I quickly explained to him that we were just looking to have some fun and do something no one else would do. He laughed and said we should ride in the engine; it would be safer. With that, we went forward and boarded the rear locomotive, one of five. Once inside the cab, we decided to sit on the engine floor until we were out of town so we wouldn't get caught and thrown off the train.

Moments later, the engines roared to life, and we were on our way. Soon we were in the foothills. It was time to venture up and into the engineer's and fireman's seats. The engines were working hard as the tracks out of Denver are all uphill. The smell of diesel exhaust was strong, and there was a lot of noise from the engines, but that all faded away with our excitement. The view of Downtown Denver was spectacular.

We traveled into unpopulated countryside on the side of the mountains, through tunnels and over bridges, always climbing higher and higher. At one point, to our surprise and fear, the train brakeman entered our cab. All of us were very surprised to see each other, but the mood quickly turned to laughter, and we spent the next half hour exchanging stories. As he was leaving, he turned and asked how we were going to get back to Denver.

"We have no idea," Sandy said. "Maybe a bus, hitchhike, or maybe find someone going to Denver."

He smiled and left.

Riding on a clandestine train was a real thrill. Sandy and I were experiencing real fear, at times wondering what we would do if we were thrown off the train into the wilderness. We also experienced a real high doing something that was probably illegal. But, uppermost, we were feeling adventurous. After a five-hour train ride, we arrived in the town of Bond, Colorado, at a train crew change station. As we descended the engine, the brakeman came up with a big smile.

He said, "I have arranged for you to ride back to Denver on the next freight train going east. It will be here in about an hour."

Sandy and I thanked him. What a great guy! What a feeling of relief: a way home!

"Somebody must be looking after us," Sandy said.

We boarded our train home and had a wonderful ride. We watched for other freight trains and hid on the engine cab floor as they passed so we wouldn't get caught hitchhiking. Just before we reached the rail yard in Denver, the brakeman came back to our engine and said they would stop short of the yard so we could get off. We thanked him for a wonderful ride.

Driving home Sandy said, "What a wonderful day. It was a day I will never forget. Everyone in the train crew was so pleasant, but I'm hungry, and I need a shower."

Yes, we sure did need a shower, and we looked like we had been working a coal mine for a week. Our initiation into the hobo community had been completed, and we were now officially hobos. We kissed gently and headed to the nearest restaurant.

When two people are in harmony and each carries their own weight, it is difficult to be angry and resentful. Sandy and I did not compete. We knew what our jobs were in the relationship, and generally, we let each other do those jobs without interference.

CHAPTER 7

Being challenged in life is inevitable; being defeated is optional.

—ROGER CRAWFORD

August 1963

On the second night of our honeymoon, Sandy and I walked around Durango for a while, visiting the stores up and down Main Street. It was fun to look, but we knew we had very little money to buy anything. We returned to the Strater for a drink in the Diamond Belle Saloon. Drinking each night would become a routine. Most of our friends drank and we thought life included drinking. The Diamond Belle Saloon was a bar out of yesteryear. It had a large, long bar on one wall with old wooden chairs and tables. The back of the bar had the usual nude woman picture over several glass mirrors and many bottles of hard liquor. It had been a long day, and the next day would be a long train ride, Sandy's first. After a couple of drinks, we headed to the dining room for our meal.

As we walked to the dining room, Sandy commented, "You know, Gordon, I think we just walked into the 1880s."

I think we both thought we would see Doc Holliday or Wyatt Earp walk in.

Early the next morning after breakfast, we were back at the train station. Sure enough, our steam engine that we had seen the day before was coupled to a string of bright yellow passenger cars. Building a railroad in the Colorado mountains was difficult and expensive. The builders decided to make the engines and cars smaller so they could negotiate tighter curves and steeper grades. So, when Sandy and I boarded the train, it was like getting onto a big toy. The inside of the car was small but very well decorated with brass ornate oil lamps hung from the ceiling and a potbelly stove on each end of the car for heat. If you were sitting near the stove in winter, you were usually too hot, but if you sat in the middle of the car, you were usually too cold. However, you could always open a window to even things up. We found our seats, and we were soon off to Silverton.

The Denver and Rio Grande Railroad had been built in the 1880s to serve the mines in southwestern Colorado and New Mexico. As we traveled north, following the Animas River, we soon entered the most beautiful part of Colorado, which could only be seen by train. Sheer canyons and steep cliffs dominated the landscape with mountains reaching for the heavens. I was so impressed that men, with primitive tools, could build a railroad through such unforgiving landscape. All was so peaceful and quiet, except for the clickety-clack of the train wheels on steel rails. Our engine was working hard, belching black smoke and straining to conquer the steep grade. We held hands, and for a long time we said nothing, enjoying the grandeur of this magnificent country. As part of our train, there was an open-topped gondola car where people could stand and really view the scenery.

Sandy motioned toward the gondola and said, "Let's go to that car for a better view."

It was cold riding in the gondola car, but we still enjoyed it, if for only a little while. The black smoke would sometimes whirl around us.

Suddenly Sandy screeched, "I think I have a cinder in my eye!"

She opened her eye and with a quick flick of my handkerchief corner, it was gone.

Then all of a sudden, Sandy said, "God must spend a lot of time here."

"Yes," I said. "I know I would if I could."

At that moment, Sandy pointed to something on the right of our car and said, "Look, there's an eagle in the tree over there."

Sure enough, a bald eagle was sitting atop a lone tree.

"That's a sign of good luck," she said.

I agreed.

The very first train arrived in Silverton, Colorado on July 4, 1882. We arrived a few years later. We raced around town exploring the old buildings, stores, and attractions. Silverton is nestled in a valley surrounded by mountains. If you looked carefully, you could see many abandoned mines and buildings dotting the hillsides. We had a quick lunch and were back on the train to Durango for another night at the Strater Hotel. We were so happy.

Sandy and I had a day we would never forget. We were so happy and full of excitement. Many adventures like this would be a part of our lives for many years to come. The next morning, we were again on our way to Silverton, this time by car, to stay at the historic Grand Imperial Hotel built in 1882. We wanted to see and experience all the history that we could. Durango and Silverton were a far cry from

Boston, where Sandy grew up. We arrived in Silverton to find a quiet little town. The only excitement in Silverton had been the train and it was long gone. At an elevation of 9,318 feet, Silverton soon took its toll on us, along with a busy day of sightseeing, exploring, and the trains. So it was dinner and early to bed for us in another historic hotel.

"Tomorrow would be a long drive home," or so we thought.

Gordon and Sandy were returning to Denver when they were stopped by a police man. The newlyweds were given a special treat. They were going to be honored guests, at the opening of a new hotel in Gunnison, Colorado, which included dinner and lodging. The perfect end to their honeymoon.

The drive to Denver would be over the Million Dollar Highway north of Silverton and through the towns of Ouray and Gunnison. We thought we would be home before dark, but there was another adventure in store for us. We arrived in Gunnison around three in the afternoon. While driving down the main street, I saw a police car attempt to stop a car ahead of us without success. I commented to Sandy that it seemed odd. We drove by the police car and thought nothing more of the incident until the red lights of the police car came on behind us. Sandy was startled and a little afraid.

"What have we done?" she asked.

"I don't think anything," I replied.

As the policeman approached the car, the tension began rising. Was this going to be an unhappy ending to a wonderful honeymoon? Not to be. I rolled down my window.

"Welcome to Gunnison," the policeman said. "I would like you to be our guests tonight at a new hotel resort that just opened."

Was this luck or something else? Was someone looking over us?

That night, we became a part of the opening celebration for Gunnison's newest hotel. We were wined and dined and treated like a king and queen. What a fantastic way to end our first few days together as man and wife. The next morning after breakfast, we headed to Denver and to the start of a new life.

Chapter 8

Kindness in words creates confidence. Kindness in thinking creates profoundness. Kindness in giving creates love.

—Lao Tzu

August 1963–January 1964

In the beginning of our journey together, life for us was simple. We were working at jobs we both loved, preparing for a new baby, and having fun along the way. Sandy was a hospital nurse, and I was working for my father in the family business. My father owned an apartment house, and he offered us newlyweds an apartment with reduced rent. The apartment would need furnishing, so the search began. With a limited budget, we worked very hard to find the best deals. Fortunately, many of the items we needed were given to us as wedding gifts. We called our friends, searched in the newspapers, and visited the Salvation Army to find other things we would need. The apartment soon began to take shape. There were so many small items needed: towels, bed linens, pillows, and all the small items needed in the bathroom. Then it was onto the kitchen with pots and pans, kitchen utensils, spices, and food. Soon we had a new couch and chair for the living room, a bed, which came first and, lo and behold, a bassinet for the new baby that we found on sale. There was still five months before the baby was to be born, and that gave us time to find all the things a baby would need. Conversations with our mothers helped a lot.

The doctor had said that we should expect the baby sometime in January, and we wanted to be prepared. Everyone was so excited to see the new baby, and we all wondered if it would be a girl or boy. We were the first couple among our friends to get married and have a baby on the way. That would change, as several of our friends would soon be forced to get married also.

In the 1960s, life was generally good and a lot of fun and quite simple. Of our many good and close friends, Brian and his wife, Carol, were the closest. They were married shortly after we were, and the four of us remained close. We attended many dinners and parties where the alcohol would flow. Drugs were never a part of our group for two reasons: one, they were illegal (and to be arrested with drugs would jeopardize Sandy's nursing career and my flying licenses) and two, who needed them? We had alcohol. There were also many clubs, and we belonged to several of them. We belonged to the Denver Pilots Club, the Shrine Air Patrol, my railroad club, and the Denver Society of Model Railroaders. Each would have their parties, and Sandy and I would always attend.

Sandy and I shared chores at meal time: she cooked, and I was the head dishwasher and maid. Since I did not know much about cooking, this arrangement worked out well. It was a time when going out meant dressing up. I loved to shop for Sandy, and we would often go together to the local department store.

"Gordon, when I dress up, I feel so elegant and special. You know, we make a beautiful couple," Sandy would often say.

I was proud of her, and she was proud of me. When we went out, it wasn't uncommon for people to say, "You two make a stunning couple." And we both agreed.

After our first Christmas, we settled down to a cold and snowy January. It was early in the afternoon. Sandy was at home, and I was in my office when she called me. She said I should get home as soon as possible because she was sure the baby was on the way. Without hesitation, I grabbed my coat, jumped into my car, and headed home. When I arrived home, Sandy was waiting with her coat on and a small suitcase in hand. My heart was pounding. I was so excited and scared. We held hands all the way to the hospital, and I was so amazed by her calmness. I guess if you are a professional nurse, you know all about babies. I drove up to the front door of the hospital and dropped Sandy off. I parked the car and ran back to the hospital, only to find Sandy sitting in a wheelchair about to head to the delivery room.

All I had time to say was, "I love you, and I will be waiting."

She said, "I love you too."

We were both excited, scared, and happy. The big day had arrived. I called both parents and told them to be on standby: the baby was coming. We were all praying for a good delivery. Both parents asked me to call when we knew all was well and to let them know if it was a boy or a girl.

In the 1960s, it was uncommon for a father to be in the delivery room when the baby was delivered. I later learned, from the doctor, that expectant fathers are so excited, nervous, and unsettled the doctors feared fathers might scare away the stork. After she was taken to the delivery room, I slowly walked to the waiting room but diverted to get a cup of coffee to settle my nerves. This was one of those times when I called upon God to watch over Sandy and our new baby. I felt happy that I did not have to be alone.

"Please," I prayed, "make the delivery easy."

I asked God to watch over them and bring them home happy and healthy. My prayers were answered. The doctor appeared in the doorway of the waiting room, wearing a white surgical suite and a big smile.

"Mr. Calahan," he said, "you are the father of a blue-eyed baby boy. Congratulations."

"Thank you so much," I said. "And thank you for taking care of our new mother, Sandy. How is she?"

He said that she was doing fine and would be in the recovery room for a while and then transferred to her room. He said she would call me when she was settled. For me, the fear and anxiety were over, replaced with joy and happiness. I was a father. A lot had gone on in just a few short months, orchestrated like a beautiful symphony. At the time, I never thought about the many things that had to come together to make this wonderful event take place and how each event was perfectly timed with very little input from me.

As the news of this monumental event wore off, I thought, "This calls for a celebration." I remembered a liquor store across the street from the hospital. I ran over and bought a bottle of Lancers Wine, Sandy's favorite, and two wine glasses. What was I thinking? I returned to the waiting room, and about an hour later, the phone in the waiting room rang.

"Hello," I said.

"Gordon, is that you?" Sandy asked.

"Yes," I said. "How are you?"

"Doing fine," she said. "You can come up now."

When I entered her room, I saw that the girl who had entered the hospital was now a radiant and happy woman and mother. She was tired from the delivery, but she still looked gorgeous, and I remember leaping to the bed and giving her a big hug. We kissed like never before. It was then that I remembered that she had just been through a major experience, and I asked if she was OK.

"I have never been better," she said.

She was surprised when I told her that I had some wine to celebrate with. Sandy laughed.

"You know that is against hospital policy."

"Let's not get caught," I replied.

As we sipped our wine, she told me about the delivery. I am not good around blood and sick people, and as she talked, I began to get dizzy. Her voice became fuzzy.

"Gordon, are you all right? You look as white as my sheet. Come, lie down next to me before you pass out."

What a hero I was: she was now taking care of me!

"I think it was the wine," I said to save face.

"Sure," she said.

"What a woman," I said. "Always looking after her man."

Donald, our second son, would come in a couple of years. The drama of the second child's birth was considerably less.

CHAPTER 9

Kindness is the language which the deaf can
hear and the blind can see.

—MARK TWAIN

The way we feel about ourselves is how we present ourselves to the world. The way we talk to ourselves is the way we feel. Let me share some thoughts about how we talk to ourselves and the voices in our heads. I assume we all hear voices in our heads. Does anyone know who these voices are? Where do they come from? If those voices are me, then who are they talking to? For years, I was baffled by the voices in my head. But now, I think I have come to know who and what the voices are.

The first voice, I will call *me*. I am the one who implements the desires, missions, goals, and dreams my soul comes up with. Simply, I am the bus driver. I drive the bus when and where I am told by my soul. My passengers are the memories and dreams from my past and the fantasies in the future. I don't make decisions. I don't have self-will. I only follow the rules of the road. It is a simple job for the *me* voice.

The second voice in my head is my *soul's* voice. This soul's voice directs my life and how I perform my life. He or she is in charge of my life journey. He or she passes information to *me*, the bus driver. Simply, it is like making a movie or a stage play. My life will be as good or bad as the *soul* voice directs. So, the *soul* is the voice in our head that we hear most of the time. It is trying to run our show by utilizing the information that it has accumulated. The soul itself is always open to change and to learn new things, although that change could be good, bad, or a number of things in-between. I can sometimes see a person or myself act strangely, or differently, when I am around other people. I may act out differently, not the Gordon people know, and act in a fashion I don't understand. I believe that this is the soul calling on God for information and guidance. I can use the information to improve or further my education on Earth, I try not to judge what I have seen or done. I only know a change may be coming, and I should be ready to change. If I have goals, then new behavior may be necessary to accomplish my goals.

I believe the soul is our connection to God (or a universal being of your choice). The soul is the animating principle that makes things come alive. It is the carrier of the life force, which is synonymous with movement and breath. The soul is also the emotional or feeling aspect of our being. It is our inner character: that which makes us unique. We can sense this inner character in others by looking into their eyes, which are often referred to as "the window of the soul." Each of us has our own individually unique soul, which lives in the Spirit World when not in a material body. When a baby is born, that first moment when it takes its first breath is when the soul enters the material body.

It stays until death, at which time it returns to the Spirit World, or it may linger on Earth for a period of time. I believe the soul may stay on Earth for a short period of time after our bodies die to provide assistance and/or maybe learn from other souls residing in material beings. Some people see these souls as ghosts. An interesting thought, don't you think?

Many people believe the soul comes to Earth to carry out a mission, assigned by God or a mission the soul wants to experience and to further its education. Hopefully, it will leave the world a better place when it departs. I have been taught that the mission of the soul of all human beings on Earth is to contribute to creating Heaven on Earth. However, the soul comes with free will. It can live any life it wants. It can act any way it wants. If it fails in its assigned mission on Earth, it can return to the Spirit World and come back to Earth at another time, to another material body. Thus, this is what we call reincarnation and what is being referred to when we hear people talk about the soul within a person as an old soul or a young soul. What are they talking about? An old soul is a soul that has been to Earth many times and has a great deal of wisdom. A young soul is young, with limited knowledge and wisdom. Regardless of how many times a soul has been incarnated, it always has a mission individualized to its unique attributes or desires. Yet, it can be difficult to interpret its mission.

When we take control of our lives without direction from others or the spirits, we may live outside of our originally intended mission and not work toward Heaven on Earth. When we interpret the mission with certain human bias, we can create a monster. Case in point: Adolf Hitler. He believed that the world would be a better place without Jews, and he created the most hellish violence and death the world had ever known. Insanity can be reinforced and justified when many people believe the means justify the results. If we see something that we consider uncomfortable, distasteful, threatening, fearful, or ugly, we must investigate our motives to eradicate it. All situations are different, and to use the same solutions to solve a problem often doesn't work and only creates more problems. It is so important to look into a situation and make a judgment to determine if that situation is right or wrong, and if wrong, correct it before it becomes an out of control problem. This calls for great diplomacy from all parties involved. Believing I have the only answer for what is best for humanity and the world is ultimate self-centeredness. This is why creating Heaven on Earth is so difficult and why love and our connection to God are so important.

Obviously, the more training, experience, and education the soul has, the more mature the *soul* voice is and the better one's life should be. So, my past-life experiences, where I grew up, what I have been taught to believe, who my parents are, and what culture I live in will all determine the experience of the soul, and therefore, my future. A quick trip around the world will give us a picture of how many lifestyles exist and how many possible ways there are to experience life. Once we recognize who we are, then we can choose who we want to become.

If your life is happy, joyous, and free and those around you are happy, joyous, and free, then maybe no change is necessary. However, if your life is filled with fear, anger, revenge, jealousy, and loneliness, you have two choices. One, you can continue living in unhappiness, or two, you can make a solid commitment to change your life. If you take the second choice and decide to commit to change, then you must dedicate your life to learning and experiencing whatever it takes to change. I guarantee it won't be easy, and you may go through a lot of pain and disappointment. But if you stay with your plan, you will change. The suffering you have experienced will gradually go away and no longer affect you. I have worked my AA and personal growth program for over thirty-five years, and the rewards are staggering. Yes, I still have unhappy times, but I know how to work through the unhappy times quickly and return to my happy, joyous, and free life. One suggestion I have is to find someone—a teacher, a friend, or a group to practice with.

In my life, I had the opportunity to participate in several self-help personal growth programs. Generally, someone would suggest a program that they thought might be helpful to me. The strange thing was that the program was just what I needed at the exact moment I needed it. Did I always jump in and take every program? I sometimes had to think about what the program would do for me. On several occasions, I was not able to see a reason for me to take the program. As time passed, I would relent and take the program. Every seminar advanced my education, enhanced my thinking, and slowly formulated and certified my beliefs.

I was on a quest to grow professionally. It had been several years since I had received my undergraduate degree. The world of business was changing. The idea of just in time production was being introduced. Quality control was becoming more important, and the business world culture was changing with more women entering leadership roles. I suddenly began to feel I needed more formal education. The voices in my head were telling me that the world was changing and it had been twenty years since I had received my undergraduate degree. I initially discounted the idea as a waste of time. I had lots of experience and training, so I passed it off. Just a week or so after I dropped the idea of more education, I was invited to a business lunch. To this day, I don't remember why I accepted the invitation. There were over 200 people at the lunch, and I did not know anyone, so I randomly picked a table and chair. At that time, I did not know how the Spirit World worked, but I was soon to find out. I introduced myself to the gentleman on my left. I thought I had been hit by lightning when he said he was the dean of the Colorado State University Graduate School of Business.

He shared with me all about the graduate program at CSU and asked me to consider enrolling. I was overwhelmed. Graduate school had not been any part of my life; I hadn't ever given it a thought.

I remember so clearly that while he was talking, I looked up at the ceiling for a brief moment and asked, "God, is this what you want me to do?" God provides us with choices. But we have free will and can accept or reject His suggestions or directions.

I thanked the gentleman for the information, and we exchanged business cards. I told him I was only a C student in college, and he said that didn't matter to him or the program. So, I told him I would think about his offer. A week later, the dean called me and asked if I thought about the program, as it would start in about three weeks. I said yes, but I told him I probably would not pass the entrance test due to my English deficiency. I think I fell out of my chair when he said he would waive the entrance exam. I was committed. No excuses. My last thought was wondering how I was going to pay the tuition. That was solved a week later when an old customer paid an old debt. A lot of things were going my way, and the graduate degree was one of the crown jewels in my life. No way could I have seen this happen to me without some divine intervention. Two years later, I received my executive master's in business administration degree. It was only then that I realized what I didn't know. I was street smart but not formally educated smart. The degree was going to change my life. I would be able to help people change their lives.

If you want a change in your life, know that nothing will change without teachers, therapists, mentors, and personal growth and self-help programs, to name a few. Programs will often suddenly appear when you are ready to experience them. Do not question why you should take them, just take whatever appears in front of you. The answer to "why" will become clear in time. We don't know what we don't know until we learn what we need to know. I guarantee that there is not an easy or simple path. I myself have looked and tried many simple paths with very little success. But these experiences are what refine one's soul. As long as we are searching, answers will come. And as long as we are learning, we are walking our path and fulfilling our mission.

CHAPTER 10

Once you have commitment, you need discipline
and hard work to get you there.

—HAILE GEBRSELASSIE

So far in the story, Sandy and I have been living our lives in a wonderful world of fun and pleasure, financed by our occupations. We'd had many experiences with the Spirit World, though we might not have known it. Sandy and I had been listening to the voices in our heads and experiencing fun situations from the inspiration of spontaneity: the opening celebration in Gunnison and the experience of riding as hobos on the train, for example. Things had been going very well, but could it continue? I am going to present to you two (of the many possible) ways of living a life, both of which I am familiar with and have lived.

The first way to live life is that I will listen to the *me* voice and my *soul* only. I will take control of my life and live life my way. My soul will gather information and experiences as it grows up, and upon reaching adulthood, it will venture into life, using the rules it has learned, mostly from its parents. As an adult, I will practice the rules of life that I have learned and/or the laws and rules that have proven to work or what I think will work. This is a life where I make decisions based on my experiences and what I have learned from my parents and other relationships. I assume that one plus two will always equal three. With this, I make the best choices I can to optimize my own personal outcome, and I hope my life will be happy, joyous, and free. As an example, I might think that if I become educated, I will attract a good job, or if I am successful, I will attract a good woman and have children I am proud of. Does this always work? Did Sandy and I ever look back to analyze what our parents taught us? In the beginning of our lives, we followed the paths set forth by our backgrounds and our life experiences, including the models our parents gave us.

Living this type of life may require sacrifices or compromises in our personal beliefs, values, or integrity. To prove we are right, we might sacrifice truth and virtue to win our arguments. If we are centered on our own personal growth and achievements, we may neglect others. The secret, I believe, is a balance between ourselves and the needs of others. Should our family's well-being come first, or should I focus on my own personal desires, education, and achievements? Should I choose a career based on what I learned in school or a career that I am familiar with—say construction? What about a career in parenting or relationships? I am not aware of a major university offering parenting and relationships courses. Yes, we do have psychology, therapy, or psychiatry, but do these programs solve the problem of finding a great relationship, or do they try and fix what is already broken? Sandy and I chose, without knowing it, the path of our parents. This was a no-brainer, and my parents did not know about other paths, so we did not have a choice. If we lived life successfully, we would survive. I am sure Sandy and I never looked at the anger, sadness, fear, and mistrust our parents had created for each other. You may ask, are there families and/or individuals who are happy, virtuous, truthful, and joyful? Yes, but from what I have learned in AA, they only represent 5 percent of the population.

People who are truly happy, joyous, and free are living in harmony with each other and nature. They are generally free from fear, distrust, anger, controlling others, and self-centeredness. They don't associate with people who are fearful all the time, are angry and distrustful, and lack truth, virtue, and beauty. Yes, I hear you say, there are people I know with different beliefs who associate with each other, and I know some too. Are these relationships fulfilling? Or is it the belief that this is what life demands and we have to endure it? Do we have to make sacrifices to be happy? Yes. I believe that we must be true to our beliefs whenever possible, or we will never be happy. However, to make others happy, we might have to temper our own beliefs. Sometimes we must put our beliefs aside for a moment or two, providing we don't bring harm to others. Remember, beliefs can be changed when we find out they are not working for us anymore. Please take a moment to inventory your beliefs and write about how they affect others. You may be surprised at what you find.

A second way of living requires me to call upon external forces to help guide me through life, what I call Guiding Spirits and/or God. In this way of living life, I am still controlled by my Soul Voice, but my *soul* listens to the Guiding Spirits for direction.

I am sure when the *soul* voice in your head says, "Do something," if you are listening, you may hear another voice say, "Let's think about this."

For example, I might want to buy a new car but soon realize I can't pay for it.

Of course, you might hear the soul say, "Rob a bank," but another voice might say, "Bad idea."

The soul, being in charge, makes the ultimate choice. So, who are these other voices? What are they, and where do they come from? Again, I am not sure, but my belief is that they are Guiding Spirits from the Spirit World, directed by God.

I am sure for some of you, what you just read is totally outrageous, or at best, a wild idea. In America, we generally don't believe, nor understand, the presence of spirits. However, in Japan, with a population of 122 million people, the Spirit World is a part of everyday life. Many Japanese people believe spirits reside in everything: cars, homes, trees, plants, and nearly all things. They recognize the spirits and thank them for the services they received and ask for continued good fortune. I have taken many trips to Japan, and I have learned that the Japanese people believe that many animate and inanimate things have spirits.

Have you thought of your house, car, or personal items as having spirits? Let's take a car, for example. If we keep it clean, maintain proper oil levels and lubricants, perform all the inspections, and drive it sensibly, it will always perform. We could say that the car spirit is happy. Well yes, you might say that that it is only common sense. In the Western world, we have explained it as proper or improper care of a machine to maintain its quality. But can this be explained in a different way? What if we let the oil level go below normal, fail to do regular maintenance, let the air in the tires go low, or just leave the car cluttered or dirty? Do things begin to go wrong? Have we made our car spirit unhappy, and it is punishing us? I don't have any knowledge of this being true, but think about it and watch how you might relate to your personal things if they had a spirit. I am quite sure that my attitude and behavior affect things around me, and maybe the spirits talk to each other. Is that possible? Yet, I have learned that not all spirits are easily pleased and are good. There are also bad or evil spirits that can interfere with our lives.

Sometimes, a simple purification can expel bad spirits and make our lives better. Purification is a part of many religions and cultures. Many Native Americans and shamans smudge by burning sage or other herbs to purify a space and often perform other purification ceremonies. There are cultures that chant spiritual doctrines to purify and cleanse. Some Chinese people follow Feng Shui rituals where space is "cleared" using incense, clapping, and bells. Even the Catholic religion recognizes purification and term it an "exorcism." In Japan, there are many purification rituals. I have been to Japan on New Year's Day and know that the Japanese recognize and acknowledge the good spirits at the beginning of each year as a type of purification. I have no idea why bad spirits come into our lives. Possibly they come to teach us something.

A few years back, our construction company was building a large and expensive chemical plant. From the beginning, the job was very chaotic. The people and subcontractors were not working together. There was one problem after another. I asked my wise old Japanese *kyudo* (archery) teacher what he thought. He said I probably had bad spirits on the site.

I asked him, "Can you help me?"

I was his friend and student, so he said yes. We arranged a Sunday morning for him to come to the job site. Upon his arrival, he immediately felt the presence of the bad spirits. He performed a purification, and the following Monday morning there was a complete and immediate change in the environment. Suddenly, the workers began working together, and the project moved forward with very few problems. I asked the workers if they could feel the change, and most said yes. This was my first direct experience with the Spirit World but not my last.

Looking back on Sandy's and my life so far, I believe we can see some influence of the spirits. However, having a belief in spirits is not a prerequisite to living a great life. There is also a strong belief that our lives are controlled by good luck or bad luck. I can subscribe to either belief. I don't know which is true. Believing in the Spirit World, for me, has been a lot more fun, and my Guiding Spirits have directed me to make better choices in life than I ever could have alone. With belief in luck, one is subjected to a fate out of one's control. However, believing in the Spirit World allows you to have the power to change your experience and work with the spirits for a better life.

CHAPTER 11

The wild grasses that grow along the riverbank will spring
back if they are trampled upon, but the delicate flower
of our love cannot survive such harshness.

—KANJURO SHIBATA

Not only are there spirits existing in objects and places, there is a group of spirits that each human soul is tied to during his/her life on Earth called Guiding Spirits. The Guiding Spirits come from the Spirit World and are teachers, coaches, advisers, and the spirits of wise men and women sent by God. They don't have free will and only communicate the rules of God. They only tell us what they know as truth from God. They may reside or communicate from inside our heads as guiding voices and advise the soul/spirit of each person. There are three basic Guiding Spirits.

THE DIVINE SPIRIT (OUR CONSCIENCE)

There is a belief that says, "Man is the child of God, and that God is enshrined in man."

This means essentially that humans are charged with a mission by God agreed upon by our soul/spirits and, when born into this world, we are given a part of God's Spirit. This part of God is the Divine Spirit, which is pure awareness (or our consciousness). The Divine Spirit is impersonal and is lacking individual characteristics. Unlike the soul, the Divine Spirit doesn't evolve. It is the best part of one's self, the seat of one's utmost integrity. It acts like an impartial observer and is forever peaceful and serene. It is unmoved by our personal joys and sorrows. The Divine Spirit is like the light of the moon, which is a reflection of the light of the sun or pure divinity/God. Each borrows light from another source: the moon borrows light from the sun, and the Divine Spirit borrows light from God. The soul is gifted with this natural wisdom of the Divine Spirit and is inclined toward good. However, a soul can also become restrained by ignorance and dominated by selfish desires and reactive compulsions. This is a part of free will. The soul is a vehicle for embodied experiences. Yet, at its essence, a soul is a reflection of divinity. Our Divine Spirit, as an aspect of divinity existing beyond time and space, patiently waits for us to rediscover its eternal presence deep within our souls. The Divine Spirit has the ability to communicate directly with God.

THE GUARDIAN SPIRIT (KNOWN AS THE ANCESTOR SPIRIT)

The Guardian Spirit is a discarnate being living in the invisible spiritual world that is assigned to guide and protect a person living in the physical world. It is similar to a Western concept of a guardian angel. This spirit could be selected from one's individual ancestors, whose job is to accompany and watch over the soul/spirit until his or her physical death. The Guardian Spirit has the responsibility of encouraging the soul to behave in a virtuous manner and pointing it in a higher direction. The Guardian Spirit supports the soul's spiritual advancement. This spirit often communicates to us through symbolic dreams, creative inspiration, and through the silent voice of our subconscious.

Guardian Spirits can communicate with us through our dreams, or if we have a premonition that something is going to happen, that is the Guardian Spirit trying to tell us something. Dreams created by Guardian Spirits are often allegorical or metaphorical and may require specialized interpretation by others. I studied with a Jungian dream therapist. We studied my dreams for over a year, and I found my dreams were following the path of my life. As my life was full of obstacles, my dreams were also revealing these obstacles. For example, one dream showed me at a train station. For about two weeks, my dreams repeatedly showed me walking up and down the train platform. I was afraid to get on the train when it stopped.

My therapist said, "As often as you can remember during the day, repeat the phrase: 'I am not afraid to get on the train.'"

Finally, I had the dream of me getting on the train. I believe this correlated with my Guardian Spirit's encouragement to move forward in my waking life. Life is full of opportunities, yet many of these opportunities are fearful or just plain scary. Sometimes a little support and love is all you need to make the most out of life.

Because of their higher vantage point from the Spirit World, Guardian Spirits can see what the future will bring and can provide protection and advice to us. They also contribute to our good fortune by various, seemingly magical, means. The effectiveness of this guidance depends on our inner purity, as well as our receptivity to the higher influence.

THE INSTINCTIVE SPIRIT (OUR ANIMAL INSTINCTS)

To protect and ensure that humans continue to reproduce and grow, we are given basic instincts. We are permitted what I call "fleshy desires," a desire for contact with flesh, an attraction that leads to intercourse. Why we have fleshy desires, I don't know. My best guess is that it is a carryover from prehistoric times when man may have been more animal and had a drive to make sure the human species survived. Thus, we have an instinctive desire to mate and produce offspring, feed and nourish ourselves and our family, and to protect ourselves from harm. In the human world, as in the animal world, we position ourselves to attract a mate with the whole purpose of either producing a child or deriving pleasure. The process can be beautiful and loving or brutal and uncaring. There is an aspect of pure desire, love, or pleasure that can be derived from sexual intercourse, but the basic desire is controlled by the Instinctive Spirit. The Instinctive Spirit is responsible for our physical body, activating its various physiological processes, our automatic reflexes, and our sensory perceptions. It is also responsible for our respiratory, digestive, circulatory, and nervous systems. In the human and animal world, we are driven by the instincts relating to food, sex, and territorial defense.

What separates humans from the animal world is the human ability to create and appreciate such things as complex languages, music, science, mathematics, art, and poetry, among many other things. Animals have a well-developed sensory perception but limited mental capacity. The same is true for the Instinctive Spirit. The Instinctive Spirit tends to be selfish and has little sense of ethics or morality. The Instinctive Spirit can operate in a manner similar to the Freudian concept of the Id, which is driven by lust and aggression and may be compulsive and automatic. It may gravitate toward the lower emotions of hate, anger, resentment, jealousy, depression, sorrow, and fear and languish in lust, ambition, and greed. This can sometimes create a paradox for human beings, as we are driven by these desires but are often mitigated by certain logical and moral inclinations (influenced by the Guardian and Divine Spirits).

Despite its lower tendencies, the Instinctive Spirit performs a useful and needed function: the survival of the human body. It can provide healthy boundaries, the aggressiveness necessary to defend ourselves from harm and to acquire what we need. Without these instincts, we would not have the motivation to eat, procreate, or succeed in the world. The Instinctive Spirit is not an enemy to be attacked or conquered, nor is it an evil to be annihilated. Rather, it needs to be tempered by our conscience, which is, in its purest form, the Divine Spirit. Sometimes the Instinctive Spirit will respond best to compassionate understanding rather than judgmental repression, but other times, if it is too wild and impulsive, then it must be kept on a tight leash. The Instinctive Spirit is an important part of our lives, but in order to guarantee true happiness, our main interest and concern should be the spiritual development of our soul/spirit. As our Instinctive Spirit can urge us toward vice, our Guardian Spirit urges us toward virtue. Therefore, what is necessary is to help increase the power of the Divine Spirit, which is the way to conquer the fundamental cause of these vices.

In order to see how these three spirits have a unique influence on our lives, let's examine the topic of "perfection." When the Instinctive Spirit is controlling one's life, perfection can manifest as self-judgment and demanding impossible things from others. Perfection can also be a reaction to fear. Will people like what I create, or will people criticize me for not creating something correctly? Are there consequences if the person I am trying to control does the wrong thing or responds incorrectly? However, when the idea of perfection is under the influence of the Guardian Spirit, it can be a guide for one to find what is perfect for their own unique path. In this case, the notion of perfection will lead us to find a teacher or to be the best that we can be in any given situation. When the idea of perfection is harnessed by the Divine Spirit, it creates beauty, harmony, joy, and happiness. It can manifest as a work of art, a flower arrangement, a musical masterpiece, a beautiful home, or even a nice dinner. A harmonious combination of all three Guiding Spirits could be a healthy amount of self-judgment so that we can be the best that we can be and create beauty in the world. In any situation and with any idea, there are always multiple manifestations possible.

Knowledge about these three Guiding Spirits is the key to finding the right balance of them in your life. In any given situation, there is always a force for self-preservation, one of guidance, and one of utmost virtue and divinity. It is your choice where your emphasis is placed and what influences you want guiding and impacting your life.

CHAPTER 12

The purpose of life is to live it, to taste experience to the utmost, to reach out eagerly and without fear for newer and richer experience.

—ELEANOR ROOSEVELT

1964–1974

Up to this point in our story, Sandy and I have been simply reacting to challenges put in front of us: a marriage, a new baby, and a new home to organize. Having completed the basics, we were ready to start living our lives.

When the baby was born, Sandy was fortunate to connect with a pediatrician at her hospital. The pediatrician would become a part of our lives for the next several years.

One of the first things she said was, "The baby comes to live with you, Sandy and Gordon; you must not live the baby's life." She also said the baby will always adapt to your lives, within reason. "Live your life the way you want to, and the baby will join you," she said.

Thinking about this, we had the opportunity to go to a party at the house of one of the members of our railroad club. The weather was cold and a bit snowy, but we bundled up Rich and off to the party we went. Our pediatrician was right. Having fed and changed Rich's diapers, he slept like a baby should, in the guest bedroom. We enjoyed the party and returned home around two in the morning. This would be a common occurrence until the boys were able to have babysitters. It was a time when Sandy and I began drinking more. For those of you who have drunk in excess, a strange phenomenon happens. As we drink more, the body adapts and, without realizing it, our bodies will demand more liquor to attain the high we want. Why this happens, I don't know. Another strange phenomenon is that the body will continue to change even though we stop drinking. So, if I needed three beers to get high when I stopped drinking, I would need four or five to gain the old high if I started drinking again.

Sandy and I talked a lot about working. Much of her life would be working at the hospital. She loved helping people recover from their illness or surgery, and she was very good at it. Sandy would say that if a patient was to recover quickly, they would need love and caring. Yes, the drugs helped, but a loving and caring nurse and family could do wonders. I knew the hospital and nursing would always be a part of Sandy's life, next to me and our children, who always came first. Sandy and I talked a lot about sharing the responsibilities of the household and raising the children. Sandy liked working the three-to-eleven shifts at the hospital and enjoyed being with the boys in the morning, then taking care of the house with a few moments of quiet time.

We decided to split the responsibility of child care: she would take the morning shift, and I would take the evening shift. The hospital that she worked at had a nursery. She would often take the boys to work with her, and I would pick them up after I finished work. This arrangement allowed Sandy and me to have dinner together several times a week at the hospital cafeteria. I learned a lot about babies, and I practiced on Rich, so when Don came along, it was easy. They would go to bed around seven thirty, allowing me personal time in the evening. The boys soon learned that there was no negotiation about bedtime. They soon learned that Sandy and I were in charge and no amount of crying, fussing, or acting out would change who was boss, and bedtime was not negotiable. I also believe children should have their own bedrooms. This encourages independence, and Mom and Dad are free to spend time together without disturbing the baby.

Since a nurse doesn't have regular days to work, I would often take care of the boys all weekend when Sandy had to work. We were also lucky to have my parents nearby, and they would babysit when I had evening meetings or other engagements.

Sandy and I always enjoyed doing things together, although we sometimes disagreed on what we should do. We both had common interests, and when time permitted, we would explore other activities. We both loved flying, although she never had an interest in learning to fly. She said she did not need to learn to fly, as I did a good job of taking care of the airplane and getting us to our destinations. I was proud she had such confidence in me, and I tried to never let her down. *Bonnie*, our airplane, never let us down either. There is a saying that, "When you fly an airplane, at some time you will make a stupid or bad decision and will make a deal with God to protect you and get you out of stupid mistakes and/or bad situations." God knows humans are not perfect.

Flying with the family was a common occurrence. The family would travel all over the United States and there was always the Saturday lunches at some local airport.

I remember a trip to New Orleans one weekend. Sandy and I loved New Orleans blue point oysters and the fine dining. There was a restaurant, I think called Acme Oyster House, where we would sit at the oyster bar and eat a dozen or more oysters at a time and wash them down with Sazerac, a New Orleans signature bourbon drink (named because of the Sazerac de Forge et Fils brand of cognac brandy that was its original main ingredient). We would enjoy several Sazerac cocktails and many oysters.

The weather was good flying down but turned a bit cloudy on our way back home. Sandy wanted to see New Orleans and the Mississippi River from the air. On the way home, it was early afternoon when we finally headed to Lakefront Airport. We loaded *Bonnie* for the trip home.

I called New Orleans Ground Control for takeoff instructions.

"New Orleans Ground Control bonanza 11ED at the terminal, requesting taxi instructions to active runway, I have current weather, over." (11ED was our airplane call sign.)

"Bonanza 11ED, New Orleans Ground, you are cleared to Runway Twenty-Seven and hold."

Ground Control also gave us current winds, barometric pressure, altitude, transponder code for identification, and radio frequencies we would need. I acknowledged the transmissions and taxied to Runway Twenty-Seven. Once at Runway Twenty-Seven , Sandy read off the takeoff checklist. We checked the engine and all related interments and fight controls. All were in the green.

"Checklist complete," Sandy said, and so I called New Orleans Tower.

"New Orleans Tower, Bonanza 11ED, Runway Twenty-Seven ready for takeoff; we request a left turn over the city and then north up the Mississippi River."

"11ED is cleared for takeoff, left turn and Mississippi River departure approved. Have a good flight," the tower replied.

"11ED cleared for takeoff, thank you," I said.

We headed down the runway with full power and very quickly we lifted off.

"Gear up," I said. Sandy raised the gear up switch.

After takeoff, we turned south until we came to the city. We could see Bourbon Street and all the buildings, even the trolley. We reached the river, which was dotted with towboats and several large ships. We saw a tugboat pushing twenty or so barges up the river. We followed the river and soon turned north. The clouds were slowly getting lower, and I knew we would soon be in trouble, so we headed up and began flying instrument flight rules (IFR) instruments. Well, my thought was to get on top of the clouds and find clear weather, but that was not to be. I knew I was not on an airway, but nevertheless, I could have been in violation of some FAA flight rules.

Sandy smiled at me and said, "Guess we will need an IFR flight plan."

"Yup," I said.

I pulled out our flight maps and plotted a course. I turned to Sandy. "You know, flying in the clouds and not knowing if anyone else might be there is a little disconcerting," I said.

She again smiled and said, "Ask God for a little clear weather; he usually listens to you."

"Good idea," I said.

So, with a moment of embarrassment, I looked up, and I said, "God, could you give Sandy and me a little clear weather while I get my IFR flight plan?"

Yes, the weather cleared for about ten minutes, and I called New Orleans Center to get my IFR flight plan. Sandy grabbed two notebooks so we could write down our clearance. Working together, we knew we would get the clearance correct and not miss anything.

"New Orleans Center, this is Bonanza 11ED," I said.

"Bonanza 11ED, New Orleans Center."

"New Orleans Center, Bonanza 11ED is forty miles north of New Orleans over the Mississippi, squawking 1200. Would like to file an IFR flight plan to Kansas City, Missouri. I have current weather," I said.

I gave the controller our exact location, and since we did not have enough fuel to get to Denver, we would need to stop en route.

"11ED go ahead," New Orleans Center said.

"This is 11ED, based at Jefferson County Airport, Denver, Colorado," I said. "We are a V tailed Bonanza 35. Requesting direct to

Kansas City Airport at 8,000 feet. Air speed 130 knots. Estimated time: four hours, thirty minutes. We have six hours thirty minutes of fuel on board. There are two souls on board. Aircraft is blue and white. Pilot's name: Gordon Calahan, Lakewood, CO, phone number—over," I said.

"Stand by, 11ED."

A moment or two later, New Orleans Center called back and gave us our IFR flight plan as we had requested, along with radio frequencies we would need to talk to other centers and a new squawk number. A squawk number is four digits long and is transmitted continuously to air centers. As we flew to Kansas City, it was used to identify our airplane and its location. For identification, Sandy had copied the plan, and so had I. We compared notes, and they were alike. Can't beat a good copilot, and she was sexy too. The clouds came back, and we flew IFR all the way to Kansas City.

I know you, the reader, might ask why didn't I ask God for clear weather all the way to Denver? The answer is simple: all I needed was ten minutes, ten minutes to stay legal; the rest I could handle. As an instrument pilot, I was qualified to fly the plane in instrument weather without an autopilot. But the autopilot allowed me to engage with Sandy. These were wonderful times. Generally, we talked about our trip and where we might go on our next trip, or what was on for next week's activities, or how the kids were doing. Sometimes, we liked to sit quietly and just hold hands, and I guess meditate. My job was to monitor the airplane instruments and make sure the autopilot was doing its job.

On the way to Kansas City, we were both relaxed and very content. We climbed to our cruising altitude, turned on the autopilot, and sat back to enjoy the smooth flight, although all we could see were clouds. It was going to be a long flight. I had just reached down in my flight bag for the Kansas City approach plate. As I turned toward Sandy, I noticed she had just unbuttoned four of her five buttons on her shirt. We both smiled and gave each other a big long kiss. Getting "all natural" in the cockpit in *Bonnie* was easy, but making love in a small cockpit can require a little imagination. We figured it out.

Sometime later, I said to Sandy, "God sure provides us with a wonderful life."

She kissed me and said, "I wholeheartedly agree."

The weather cleared before we reached Kansas City. We landed, fueled, had a big lunch, and then it was off to home.

Over the next few years, Sandy and I would fly all over the US. We made five trips to Boston and New York to see her parents. I was a Mason and belonged to the Shriners and was a member of the Shrine Air Patrol along with my father. As a group, we would fly to different cities over a weekend, just for fun. Sandy and I enjoyed taking a Saturday to fly somewhere locally for lunch, maybe Aspen, Cheyenne, Wyoming, or Colorado Springs. On the way, we would buzz the antelope in Wyoming, and sometimes we would look for a train and make a bombing run like the fighter planes did in World War II. Weather and wind permitting, we would fly the mountains and valleys. Often, we would fly down a valley, looking for elk, deer, or mountain sheep.

Bonnie was an intricate part of the Calahan family, sometimes acting like a family pet, always wanting to be involved in the family adventures. She would become the magic carpet that would fly the Calahan's to exciting and exotic places.

In time, Sandy and I thought it might be fun to learn to parachute. This was something that we both talked about and agreed that there was some risk, but it was small. So, it was on a Saturday afternoon that we flew *Bonnie* to an airport where there was a jump school. We talked to the instructor and made arrangements to attend a parachute jumping class. The class lasted several weekends, and we learned all about jumping out of a perfectly good airplane. It was near the end of the last class that we were practicing the use of our reserve parachute in case the main chute failed. I remember the instructor saying that if the main chute failed, the first thing was to release it and then pull the ripcord on the reserve. When Sandy tried what we called the "cut away," she became confused. At that very moment, the instructor said, "Sandy, if this had been for real, you probably would have died."

*As the family grew older, Gordon and Sandy's sons
Don and Richard would become pilots. Don would
lose interest in flying, but Richard loved flying and
would become a corporate jet pilot.*

I saw for the first time; Sandy was scared and confused.. I believe these are the times God or our spirits tell us we have gone far enough and it is not necessary to go any further.

She looked at me and said, "I think I have met my limits, but you must go on."

I knew at that moment I had married a one-of-a-kind woman. She never jumped, but she would ride up in the jump plane and watch me jump. She always went to the jump zone with me to be with our jump friends. Our boys always went too. Saturday night would find all the jumpers and family partying, another time of hard drinking.

Sandy's love for flying brought us closer together, but this was not the case with my parents. My mother hated the airplane, for what reason, I am not sure. And so, my father did most of his flying by himself. It was sad and led to a lot of arguments between them. My mother's hatred may have been because she did not trust dad's flying ability or that he spent too much money on the airplane that could have gone to other places, although she had everything she wanted. Or maybe it was jealousy. Flying was something she could not control, and therefore, she would not accept it and wanted Dad to stop. He never did.

I believe the glue that keeps a marriage together and loving is trust. However, trust must be earned and always reinforced every day. It is like expressing love; a man or woman in a relationship must tell his significant other that he or she loves her or him and mean it, every day. If you men don't believe this, ask any woman. I heard a story about a man who came home from work one day after several years of marriage. His wife asked him if he still loved her.

He answered by simply saying, "When we were married, I said then that I love you, and if that ever changes, I will let you know."

This is not a way to a happy marriage.

CHAPTER 13

A true friend never gets in your way unless
you happen to be going down.

—ARNOLD H. GLASOW

Sandy and I had a lot of friends. Some were close, and others were now and then. Of the closest were Brian and his wife, Carol. We would spend many dinners and outings together, and as time went by, Brian, Sandy, and I became very close.

There is a great love story called *Camelot: The Story of King Arthur, Queen Guinevere, and Sir Lancelot.* King Arthur wanted to create a group of knights that would go out into the world and right wrongs and create truth and virtue. Sir Lancelot came from France to be a part of the group. Sir Lancelot became the bravest and the best of all knights. He soon became the king's favorite. He also attracted the interest of Queen Guinevere, who found him quite delightful. As time went on, the three became very involved—just how involved varies as to what books you read about Camelot, but generally there was a strong love between the three. In some versions, Guinevere and Lancelot were lovers, and Arthur was left out. Much of the story was written 500 hundred years after Arthur's death, and there are some historians who believe Arthur never existed. Others believe Arthur did exist and created the roundtable and a form of Heaven on Earth. Yet, whether Arthur was real or not is not important. His story lives on after 1,500 years as a story of love, chivalry, truth, and virtue. He created a happy kingdom, which only ended when greed and power intervened and divided the kingdom, resulting in a war. The King Arthur story doesn't have a happy ending. Arthur dies in battle with a broken heart, Guinevere retreats to a convent, and Lancelot dies a poor man. However, some people believe Arthur will someday return to Earth when mankind approaches self-annihilation and bring back Camelot.

One question that King Arthur's story poses is: Is it possible for three people to love each other without jealousy, fear, or distrust? I am sure the therapists today could provide books full of answers as to why it would not work. I like to look at it this way: growing up, many of us never received the love we fully needed. How much love is necessary? I don't believe there is an answer because we are all different. Some people don't even know they are suffering from a lack of love, or they are afraid to risk the love they have in order to find more love or a better life. They can't trust others who are willing to give love unconditionally. Some people have a hard time accepting love from others for fear of being controlled or manipulated. I believe that real love is always unconditional and should not be used to gain power or control over other people. I heard a story about a baby, deprived of love and only fed food and milk, who did not survive. Is this true about adults? I don't know. In the land of Camelot, there must have been a lot of love, trust, balance, openness, and a lack of jealousy between Arthur, Guinevere, and Lancelot. However, in a story, we can make anything happen. But in real life, is this possible?

Brian, Sandy, and I had a strong love for each other. We did something that most people would say couldn't be done. Our love was unconditional. Brian knew he would never leave his wife, whom he loved, but he was a big part of our lives. Getting together was not a regular occurrence though: occasional dinners, parties, and a couple of weekend trips. It was a time for sharing and supporting each other. Liquor was always involved. For those who have experienced unconditional love, you will understand. Was it a good thing? Did it interfere with our lives and the life of Brian's wife? I don't know, but I am sure it had an impact. I am sure some of you are asking and would like to know: Was sex involved? On a couple of occasions, yes, but it was not a common thing. A little too much alcohol, and things would get out of control. Sometimes we pushed too hard and too far to see what the experience would bring and what pleasure we could enjoy. Sometimes we let our Instinctual Spirits take control, and it got out of hand, but we all got some extra love that we each hungered for.

In today's world, we all have our personal beliefs about love. I am sure we all see this love affair a little differently. Maybe the three of us were influenced by the strong women's liberation movement that was going on at that time. Sandy was a strong woman and wanted freedom to do what she wanted, the freedom to experience being a full woman. I was totally confused, but I had to admit, it was intriguing. All of this was new to me, and I did not have any definitive answers about the modern woman, and twenty-five years later, it can still be confusing. Yet, I supported her quest to explore the life of a modern

85

woman and the freedom to live her own life, the freedom to make choices. She worked hard to intertwine the modern woman into our lives so that we all got what we needed. And one thing is certain: we all needed a lot of love.

CHAPTER 14

Be faithful in small things because it is in them your strength lies.

—MOTHER TERESA

December 1981–May 1982

B en and Ann had been occasional friends in the beginning of our married life. But it was at a friend's party one evening that Ben, Ann, Sandy, and I found ourselves in a conversation about fun things to do. All of us were very active and always looking for new adventures to partake in.

"Have you ever been to a nudist ranch or club?" Ben asked.

"No," Sandy said. "That is way outside of our box, but tell us more."

She then asked if Ben or Ann had been. To Sandy's surprise, Ben said that they were members of the Mountain Air Ranch just west of Denver. I knew that Sandy was slowly becoming very interested.

Sandy loved to be in the outdoors, especially in the mountains. And she often would sunbathe topless in our backyard at home. The sun was Sandy's main source of energy. In the winter months, she would long for the hot, sunny days of summer.

Later in the conversation, Sandy said with great interest and enthusiasm, "Tell me more!"

Ben explained that the Ranch was family friendly and that sexual activities or expressions were not tolerated and would result in dismissal from the Ranch.

"Does everyone go naked or do some people wear clothes?" Sandy asked.

Ben answered that cloths were not allowed. Sandy then wanted to know more.

"What do people do? Just lie around naked?"

Ann was quick to answer. "There are many things to do. There is a swimming pool, volleyball courts, and a hot tub. There is a very nice lodge with a snack bar, restrooms, and a large open area with a fireplace where people can gather in the winter."

Ann also explained that there were parties with live bands for entertainment and dancing. It was a place to meet other people with like-minded interests. After Ann finished, Ben asked, "Would you like to go up with us sometime?"

I had been quiet during the conversation, as I was probably distracted with visions of beautiful women and muscular men laying around the pool and grounds.

Sandy turned to me and with a big smile said, "I would like to go with Ben and Ann to the Ranch." I sensed apprehension and a small bit of fear in Sandy's voice. This was something totally foreign to us.

Without thinking, I immediately said, "Sure, that sounds like fun. When can we go?"

Ben answered, "We are going next Saturday night to the annual New Year's Eve dance. Would you like to join us?"

Without a moment's hesitation Sandy said, "Yes, we would love to go."

The excitement of a new adventure replaced the apprehension and fear.

And so, the life of a nudist began. It would be a large part of our lives for the next several years.

Sandy was excited, but the apprehension had returned. All week long she was a bit edgy, but she said she was very much looking forward to the weekend at Mountain Air Ranch. Ben and Ann arrived late Saturday afternoon to pick us up, and we were ready. The drive was less than an hour, and the weather was perfect, clear skies and not too cold for December. We drove southwest of Denver to South Deer Creek Canyon Road, a road that snakes up into the mountains, until we found Mica Mine Gulch Road, which led to the Ranch. Mica Mine Gulch Road was a poorly maintained road, and I began to wonder what we had gotten into.

Surviving the bumps, ruts, and packed snow, we finally came to the Ranch gate house, where we all signed in. We then drove less than a mile to the main facilities. It was just as Ben had described it. The pool was large, and the clubhouse overlooked the pool. Ben parked and looked back at Sandy and me. Overcoming any thoughts of turning back, we looked at each other and ventured on.

"Time to join the crowd," Ben said.

He and Ann started for the clubhouse. Sandy looked at me and, with that big look of apprehension, we joined Ben and Ann. It had become colder, and all thoughts of a nudist camp with the sun shining down and people lying around the pool disappeared. And this was going to be a nude dance? My mind couldn't quite comprehend people dancing nude, but that would change momentarily. I somehow thought it would be fun.

Entering the lodge, we were confronted with a small undressing room. There was wood paneling on the walls, several wood benches, and a row of clothes hooks to hang our clothes. Several people were in various stages of undress.

Sandy looked at me as if to say, "What do we do now?"

I gave her the look back that said, "Go with the flow and see what happens."

We made it through the transition, and soon, we were in the main lounge. A band was setting up, and there were several people seated and drinking. We followed Ben to a table where several friends waited, and we sat down. We had brought our own beer, and I reached into the cooler, grabbed four beers, and opened them. There would be many more.

Sandy and I were overwhelmed, curious, and excited. I reached over and grabbed Sandy's hand and squeezed it gently.

She turned and smiled, and we both exchanged that look of, "I love you and this is going to be fun."

After a little while, the band began to play. Sandy and I watched for several long moments and finally joined the other dancers already on the dance floor. Sandy had worn a pair of white snow boots about a foot high, decorated with fur around the tops. It was the cutest thing I ever saw, reminiscent of a dancing snow bunny.

There was something magical about two naked bodies dancing and touching each other without the restriction of clothes. Later, Sandy said that it was indescribable and she had never experienced such closeness. We danced with Ben and Ann and several other people, but we both agreed later that we really just wanted to be with each other.

The drive back to Denver was very peaceful. Sandy nestled into my arms, and we both agreed we'd had a wonderful time.

"I think something was missing though," Sandy said.

"What?" I asked.

"Dress up," she said. "I miss wearing the beautiful dresses you and I bought."

"Yes," I said.

"You remember how much fun we had picking them out?" Sandy asked. "You sat for an hour while I tried on one after another until we both agreed on two dresses. You were so patient with me."

"Every dress you tried on looked great," I said.

"Next year for New Year's Eve, I would like to dress up and go to a nice restaurant for dinner," Sandy said.

I agreed. After a few quiet moments, she asked, "Are we going to join the Ranch?"

I told her we could if she would like to. We did. We added it to the list of our adventures: train hobos and nudists.

The warm weather of spring finally came, and for the next few weeks, Sandy and I would head to the Ranch often. We had finally adjusted to ranch life and the love of being in the mountains "all natural." The pool had opened in May, and nature's love began coming out of hibernation. There were many old members and a few new members of all ages enjoying the beautiful surroundings.

One day, Sandy and I had arrived late in the afternoon. The pool was crowded, but we were able to find a couple of lounge chairs and settle in. We had a cooler full of beer and were resting peacefully when a couple, maybe ten years younger, walked past. They stopped and introduced themselves as Nancy and Dave. Nancy, an auburn-haired woman, was smiling pleasantly, and we all talked for only a moment. I later thought that I had a strange feeling about Nancy. It was as if Nancy's spirits and my spirits were checking each other out, but I let the feeling pass and would not remember the experience until many years later.

Chapter 15

*Every day for a week, do something new, something you have never
done before. I will bet in one week's time, your life will change.*

—Tom Willhite

September 1982

The summer went by quickly at the Ranch. The Labor Day dance
was about a week away, and Sandy and I decided to try another
dance. Sandy told me she loved the beauty of the Ranch and especially
lying in the sun and taking in the sun's energy. She also liked the people
because they seemed natural, and I agreed. It was fun to walk the trails
and enjoy the flowers, the plants, and if we were lucky, one of nature's
creatures. We would find a quiet spot and just sit, usually holding
hands and talking about the things we had done and the things we
were going to do in the next couple of weeks. The boys were growing

up and starting to go out on their own. Rich had joined the Colorado Air Guard, and Don would soon follow. Rich was in college, and Don would finish high school in two years. They were always a topic of discussion. We talked about their future. Both boys had worked for Calahan Construction during the summer and showed a real interest in joining the company after college, which they did. They would be the third generation of Calahans in the construction business.

Sandy and I had created a lot of trust in our marriage, and we each knew our jobs well. We seemed to know and understand each other's needs and goals. We assisted each other in achieving these needs and goals by listening to each other. There was no need to control each other. We both made mistakes, but that is life. We usually laughed it off or made a simple comment like, "That's funny." Controlling each other is only a way of saying, "I know better." This leads to anger, fear, low self-esteem, and resentment, which will harm any relationship.

On the day of the Labor Day dance, we had one of these discussions, then quietly walked back to the Ranch house and settled in for a little dinner before the dance. We were hungry, and we also knew there would be a lot of drinking, so we wanted a full stomach to be ready. I opened the door; Sandy went in, and I followed. I couldn't believe my eyes, and I was somewhat shocked, but there sitting on the dressing bench was General George and his wife, Kathy.

All I could say was, "Is that you, George?"

It was a dumb question because I knew it was. Sandy had not met George and Kathy and had that look of, "Who are these people?"

I introduced them to Sandy, and we agreed to have dinner together.

George had married Kathy, a longtime friend, twenty or so years ago. Kathy was twenty years younger than George. She was the same age as Sandy and me, which would have been about forty-two at the time. Both George and Kathy had taken care of themselves. Kathy was about five-foot-nine with brown hair and a slender body. George was also in good shape; however, he had put on a little weight since I had last seen him. But he still had the look of a brigadier general. His shoulders were strong, and he walked with a look of authority.

To say the least, the three of us were totally surprised to see each other.

We all exchanged the usual, "I never expected to see you here. What's been going on with you, and how have you been?"

We then ambled to the dining room, four naked friends. George and I talked about old times in the Air Force and how I had taken care of his plane. George told Sandy that I had been one of his best mechanics. We talked about the times we hung out together at the Denver Pilots Club. I added, for Sandy's benefit, that George had served in WWII and had flown fighter planes over Europe. Kathy said that they had met years ago and, over time, had fallen in love. It was the second marriage for both of them.

Sandy and I also updated George and Kathy on our past twenty years. We talked about our nearly grown children, the Ranch, and how much fun it was now and then.

The conversation turned to the present, and George said he had retired from the Air Force and was enjoying traveling and playing golf. He said he had bought a new boat about three years ago and was enjoying his love of boating. Sandy asked where the boat was, and he told us it was at Lake Powell and asked if we would like to join them sometime on the boat. Without hesitation, Sandy said, "Yes, when?"

That was Sandy. Something had connected us.

George told us that they were going to Lake Powell in three or four weeks, and they were planning to stay for two weeks.

Sandy looked at me and asked, "Can we go?"

I thought for a moment. A trip like this would be fun, and I had always liked George, so I said yes.

Sandy smiled and said, "I can get the time off in three weeks, how about you?"

I replied that it was workable. George remembered our Bonanza, *Bonnie*, and asked if we still had it. I replied yes, and he asked if I had been to Lake Powell. I said yes. There are two landing strips, Bullfrog Marina and Hales Crossing Marina, and I had landed on both.

"We will be at Bullfrog," George said. "Buzz the marina, and I will come pick you up at the airport."

We checked our calendars and arranged a time, weather permitting. Flying to Lake Powell required good clear weather, as Lake Powell is off the airways and there are no instrument approaches to the airport.

Sandy always connected with people. She had a way of knowing who she liked and who she was uncomfortable with. Today, I know she was an old soul, one who had made the journey to Earth many times. She was always grounded and had a calm way about her. She knew the mission or lesson she wanted to learn while here on Earth. This would be important, as George, Kathy, Sandy, and I made an instant connection.

Three weeks went by fast, and the day of departure finally arrived. It was early in the morning when we drove to the airport. There was a slight bit of tension in the air, as flying and spending time with new/old friends was always unpredictable. However, planning for a trip in *Bonnie* required a lot of preparation, which occupied our minds: checking the weather conditions, filing a flight plan, and making sure *Bonnie* was ready to go. The flight would take about two and a half hours, depending on the wind that generally would blow from the west. Sandy and I were getting excited, and as we pushed open the hangar doors, we saw *Bonnie* looking like the queen she was.

I could feel her spirit asking, "Where have you been and where are we going?"

"Hi, *Bonnie*, we are going to Lake Powell," I said out loud.

Sandy looked up and asked, "Are you talking to *Bonnie*?"

"Sure am," I said.

Sandy just smiled.

With clearance to go, we turned onto the runway. We were soon at full power and lifting off, gear up—"Climb, *Bonnie*, climb, we have some high mountains to go over!"

Heading west out of Denver are the Rocky Mountains, an impressive range. Having flown over them many times, I headed to the low point, Corona Pass, where sixty years before trains would cross the Rockies. We reached our cruising altitude of 14,500 feet. We were on oxygen until we could descend to a lower altitude. We crossed over Winter Park Ski Resort and the town of Kremmling, headwater of the great Colorado River. Next came Glenwood Canyon, the towns of Glenwood, Grand Junction, and Moab, Utah. I knew we were getting close to Lake Powell.

"I see it," Sandy said excitedly, "the north shore of the lake."

Moments later, we were over the lake. George had said, "Buzz the marina; I will come pick you up," I descended over the lake and headed north toward the marina. Dropping low over the water, so George could see me, I buzzed the marina.

"They saw us," Sandy said. They were both waving.

We landed and were tying *Bonnie* down when a light green pickup truck with a forest service logo on the side door pulled up. A tall man dressed in the green uniform of a forest ranger walked up and introduced himself.

"Flying a little low?" he asked.

I knew I had been, but I hoped for the best.

"It was hard to tell over the water," I commented.

A dumb answer. The ranger, of course, didn't believe me.

"I should write you a citation," he said. "But I did not see you; I only heard you."

After a little more conversation, concluding with, "Next time pay more attention," he left.

George drove up, got out of his car and with a big smile on his face, and said, "What was that about? Flying a little low maybe?"

"Not *that* low," I responded.

"Yeah," George said. "I actually thought I might have to open the front and back door on the boat so you could fly through."

"Yeah," Sandy said. "Cool, don't you think?"

We all started laughing.

CHAPTER 16

When we seek to discover the best in others, we
somehow bring out the best in ourselves.

—WILLIAM ARTHUR WARD

September 1982

A short drive later, George's boat came into view. Kathy was standing on the deck and walked up to meet us.

"Good flight?" she asked.

We said yes and all exchanged hugs. George's boat was white and about twenty-eight feet long. Carrying our gear, we climbed on board. George directed us to the forward cabin. To get to the forward cabin, we descended a ladder and found we were in the galley. The galley was small but contained all the things needed to cook meals. It had a propane stove, refrigerator, sink, and countertops. Also, there was a table and benches where we could eat if the weather was bad and we were forced below deck. Two steps forward past the head (restroom), and we were in the forward cabin. There were two bunks on each side of the room, curved to the bow, and a small storage closet. The room was just large enough for one person to change clothes.

After stowing our gear away, we went back on deck. Kathy showed us their cabin, which was amidship under the top deck with about four feet of head room. At the rear of the boat was a nice roomy and open deck with a removable table and built-in benches to sit on or lie on.

I heard Sandy say, "This is perfect, I know where I am going to hang out." I think she was really looking forward to the trip.

Back on the dock, George and I loaded the rest of our provisions. He then instructed us on boat emergency procedure and where the life jackets were stored. George then headed to the helm, and I went back to the dock. Soon, I heard the sound of the engine starting, and I knew we were about to cast off. I was standing near the front of the boat on the dock, ready to release the lines that were holding the boat to the dock. At his signal, I first released the bow line and then the stern line. I pushed the boat away from the dock and jumped on board. Lastly, I stowed the lines and fenders (the round rubber tubs that hold the boat away from the dock to prevent damage).

We were off, slowly heading to open water. I climbed to the helm, sat down next to George, and asked where he planned to spend the night. He said there was a quiet and secluded cove not far away where we would have complete privacy. This was important, as I soon learned. About a mile out from the marina, George slowed the boat, stood up, and took his clothes off. Kathy followed suit. I turned and looked back on the stern deck to see Sandy already natural and lying on one of the benches. I supposed that it was my turn, so I joined the others.

As I looked out over the lake, I could see the beautiful sandstone mountains, which had been eroded by the wind and the occasional rainstorms. The colors were breathtaking: light tan, brown, red, and in some cases, a combination of all three. The sky was a deep blue with a scattering of white fluffy clouds. There was not a tree or bush to be seen. For the first time in my life, I thought God has created all this beauty and not hidden or covered any of it. I also thought of how this could equate to the human body, if we were open to it. Over the past hundred years, we have slowly shed our clothes to the point that now only a tiny bikini is needed in public. I know that clothes make a statement, and that is also wonderful. But here were four people, exposed all natural, soon to join the landscape and blend in as their forefathers did 100,000 years ago. What could be more beautiful?

I was shaken out of my daydream by the engine going idle and George calling me to man the lines. We had reached our cove for the night. I secured the bow line to the boat and waited as the boat slowly approached the shore. The sound of the bow siding on the sand meant, "Jump!" I did, and on the shore, I located a large rock to secure the bow line to. George was standing on the stern with a line in each hand attached to each side of the boat. He tossed each line so I could attach them and keep the boat perpendicular to the beach. I looked up to see we were surrounded on three sides by gently climbing cliffs.

It was late afternoon, and the sun was beginning to set. It was time to do our final chores and prepare for dinner. Sandy and Kathy were in the galley starting dinner.

I called, "Do you girls need any help?"

Earlier in the day, I had asked Sandy and Kathy what they would like for me to call them when addressing them both? They both said, "girls" because it made them feel young.

On George's boat we all agreed that the girls would work in the galley preparing meals and handling cleanup. We boys would handle the rest of the chores, which included bartending, provisioning, boat maintenance, fueling and piloting the boat, head cleaning (toilets), and any other job that had to be done.

George headed to the bar and soon had a pitcher of martinis and a bottle of wine for dinner. Shortly after, the girls appeared carrying plates with dinner, consisting of broiled salmon, rice, carrots, and a dinner salad. These were impressive women. When dinner finished, we cleaned up and tidied the boat. We relaxed, finished the wine, and realized it had been a long day and we were ready for bed. Sandy and I headed forward to our cabin, and George and Kathy went to their cabin. It had been a wonderful day.

The forward cabin, as I mentioned, was very small. Sandy went in first, and I followed and closed the door. Sandy turned and wrapped her arms around me, and we kissed for a long time. Being natural, without clothes, I could feel Sandy's warm and sensuous body and her soft breasts against me. We both knew that what was coming next was fueled by our Instinctive Spirits, who were in full gear.

Later, lying together, I said, "You know, you are more beautiful today than you were when we first met."

She smiled, and I said, "We are so fortunate that life has given us many wonderful things and exciting experiences with many outstanding friends."

She paused and added, "Yes, I love George and Kathy. George is so powerful, yet so gentle and caring. He really loves Kathy a lot. It is a real joy to be with them. I also love how comfortably we all four work together."

With that, we were soon fast asleep.

In the morning, the smell of coffee drifting into our cabin slowly woke us up.

Sandy looked over at me and softly said, "That smells wonderful."

We got up and walked to the galley. We picked up coffee and went up to the aft deck, where George and Kathy were sitting. We all had big smiles on our faces, and we exchanged the usual: "How did you sleep? Was the bunk comfortable?"

The conversation then turned to the weather and the beautiful, yet rugged, landscape and finally to what was for breakfast, which was not a priority yet. When on Lake Powell, nothing moves very fast. It is perfect to relax, read a good book, swim, enjoy the sun, and share with good friends. For the next five days, I vowed to comply.

After breakfast, we decided to go to Escalante Canyon. Escalante Canyon is south of Bullfrog Marina and is one of the most beautiful canyons at Lake Powell. We arrived around three in the afternoon and slowly proceeded into the canyon. The canyon is narrow in most places and only wide enough for two boats to pass. Sandy and Kathy climbed onto the front bow and leaned back to enjoy the trip. The canyon walls are steep and high and every turn presented a new display of colors on the rocks. This had to be God's studio where He created a natural display of color and texture.

I heard Sandy say, "I see a face!"

"I see a buffalo," Kathy added.

And with a little imagination, each figure was visible in the rocks. The colors ranged from dark coffee to auburn and many shades of rosy red. For accent, there were lines of black, turning and swirling in all directions.

Approaching the end of the canyon, we could see an open inlet where there was just enough room to turn the boat around. We paused, silenced the engine, and for several minutes quietly enjoyed the surroundings. True beauty like this little inlet and Escalante Canyon do wonderful things to the mind. I truly believe God wants us to see and enjoy all His creations whenever possible and create our own beauty. We create beauty in the way we dress, and in our homes, and in the places we inhabit so that other people can enjoy infinite joy and happiness also.

Time was running short, and we had to find an inlet for the evening. Powering up, we headed back down the canyon. The sun was lower in the sky, and it was casting shadows on the rocks, which changed the colors. The return trip was a whole new show. Clearing the canyon, George said he knew of a cove that would be a little different, just minutes away. We turned into a small opening in the rock wall, and there it was: Shangri-La. Ahead we saw small trees, shrubs, and grass covering the shoreline. Somehow, in this vast desert, water had traveled underground and finally surfaced in this small cove, nourishing the plants and creating a small paradise. We tied up the boat and were partaking in our evening libations when I asked if anyone had heard the story of Shangri-La? The answer was no, and both Sandy and Kathy asked for the story.

CHAPTER 17

Love doesn't make the world go around.
Love is what makes the ride worthwhile.

—FRANKLIN P. JONES

September 1982

There is a story that originated in China about a fisherman. This fisherman would fish a river near his village every day. He would bring home fish for his family and other villagers. One morning, he was rowing downriver when he noticed a small cove that he had never noticed before. All the indications pointed to the perfect fishing spot, and he wondered why he hadn't seen it before. Changing course, he entered the cove, which was surrounded by lush trees and foliage. He was awed by the beauty. The fisherman was ready to start fishing when he noticed an opening in the rock wall. Curiosity distracted him from his fishing, and he jumped ashore to investigate what treasure he might find hidden in the opening. The opening turned into a short tunnel. Light from the other end of the tunnel illuminated his path. Emerging from the tunnel, he could see what he thought was an imaginary paradise. It was a remote exotic utopia, a faraway Heaven on Earth, beautiful and tranquil.

Before him was a path, twisting and turning down the mountain to a village. The village was named Shangri-La. He saw many people working together; all were happy, joyous, and free. They had learned to work together, to help each other, to create beauty, and most importantly, to make sure the beauty was maintained.

The fisherman was overwhelmed, and his only thought was, "These people have become enlightened. I must bring my family and the other villagers to see what I have found."

He returned home and told everyone who would listen the story of Shangri-La. Later, he returned to look for Shangri-La, only to find the opening and the village were gone. Sad and disappointed, he headed home. On his way home, he met an old and disheveled monk. The monk explained to him that the village of Shangri-La had ascended into Heaven. He said that the people of Shangri-La would watch over humanity and would return to Earth if needed.

I do wonder if Shangri-La and Camelot are similar stories from different parts of the world? One thing is certain, they both live in the hearts of many people. (If you are interested in learning more, there is a book and movie called *Lost Horizons* about Shangri-La.

After I told the story we all sat quietly for several moments, trying to comprehend such a story.

Then George broke the silence and asked, "Do you think we should start dinner?"

To Kathy and Sandy's surprise, I said, "Let us boys cook tonight.

Is spaghetti OK?"

They agreed and wished us luck.

Dinner turned out well, and we relaxed and enjoyed the magnificent cove that we had found. The sky was inky black, dotted with thousands of stars that were only visible with the total darkness.

"Look!" exclaimed Kathy.

A shooting star raced across the night sky, coming from somewhere and going to who knows where.

Then Sandy said, "We are so insignificant; yet, we are so important to our world."

It was George who then said, "The show is magnificent, and I have enjoyed another wonderful day, but I think I am ready to turn in."

He looked at Kathy, she smiled, and they both headed to their cabin.

Sandy and I relaxed and sipped the last of our wine. We were nearing the end of our stay on the lake, and I think Sandy wanted to enjoy every last minute possible.

The evening was turning cool, and Sandy said, "We need a blanket!"

"Yes," I said, and I went to our cabin to get one. I returned with the blanket and two pillows. I covered Sandy with the blanket, lay the pillows next to her head, and then wiggled in next to her. The blanket was just what we needed to say warm.

With the pillows under our heads, Sandy said, "Let's sleep here tonight."

"Sure, it's perfect," I replied.

Sandy and I were still wide awake, tired, but not ready to go to sleep.

Sandy was looking up at the stars when she said, "You and I have a wonderful life. We make each other's dreams come true. We support each other so we can each experience and live our own personal dreams, jobs, hobbies, or other endeavors. We balance our time carefully so we each have time for ourselves and each other, but the most important thing is trust. We are open about our needs and desires. Sometimes, I don't know why you need or want something, but that is not important, and you might feel the same about my needs or desires. What is important is walking the path to fulfillment. The path may be easy or hard, but together, we can accomplish anything."

I was in total agreement with what she said, and so all I did was listen.

"This was heavy stuff for an old cowboy," I often said.

One of the gifts a woman has is the ability to collect information, process the information, and implement what they have learned into a plan. I think they are able to do this by networking with other women. When Sandy and I are in agreement on a plan, she expects me to implement the plan, and she stands back, offering suggestions and guidance when I ask for it. The plan may not go as she envisioned it, but that is not important as long as the plan comes to fruition. Most rivers will flow to the ocean, no matter what the obstacles or the path.

Sandy relaxed, and for some unknown reason, I knew she had more to say, and she did.

"Gordon," she said, "George and I were talking about sex in a marriage."

If I had not been paying complete attention to her, I was now.

She said, "George and Kathy are extremely dedicated and committed to each other. George said he was able to provide for her in every way but one, and that is sex. He said that his age and a heart attack had cut him short. He reminded me that Kathy was twenty years younger and he felt that she was missing out on an important part of marriage: sexual pleasure. Kathy said that sex was not important, but George persisted and asked if she would be interested in spending a little time with you. She answered that she had a passing fancy but no romantic interest, but maybe a little time together would be fun."

I asked Sandy how she felt about Kathy and me. She replied that she was a woman the same age as Kathy and understood Kathy's feelings as her own.

"Kathy is a beautiful woman," I said, "and I like her as a friend, but you know I am committed to you."

Sandy smiled and said softly, "Life is complicated, and we don't always have the answers to every question." She looked at me and said, "It just feels right."

Sandy and I were connected by love, and that love was still strong after many years of marriage. The same could be said about George and Kathy. If we can go beyond jealousy and fear and trust our feelings, beautiful things can happen. I know there is a risk that things could go wrong, but life without risk can become boring and mundane. This may be acceptable to some people, but for those of us who ride in the heavens, we find great joy and happiness in loving, trusting, and committing.

So, it happened the next evening. We finished dinner, and we all felt a bit of sadness, as this would be our last night on the lake. The sun had set, but it was warm, and the world around us was very peaceful. George said that he felt like a walk and asked Sandy if she would join him. She said yes, George grabbed a lantern, and they went ashore. They were only visible for a moment, and then they disappeared into the darkness. I felt like I had just bid my best friend goodbye. I was looking into the darkness when a gentle hand grasped my hand and a warm feeling rippled through my body. Kathy and I descended to the aft cabin.

I think it was about an hour later when Sandy and George returned. Kathy and I were sitting on aft deck as they stepped aboard. We greeted each other with big hugs and smiles.

George said, "I think it is time for bed."

Flying home, Sandy and I talked about our boat trip with George and Kathy and how wonderful it had been. Our friendship was becoming very intimate.

Sandy said, "I haven't been with a couple that I enjoyed so much. Do you feel the same?"

I thought for a moment and replied, "There is something magical about the four of us. There is a strong trust, a gentleness, and a sense of calm."

Sandy responded, "I think we are going to spend a lot of time together. We have a lot in common."

"I feel the same way," I said. "George and I also love flying together."

Yes, the four of us would have many adventures together traveling or just having a quiet dinner together.

CHAPTER 18

Challenge yourself every day to do better and be better.
Remember, growth starts with a decision to move
beyond your present circumstances.

—ROBERT TEW

As I look into the world of Gordon and Sandy, I can see how the Spirit World works. Our lives were full of adventures, shared equally and together as we lived each day of life. There were disagreements and times when surviving was difficult, but we always made it through. I believe our joy, successes, and happiness were orchestrated by our spirits, and our love for each other was never in question.

The spirits often have a tough time keeping our lives together. Our Instinctual Spirit spends most of its time mapping out a plan for life and collecting and learning tools that will enable us to survive. These tools and survival skills are mostly learned from our parents.

As a child and young adult, we study how our parents live their lives, and we store the information for future use. We logically think that if these principles worked for our parents, it will work for us too. Take a moment and see how much you are like your parents and realize that in many cases we will marry or have married someone like our parents, be it a mother or a father. This is understandable because this type of person is familiar to us. We see our mate as someone who will fit into our life, per the game plan we have envisioned. If we see life was hard for our parents, than more than likely, we accept that it will be hard for us. We may even learn to tolerate anger, losses, hard times, a lack of love, and fear. We don't understand that life can be happy, joyous, and free because we never learned that game plan from our parents, and we find it difficult to change or see another path.

I grew up with parents who were loving and caring. They believed in always learning and growing. My parents enjoyed many of the beautiful things in life. I had adopted many of the principles that make life wonderful. Yes, there were trust issues on my mother's side and a lack of education on my father's side. He had quit school in eighth grade to work in his father's store. Alcohol was always present.

Sandy and I both grew up with alcohol as part of our parents' lives. As children, we often see things happening that we don't understand. We see alcohol consumed by our parents as a part of life. As we grow older and begin to implement adult behaviors, such as consuming alcohol, we find that it is pleasurable. We feel good and may gain self-confidence. No one gives a play book or rule book about alcohol and how it affects our lives. We start out slow, a couple of drinks will usually satisfy our need to be happy. But alcohol has a deadly secret. As time passes, our body will adjust and compensate to the chemical reaction alcohol provides. The problem is that our bodies slowly require more alcohol over time to give us the pleasure we desire or to maintain the high or experience we want. This begins to affect our daily lives.

As children, Sandy and I watched our parents change as they drank more alcohol, usually in a negative manor. Children and young adults usually see the change subconsciously and make mental notes like, "The more we drink, the more problems we have." Children are able to see things as they are. But children think that that's the way life is and that alcohol has to be handled. There are a few people who see that the alcohol is affecting their lives negatively, and they plot a course to change. To make a change may require total abstinence. When the alcohol stops, we see our lives clearly and realize we may have to change our behaviors and the way we live. In some cases, this is an overwhelming challenge and is not doable alone.

Sandy soon saw something in her life that she did not like. She said she was drinking too much. I had no idea what that was, and maybe Sandy didn't even know, but she wanted to find out. Sandy and Gordon were always experiencing and learning about life. Giving up alcohol may have been another experience Sandy wanted try. She may have seen the writing on the wall and said to herself, "I don't want to be like my parents."

Her choice was to join Alcohol Anonymous (AA). Sandy and I talked about the program, and Sandy said that this was her problem and that it was OK with her that I did not stop drinking. This made sense to me. Yes, I was drinking, and often more than I should have, but I had a group of friends who drank like me, and that seemed normal. I couldn't see that drinking was affecting our lives. My mother and father may have not drunk as much as Sandy's mother and father, so the urgency for me to stop drinking was not as acute.

A new program for life can't be created with the tools we learned as a child. However, those childhood programs are chiseled in stone and will always be remembered. A new program is going to challenge the old, and the old program will not give up easily.

I have said that the Intuitive Spirit will work hard to change your life if you want. However, I believe there may be a Rogue Spirit that will challenge the Intuitive Spirit. Both spirits are only interested in keeping us alive and helping us to achieve our goals or dreams. If one is based on truth, virtue, and beauty and the other is based on self-centered power, greed, and control, which do we choose? I am now faced with confusion, indecision, fear, and conflict deep within my subconscious.

Is it possible, as this conflict escalates, that we use more alcohol to stop the turmoil and confusion in our subconscious that is slowly moving to our conscious mind? There is only one way to stop these two diabolical nightmares, and it is to stop drinking and challenge each program. We then can choose the path we want to take. There are consequences to each. Remember the childhood behaviors are proven to work, whereas the new program is untested. Can we persevere until our new program proves successful?

Sandy attended an AA meeting and found a sponsor to help her work the program. Gordon and Sandy talked about what she was learning in AA; however, I was not a part of her program. This was her program. This was the first time we did not work together. We still went to parties and enjoyed our adventures as usual, but Sandy did not drink. This was the first time that I did not understand what she was trying to accomplish and what my role might be. All I could do was sit back, watch, and wait.

Chapter 19

Ninety-nine percent of failures come from people who make excuses.

—George Washington

January 1984

Almost two years had come and gone since Sandy had joined AA. Sandy and I talked about taking a vacation, something we hadn't done in the last two years. We searched vacation packages and came up with a windjammer sailing adventure. The ship was based in Grenada, and the trip would be a week long. We booked reservations, and in two weeks, we would be heading to Grenada for some sun and fun. We were both excited.

The flight to Grenada would require a stop in Miami, a change of planes, and a four-hour flight arriving in Grenada late in the evening. On the plane, Sandy was in one of her playful moods, and after dinner, she talked about how fun a sailing ship would be. The airplane's cabin lights had been turned down and most of the passengers were resting. Sandy grabbed my hand.

"Come with me," she whispered.

She led me into the forward restroom, closed the door, and kissed me passionately. You can guess what came next. We tidied up and opened the restroom door, and to our surprise and embarrassment, six people were in line waiting for us to finish. We laughed, the passengers smiled, and we retreated to our seats.

All Sandy said was, "We did it again."

The next morning, we headed to the marina where the boat was docked and checked in. Our cabin was small, with bunk beds and a small chest.

"This is just like George's boat," Sandy remarked.

But this is what we expected. A windjammer boat is very intimate. We headed up on deck to check out the rest of the boat. The deck was crowded with deck chairs. The crew was preparing to leave, stowing gear and taking on provisions. From the deck, we could see the town of Saint George. It was picture perfect with rows of houses, shops, and stores all painted in different colors. Below deck was the galley, the dining room, a sitting area where passengers could group together or just sit and read, and a bar. At the end of the bar was a large cage with a parrot in it. I asked Sandy if she thought the captain might have a peg leg and an eye patch. He didn't.

At about two in the afternoon, the lines were detached, and we headed to open water as the song "Amazing Grace" played over the intercom. We both commented on how the sound of the music was so peaceful. The sky was clear except for a few scattered clouds, and there was a light wind. With not much wind to speak of, how were we moving? The ship was equipped with a diesel engine, which would be used for most of the trip to keep us on schedule. We were scheduled to visit four different ports, where only smaller ships could dock. Clearing the harbor, the sails were unfurled. It was the most beautiful sight we had ever seen. We were under sail, as ships had done for hundreds of years. But on this ship, the sails could be furled and unfurled automatically. No one had to climb the mast.

Sandy and I both knew we had chosen the perfect vacation. Somewhere around six that evening, we heard the first call to dinner. All the meals were served buffet style. Many selections of meat, fish, vegetables, soups, salads, and the trimmings were presented. For the 125 passengers, it was a sight to behold: nearly everything a person could want. And to top it off, the bar was always open from eleven a.m. until twelve midnight. The evening was a wonderful time for the passengers to get to know each other, socialize, and relax. We would be at sea most nights of the trip. For the next seven days, we would visit remote towns and enjoy the cuisine, entertainment, shopping, and hospitality of local people. Each day and night were a new adventure. We also had a lunch and a dinner on a beach for a break in our routine. If you wanted more adventure, you could swim or scuba dive. The days were warm, and the passengers were delightful. I remember one night the wind had picked up and the helmsman said we were sailing without the engine. During the day, the helmsman would let the passengers steer the boat, creating a not-so-easy job of staying on course.

The trip had been delightful. We made new friends and had a down-right good time. It was the last night on the boat, and the captain had arranged a special dinner. The dinner was going to be a costume party, and Sandy and I had prepared for it. We were going to dress up as Romans and had planned to use our bedsheets as the base costumes. I had brought along some Roman senator accessories, mainly the typical senator's crown. We decided to decorate Sandy's costume with flowers, and so at our last port stop, we picked up a bouquet of flowers. Sandy, as usual, wanted to be a bit outrageous. We arranged the sheet so that her left breast would be uncovered. We fashioned the flowers into a sash, which would come up her back, over her shoulder, across her chest, and cover her other breast.

The finished costume looked outstanding and very sexy. Up in the dining room, we joined the party, which was well underway to becoming a real bash. Earlier in the trip, we had made friends with a couple, Frank and Judy. Frank was tall, brown hair and blue-eyed, and quite handsome. Judy was blond with brown eyes and slightly shorter than Frank, with a trim and slightly muscular body. They had already secured a table, and we joined them.

We all ordered drinks, and Sandy ordered a virgin Mary. Dinner was served by the crew, and it was, as the captain had promised, out of this world. We had our choice of steak or fish, and Sandy and I ordered steaks, which were served with all the trimmings. We ordered champagne to celebrate the successful trip, and the server returned and filled all four glasses.

"A toast," Frank said, "to good friends."

To my surprise, Sandy lifted her glass.

"On this special occasion, I am going to make an exception and drink to the four of us."

I was completely caught off guard but added, "To good friends."

Sandy did not stop with one drink but continued drinking all night.

We ate and danced, and as the evening wore on, I danced more with Judy, and Sandy danced more with Frank. It was around midnight when I asked Judy if she would like to take a walk on deck and take in some fresh air. She said yes, so we excused ourselves and went on deck. The night was cool, and the lights had been dimmed except for the running lights: green on starboard and red on port, easy to remember by port wine, which is red. We walked to the bow and looked out over the deep black night filled with a thousand stars. We were alone, two people in paradise. Judy turned toward me, and we kissed, long, hard, and passionately. I could feel her warm body telling me she wanted more, and I suggested we go to her cabin. Somehow, all four of us knew that tonight we would switch partners. We were well motivated by the many drinks and knowing that this was the last night on the boat. The next day, we would go our separate ways and head home.

Judy was very passionate, and she wanted to take full advantage of the situation, which we did. I remember falling asleep for an hour or so and then waking up, confused as to where I was. I then realized I was with Judy, not Sandy, and I wanted to leave. I dressed and went to the dining room to look for Sandy, but she wasn't there. I then went to look for her up on deck. No Sandy, but I saw Frank asleep on one of the lounge cushions. I turned and quickly headed to our cabin. I opened the door to our cabin and undressed as quietly as I could but not quietly enough.

Sandy woke up and smiled. "Come to bed, you Roman gladiator," she said.

The bunk was small, but I managed to squeeze in next her. Half asleep, she asked, "Did you have a good time?"

"Yes," I answered. "How about you?"

She laughed. "He was too drunk to do anything, but I have you now."

CHAPTER 20

*Nearly all people can stand adversity; if you want to test
a person's character, give them power.*

—ABRAHAM LINCOLN

January–February 1984

The spirits had worked overtime scripting all aspects of the boat party. Sandy and I were now facing some real changes in our lives. Neither of us had any idea how to make these changes, but we knew change was needed. At the time we did not know it, but the spirits had already worked out a plan, thank God. All we could manage the next morning was trying to cure our hangovers and putting things together for the flight home.

The flight back home was very subdued, and both Sandy and I were doing a lot of thinking. We both had pushed ourselves to the limit, and a change was in order. Sandy had called her sponsor, Carol from AA, and made arrangements to meet at our house the evening we arrived home. The fall weather had settled in, and the evening was cold when Carol arrived. We talked about our trip and the drinking. Sandy said she just wanted to have fun and be a part of the group. She felt left out and was tired of being sober all the time. The Rogue Spirit had won out.

Sandy and I knew what was coming next as Carol laid out our options. Sandy could go back to AA and try to stay sober, or she could give up and go back to drinking. Sandy also had the option to go into a treatment center for addiction for the next four to five weeks. Sandy knew she had a problem with alcohol and said she wanted to do what was necessary. On Monday morning, Sandy went to the hospital, where she worked to arrange time off and to check her insurance availability. She found out that she was covered by the hospital insurance, and the decision was finalized. Sandy would go to a treatment center.

Carol had talked to a treatment center she knew of in Estes Park, Colorado, which is north of Denver about sixty-five miles. She arranged for Sandy to be admitted. We left the next morning for Estes Park, the weather was clear and still cold. As we drove, we talked about the things I needed to do in the next couple of weeks. We had talked to the boys and told them about our plans; they understood. We also talked about our life up until now and what might have gone wrong. We had no answers. We both agreed that we could and would overcome the problem of addiction and alcohol.

In the movie *Top Gun*, Val Kilmer, call sign Iceman, and Tom Cruise, call sign Maverick, were in a flight of two airplanes. Iceman was the leader, and Maverick was his wingman. They encountered an enemy bandit, Michael Ironsides, call sign Jester. Together, Maverick and Iceman engaged Jester, at which point Maverick decided to go on his own and was shot down. Thus, the term: "Never leave your wingman." When Sandy made the decision to work AA, I was her wingman. Initially, I had chosen not to follow. That was a mistake I would not make again.

We arrived at the center, and Sandy checked in. It was time for me to leave, and with tears running down our cheeks, we kissed and hugged each other and said goodbye. I told her to call if she needed anything. As I walked out the door, I felt so helpless: forty-three years old and I was totally clueless as to the future and what was going to happen to Sandy and myself. I would soon find out.

I did not hear from Sandy for about five days, but the treatment center said she was going through a detox period. In addition to the alcohol, she had taken some pain medication, and that prolonged her purification. It would be about ten days before I could see her. When she called and said I could come up to see her, I left in a flash.

We met in the visitors lounge, and Sandy looked tired and worn out. She had lost all her happiness and joy. We talked about things around the house, which she had no interest in. We then switched our conversation to how she had been. She told me that it had been the worst week of her life. The weather had been cold and snowy, and she was very depressed. She wanted out of the center, or at least, she wanted to go to some place where she could enjoy the sun. I knew Sandy gained her energy and joy from the sun and the outdoors. I told her I would find a new center where she could regain her health, preferably where it was warm and sunny. We held hands, and she finally said that I had to go. Leaving was one of the hardest times of my life. I resolved that I would find her a Heaven on Earth where she could recover.

Crying became a habit. I was also afraid I would not be up to the challenge of recovery. I knew nothing about alcoholism, let alone the changes we would need to make in our everyday lives. Where would

I learn about a life without alcohol? I knew I couldn't drink any more. I later learned that God had sent a plan to our spirits, and they would enlighten us.

Returning home, I called Sandy's sponsor and told her that Sandy wanted out of the cold in Estes Park, and I asked if she could find a treatment center in Arizona or Texas where it would be warm. She assured me that she could, and within a couple of hours, she called back. She had found a center in Tucson, Arizona, called Cottonwood. Sandy could go down anytime. Thank those spirits.

I called Sandy and told her what I had found. I told her that I would make plane reservations and pick her up the next day, if she wanted. She said yes and was so happy that I could hear her crying. I picked her up early the next day, and we headed to Tucson. We arrived late in the afternoon. Sandy had slept during the flight down, but when we walked out of the terminal, and as the warm wind and the clear sunny sky met Sandy, she came alive. It was the first time in two weeks that she said she was happy. At that moment, I knew she was going to be OK.

The center had the typical southwestern Mexican architecture. The landscaping was reddish brown, and the soil was accented with light brown gravel and many cactuses of several shapes. Sandy fell in love the minute she saw it. We checked in, I saw a happy and friendly staff, and I knew Sandy would be well taken care of. We kissed and hugged, and I finally saw the Sandy I knew and loved. They told me not to call but to write letters for the next two weeks. If things went well, I could see her after that. Boy, was I excited! I finally felt hope and encouragement.

CHAPTER 21

Attitude is a choice. Happiness is a choice. Optimism is a choice.
Kindness is a choice. Giving is a choice. Respect is a choice.
Whatever choice you make, makes you. Choose wisely.

—ROY T BENNETT

March 1984

The two weeks passed quickly. I wrote to her every day, and she wrote me when she could. She said her days were full of classes and meetings and that she would fill me in when we next met. Yes, I would be allowed to see her after the first two weeks. I made reservations on Frontier Airlines and was on the first fight I could get to Tucson. Flying in March the weather could be questionable and unstable, and I didn't want to miss seeing Sandy.

The change in Sandy was dramatic. She was well on her way to being her old self. We had lunch and talked about her program and where she thought she would be going after treatment. She was so looking forward to a life together, and I assured her we would always be together. She told me that there was going to be a family week and that she hoped Rich, Don, and I could participate. The event would last four days and be held at the center. During the family week, we would learn about addiction, alcoholism, and the 12-Step Program. She asked if Rich and Don could attend. I told her that Don was still in basic Air Force training and that he would not be able to come, but I was sure Rich would come, and of course, I would be there as well. That made her happy. Never leave your wingman.

The weeks passed fast, and it was soon time for Rich and me to crank up *Bonnie* and head for Tucson. The weather was good for our trip. Rich and I always enjoyed flying *Bonnie*, and *Bonnie* was never happy when she had to stay at home. The first day of family week was orientated to getting acquainted with each other. It had been over a month since Sandy had seen Rich. We were joined with several other people who, like us, had someone in treatment. The facilitator presented to us the 12-Step Program and a background on addiction. He asked that we refrain from drinking during family week. Addiction and habits are strange and unpredictable, full of compromises and justifications. It was at dinner after the first day that Rich and I agreed that by saying "refrain from drinking," the facilitator actually meant "nothing excessive, but maybe one drink was fine." Talk about insanity.

The next day, we spent time planning a program so that when Sandy came home we would all be on the same page. The facilitator emphasized that there was going to be a lot of changes. The third day was similar to the first two days: more information on addiction, how we were going to see life differently, and how we would have to cope with these changes. On the fourth day, my life was shaken to the core again.

Rich and I were having breakfast when out of the blue, Rich said, "Dad, I think I am an alcoholic, and I would like to go to treatment."

It was then that I saw so clearly that alcohol and addiction are family problems. Rich was twenty-one years old then, and he would go on to celebrate his thirty-thrid year of sobriety in 2019. On that day, the last day of family week, I had my last drink.

Rich left family week and entered treatment in Cottonwood's second facility in Albuquerque, New Mexico. Never in my life was something so clear: I would have to join my family and abstain from alcohol. However, a question I couldn't answer was, "Am I an alcoholic?" It took several months to answer this, but I did know one thing: I agreed with Step 1.

Step 1 in AA is, "I am powerless over alcohol, and my life is unmanageable."

My life was indeed unmanageable, and alcohol was a big part of my life. Without any further thinking, I assumed I was an alcoholic. God had provided a chance for our family to come together and find a new way of life, and for this, I will be forever grateful. God did not take away my addiction to alcohol. He showed me and my family how to manage and create a new life that would not need or include alcohol and addictions to survive.

The program of AA is hard and demanding. It requires dedication and commitment for the rest of your life. It takes listening to teachers and attending programs so that one might see and learn a new way of life. It takes sacrifices, but in the end, the rewards are staggering and well worth the effort. Sandy and I made many new friends and learned many new things in the AA program.

A week after family week, I flew *Bonnie* to Tucson and brought Sandy home. I am not sure she if she was happier to see me or *Bonnie*! She loved the flight home, and I remember her saying that *Bonnie* was a part of our family. She was full of confidence and had a plan for our new life. She flew point, and I was her wingman. Our program included an AA meeting every day, and we always went together, more or less, for the next five years. We engaged in service work, and after a couple of years, we began to sponsor other people. Most of our drinking friends went off in other directions, which was good. We did remain friends with Ben and Ann and George and Kathy. The program did change how we looked at life but not how to give up life. On the contrary, it opened up many more opportunities, and Sandy and I participated to the fullest whenever possible.

I hope you are asking, "What are the things Sandy and Gordon did on their new path of life?" I am here to tell you. The path is amazing. Life is based on truth, virtue, and beauty. To understand the meaning of these three things would take me many years. As to what they meant, I could find only limited meaning in books. I had to live them and practice their principles in my everyday life to fully understand. It has taken me many years to find some of the meanings, and I am still learning every day. There are many related programs, workshops, meditations, self-help programs, and meetings.

The spirits would help me find teachers, and good ones, if I showed interest and was willing to give it all I had and follow directions. Sobriety is following tried-and-true rules, not creating new rules or ideas. The saying that "If a student wants to learn, a teacher will appear" is true. But good teachers will only stay if the student dedicates himself or herself to learning and practicing what the teacher is teaching. If the student doesn't continue to learn and apply himself or herself, the teacher will leave. This has proven to be true, as only about a quarter of the people who come into AA will stay sober. It takes commitment, and that is something most of us have very little of. Another integral part of AA is that the program generally can't be worked alone. Yes, there are a few people who can stay sober on willpower alone. These people say that they don't need AA to stay sober, and traveling the path alone is their best choice. I commend anyone who can stay sober alone, but I know it is a hard road to travel. Life is better with support, teachers, and sponsors.

CHAPTER 22

A dream doesn't become reality through magic; it takes sweat,
determination, and hard work.

—COLIN POWELL

May 1984

Alcoholics Anonymous has been around since the mid-1930s and is based on the 12 Steps to Recovery. Step 1 refers to our powerlessness to abstain from drinking. The second part of Step 1 is that our lives have become unmanageable. Here is where the fun of interpretation begins. "Unmanageability" has hundreds of meanings. Each person interprets his or her life based on the lives of their parents, rules of society, friends, government, and other influences. The basic rule for manageability is that one has taken charge, resulting in a life where one is happy, loving, joyful, supportive, free, and enjoying much tranquility. An unmanageable life is full of sadness, depression, anger, jealousy, confusion, hatred, revenge, and a dissolution of love.

Many people believe the answer to an unmanageable life is to abstain from drinking alcohol. There is no question that this will help and may even make life bearable. I believe we must first determine what is making our life unmanageable, which is why we turned to alcohol for peace of mind and sanity. Alcohol or addiction will mask or hide the unmanageability for a period of time, maybe even give us peace, but that comes with a high price. Usually, this leads to a continued escalation of using what we are addicted to.

The AA Step 4 is an inventory of our lives. It consists of a written list of all our shortcomings, the things that are creating problems in our lives. With this, we can find what things may have caused our addictions. We look back on the road just traveled and ask, "Where did I come from?" With this, we can see all the bumps, holes, ruts, and obstacles that made our ride uncomfortable or unbearable.

The first question is: how do we fix, smooth, and repair the road ahead? The second and more important question is: how do we fix and repair our bodies and minds from the damage of the past? For me, the answers were not obvious. However, I know that I must go on and manage the damaged road for a while, learning to make repairs and learning a new or altered way to live. I know that I must take with me, while traveling the old road, teachers, friends, and drivers who are familiar with the road I am about to go down. This is a team effort. I know I will have to get out of the car and physically repair the road. Sometimes, however, if the spirits are working with me, we will most likely find a new smooth blacktop road ahead.

But the damage to my body and mind must still be repaired or things won't go well. A plan must be formulated, outlining where I am going and how I am going to get there. I must find teachers and make a commitment to follow their teachings and suggestions. Remember, my Instinctual Spirit is always looking for an easier and softer way to change my life. So I must listen to my Guardian Spirit to find the true teachers. These teachers are the ones who will make me chop wood and carry water, over and over, until I learn to react without thinking. I may be pushed to frustration, anger, confusion, and the urge to quit, but I must overcome those feelings and push forward. I don't have to know the reasons I am doing something; I only have to trust that my teachers do. The spirits will guide me to the best teachers if I am willing to do the work.

Sandy and I knew we had a lot of work ahead of us. AA was the foundation of our recovery and new life, but AA was only one part of a complex, new life plan. The first thing that we wanted to do was find a therapist, someone familiar with the AA program. We asked around and finally settled on a woman who was very involved in AA and Al Anon (a worldwide fellowship that offers a program of recovery for the families and friends of alcoholics). Pat, as we called her, was older than us. She also had written several children's books. She was a strong woman and was a leader in the women's movement of the 1980s.

I had been attending AA meetings, and Pat suggested that I join the Men's Al Anon group to get a second perspective of alcoholism, which I did. The members of Al Anon are generally friends, spouses, and family members who are connected to alcoholics who are attending AA or to an alcoholic who they knew or were close to. Al-Anons are sometimes referred to as codependents, meaning they support the alcoholic. They generally hold a family together while the alcoholic is drinking. When an alcoholic stops drinking, the Al Anon could find themselves out of a job. As the alcoholic who stops drinking must learn a new way of living, the Al Anon must learn their new role in the recovery process as well. I did not know who I was, an alcoholic or an Al Anon. In about six months, I would be confronted by a group of older, longtime alcoholics who would explain and point out this denial and how my behavior and drinking qualified me as an alcoholic. At that time, I finally accepted that I was an alcoholic and never questioned alcoholism again.

Pat was a very strong person, and this would prove useful in getting my attention and in making me listen to her. I remember several times that she would confront my behavior. One time, I was late to a meeting with her and I told her that since I was paying the bill, I could come and go on my own time. She informed me that I had an obligation to be on time and I had made a commitment. Pat said that your word was law, and since I had made that commitment, I better never tell her to adjust to anything different. I was never late again. On another occasion, because I was tall (six foot, four inches), she told me to never talk down to a woman. She told me to always look at a woman at eye level. Surprisingly, I found this to be helpful in conversations, and it garnered much respect. She also pointed out that I often talked down to people with an air of arrogance—not a good trait. We spent a great deal of time working on this, and today I have a totally different attitude, which took several years to change and correct. Yet sometimes, I revert to my old behavior. I have to admit that I had left Pat's office many times angry and frustrated, but today I am so thankful that she was one of my mentors. The spirits did it again.

One of the big decisions in AA and Al Anon is selecting a sponsor. A sponsor is a member of the program who has had several years in the program and can help the newcomer work the steps and lead him or her through the program. I remember one early meeting with Pat that she asked if I had a sponsor. I informed her that a sponsor was very important to me and I need time to find the perfect person. She informed me that that could take months.

She suggested that when I went to my next Al Anon meeting to stand up and say, "I need a sponsor; would anyone be my sponsor?"

Why did I think I could pick the perfect sponsor? Since God directs the spirits and can arrange details like a sponsor, I would be very self-centered to think that I could do better than God or the spirits. I was reminded by my Guardian Spirit to remember Step 3 of AA: "Make a decision to turn your will and your life over to the care of God, as you understand him."

At the next Al Anon meeting, a sponsor found me. My sponsor was Chris, who had worked at an AA treatment center. I worked with Chris for several years, and at one point, he came to work for my company as an accountant.

Sandy and I were like two blind people trying to find a blank wall. We were in and out of old and new behaviors. Some parts of our lives were unmanageable. Other parts were just fine. We were loving and supportive of each other. We both were dedicated to the program and gave 100 percent, most of the time. We had pushed our lives to the maximum and tried many things, such as drinking and promiscuous sex. Drinking had become a real problem for both of us, and many of the other unmanageable decisions came while we were drinking. We knew that we couldn't drink again. We also gave up swinging, as we were told it could eventually create many problems, like distrust and jealousy.

Life was going to change in a big way. There is a saying in the AA program that when a person becomes sober, he or she will lose most of their friends, probably change jobs, and in some cases, divorce their spouses. How would our friends accept our abstinence from drinking, and could we accept their drinking? Our lives had been based on alcohol, and our friends drank a lot. I also learned very quickly that our construction company customers were generally alcoholic and that they did not want to do business with someone who would not drink. Many of our friends felt the same way. This new life was going to be very difficult, and many changes were to come, like giving up old friends.

CHAPTER 23

You are the right age, color, IQ, sex, and physical appearance to create an exciting, happy, successful life. You are the right being to make it big and to make it great.

—TOM WILLHITE

May 1984

The challenges facing Gordon and Sandy were many. They would be making new friends, finding new customers for the construction company, learning and implementing a new lifestyle, and giving up old ideas and habits. The program and path were clear, and they were both committed to it. Both Sandy and Gordon were religious and believed in God. Yet, the idea of turning their lives over to God, as stated in the 12 Steps, was a bit disconcerting. They knew God was loving and benevolent, but how would He help direct their lives? These lessons were all new.

"God is not Santa Claus or our parent," my sponsor said. "He/She doesn't give gifts of sobriety, a new car, a house, or other tangible item."

"Then what does God do?" I wondered. I found that if I believe in God, He will show me the path that leads to the accomplishment of my goals. God will show us the path if I follow the principles of truth, virtue, and beauty. But I must do the work and follow the path. It is a joint effort. For, it is not enough to just have a belief in God, we must also have a clear direction for our life or a set of goals that I want to accomplish under specific guidelines. Remember, what we ask for we will get just the way we ask for it. So be very specific.

The first thing I must do is to determine the goals I want to accomplish and the values that are important. These values are our guidelines and must be things that we won't compromise on; they are values etched in stone. These values must come before anything else. A simple value might be: I will eat breakfast every morning, and even if I run late, I will always eat breakfast. A goal to accompany this value could be anything: what I eat and when and how much I eat because eating breakfast every day is a good basis for anything. Another value could be to stay in truth and honesty or to communicate clearly to the best of one's ability. The goals and values must be clear and specific, not conflicting. The size of the goal is not important. I may set a goal that includes acquiring a new home, car, or job. Yet, goals must be specific. Having the goal of "I will be healthier" is not specific enough to be measurable and attainable. Instead, this goal could be "I will eat plant-based meals one day per week," or "I will exercise for thirty minutes three days per week," or "I will buy at least 50 percent of my produce certified organic." All of these specific goals will result in being healthier, but they are clearly attainable. The goal must also have a timeline and a set date when it is to be completed. At this point in the beginning, it is not necessary to know how you will accomplish these goals and values, but it is good to include smaller goals that may help the attainment of a larger goal.

For example, maybe you want a new house. Let's get specific. The house has to be three bedrooms and two baths, all on one floor. I want it to be Spanish in architecture, not more than ten miles from the city, and on a one-acre lot. If you want to add more details, that is good. Next, you must set a deadline for the purchase, again picking a reasonable time to move in. Once we have our goal, the next thing is finding out what we must do to obtain it. If we have limited income and can't afford the payments because of our jobs, educations, and experience, we may want to research what jobs are available that we are qualified for and that will provide the money for the payment. Will the job provide the income necessary to buy the home? Will I have to obtain more education or experience so I can obtain a job that will provide the money for the payment? Am I willing to limit other purchases so I can buy the home? What sort of down payment will I need?

If I have the wisdom to answer these questions, then I don't need outside help. But if only one question can't be answered, then where do I turn for help? Maybe a friend, sponsor, family member, or a teacher will know the answer. The question is, which one? This is the time we turn to our spirits and God and ask for help. In my life, the answers will come forth in a very short time. That person who has the answers will appear quickly and help with my questions and may even add more questions for me to address. So, how do we make all this work?

We can call on our Instinctive and Guardian Spirits. These spirits will provide us with directions, using the tools they have learned. They won't give advice but only unbiased information. The soul, on the other hand, has free will and chooses the path that it would like to explore. When a path is new or untried, the spirits may have to learn new skills and accumulate new information. I believe that these new skills are provided by God. Our Divine Spirit travels to God and is given instructions, which it brings back to the soul and Instinctive and Guardian Spirits. God provides a true and virtuous path to fulfill our goals. This path is loving, truthful, and beautiful. However, the soul has free will, so it might have other ideas, learned from other humans, which can include lying, deception, cheating, dishonesty, and even murder. Yet, the path that keeps one in virtue is always an option if we look for it.

History has examples of every path that has ever existed, and with a little time and direction, I can find a path that is suitable for me. Again, remember our soul has free will, and it can choose any path. Our job is to find the path that best fits our dreams and desires. We must also make sure the path will fulfill our desire to be happy. Hopefully, our path will include helping other people and creating an environment that is full of happiness, joy, and freedom. It must be truthful and not full of deception. It must provide the opportunity for others to obtain their goals and dreams as well. This is a big challenge and a lot of new knowledge must be found, learned, and implemented into our lives.

Yes, I know there will be times when we deviate or fall off the path and sometimes drive off the road into a ditch. These could be times when we were so focused on a goal that we failed to see other possibilities or hear the advice from our Instinctual, Divine, and Guardian Spirits. Or it could be a compromise in values or a relapse into old habits.

When we are learning a new path about life, we sometimes can be overwhelmed, confused, or just lose interest in what we are doing. The new path and teaching may not be what we think they should be. At some point, we just give up. This is where the Rogue Spirit comes forward with old behavior and says: "I told you the new stuff won't work. Here is your old behavior. You know it works, and you will survive life." The Rogue Spirit doesn't remind us that the old path will be full of addiction, anger, selfishness, fear, and everything that contributes to unhappiness and lack of joy and freedom. The Rogue Spirit is here to rescue us.

The Rogue Spirit is always ready to remind us that our past is always available and is always ready to take us back to our unmanageable or destructive past when our new paths become more work than we are willing to give or to perfect or to persevere to fruition.

Regardless of the reason, at such times, we can refer to Step 10 in AA: "Continue to take personal inventory, and when we are wrong, promptly admit it." This includes admitting it to ourselves. We can also refer to Step 9: "Make direct amends to such people wherever possible, except when to do so would injure them or others."

We may have given up our new program too soon. Going back to old ways was wrong. We may have harmed people around us and needed to clean up our mess. I have learned that it is so important to clean up the mess or problem that I have created. This is not only in my own affairs with others but to keep my house, car, and workplace clean and neat as well. The cleanliness of our environment can be an outward reflection of our relationships and inner lives and thoughts.

Please understand, I don't want to change your thinking and behaviors if you are comfortable working with your old beliefs and behaviors. I only want to offer you other ideas that may improve your life or awaken you to ideas you may not have thought of. I only want you to think, as they say, outside of the box—remembering that the instructions on how to get out of the box may be on the outside of the box, making life more interesting. I only ask that you let your mind wander and play in the world of new ideas. Ask yourself, "Could this idea help me in my everyday life" or "Could that idea explain why the world works the way it does?" Believe me, there are many teachers who know the world and ideas better than I do.

A friend once said to me, "Gordon, you are just an old cowboy who has spent most of his life on the range." I am inclined to agree.

If a person doesn't want to change, he or she won't have to read the book. I am not trying to change everyone, only those who want or need to change.

Chapter 24

The trouble with not having a goal is you spend your life running up and down the field and never score.

—Bill Copeland

Mark Twain once said, "It's not what we don't know that gets us in trouble. It's what we know for sure that just ain't so." When traveling down a new path that is unfamiliar, we will undoubtedly be confronted with ideas that are questionable to us. For example, how was the Earth created? In the Bible, we are told that God created Earth. I also understand there is a theory that Earth was created by accretion from the solar nebula and that volcanic outgassing created the primordial atmosphere and then the oceans. The fact that this is a "theory" means the scientists are not sure. There is also an idea that Earth came from a dying solar system and is a sun that was nearly burned out. Over millions of years, the crust cooled, but the interior still burns. An article in *The Denver Post* newspaper, dated March 17, 2019, states that there are three basic kinds of asteroids. The C-type asteroid consists of water, ammonia, methane, nitrogen, oxygen, and hydrogen; the S-type contains iron, nickel, magnesium, and titanium; and the third is the M-type, containing iron, nickel, and cobalt. Is it possible that our Earth, our dying sun, traveled through space and was bombed by these asteroids, and thus, gave Earth the elements we have now? Wouldn't this explain why most rare metals are concentrated in small pockets on Earth? Was the creation of Earth haphazard or orchestrated by God? I am fairly sure no one knows for sure.

I have heard that when the sun burns out, the people on Earth may have to travel to some unknown planet in another solar system and recolonize. Could it be that another star is burning out and developing like Earth did and will somehow travel near our Earth so we can jump on? If the Earth did originate as a solar nebula, then other questions are: Where did the solar nebula come from? Did it come from another solar system? If so, where did the other solar system come from? My point is, we don't know all the answers, but we know Earth exists. All of our attempts at proving any of these ideas have only led to more questions and more unproven beliefs. If you can't believe or accept an unproven belief, move on to more important subjects and beliefs that can enhance and improve your life.

If we spend our time in the past and worry about the future, we won't have time for the present. Review your past, and let it go—you can't change it. Look to the future, and make an inventory as to what you need to do today. Look at your life program, and see if it is working. If it isn't, develop changes or a new plan. Recommit to your goals, and make sure your values are strong.

Socrates decided not to become an ideologue, relativist, or nihilist, and instead, he studied things like virtue and justice that allowed people to have a better and happier life. I also believe that part of my life should be dedicated to the understanding of truth, virtue, and beauty. It is important to keep these three topics in mind and the focal point of understanding Gordon's and Sandy's recovery. In the beginning of their recovery, they were not aware that these truths would become an integral part of their program.

One of the most difficult AA steps to understand, accept, and manage is Step 1. Recall that Step 1 says: "We admitted we were powerless over alcohol, that our lives had become unmanageable." Admitting that we are powerless over alcohol is a very difficult thing to accept. Our ego is always pushing and confirming that we are OK. The ego is connected to the Instinctive Spirit, which has unlimited information suggesting that in some cases, we can drink alcohol and have no consequences or that we are not alcoholic. It says that we just need to take control of our drinking. When we drink to excess, unmanageable things can and do happen. Some of us may have woken up in the morning and realized that we had done things that we regretted and swear that we will never do them again. To our disappointment, we find that we do repeat dysfunctional behavior over and over again. I am sure as the reader of this book, you can conjure up your own disappointing, disastrous, and embarrassing experiences. Albert Einstein is credited with saying that doing the same things over and over and expecting different results is the definition of insanity. If something doesn't work the first time, it won't work the second time.

Lying, cheating, disrespect, irresponsibility, stealing, abusing, and infidelity are not limited to those with addictions. We all may fall off our paths at some point, but hopefully, we will see the problems we have created. And if we can't see and solve our problems, hopefully we can find someone who can help us make corrections. When I would fly my plane in instrument weather and use the airplane instruments to find a runway, all I needed was small changes in my flight path to make a safe landing possible. It can, at times, be beneficial to follow a tried-and-true path laid out by good teachers while making the necessary adjustments to accommodate for your own individuality.

What is alcoholism? What is addiction? It could be a disease, a learned behavior from our parents, or something we learned from experience that can make life look and feel better. Did we learn alcohol or drugs could make life manageable or more enjoyable? Yes. Regardless, it is not the substance that is the problem but the reason, belief, or behavior that caused us to turn to these things in the first place. But if we are powerless over alcohol or an addiction, what difference does it make *how* we became an alcoholic or addicted to drugs, sex, substances, caffeine, sugar, or emotions? We must put all our effort into overcoming our addictions and creating a manageable life. I find it interesting that when my soul finally admitted that I had a problem with alcoholism and that I needed to change my behavior and lifestyle, my Instinctive Spirit still continued to hold on to old behaviors. It was my Guardian Spirit that knew old behaviors did not work. It was time for change.

CHAPTER 25

Being at ease with not knowing is crucial for answers to come to you.

—ECKHART TOLLE

August 1984

When Sandy returned from treatment, she began going every day to AA meetings, and I usually joined her. As I mentioned, at that time, I was still six months from admitting I was an alcoholic, but I still attended meetings with Sandy. I recognized that although I thought I did not have problems with alcohol, I wanted to support Sandy. Regardless, I was in Al Anon. Members of AL Anon are family members, friends, or those who support the alcoholic during his drinking days and, in many cases, enable the alcoholic to continue to drink. Meeting topics were diverse and many but always focused on the problem of alcoholism. Each person would talk about his or her problem with alcohol and sometimes discuss a solution they had found. The 12 Steps were always important and talked about and related to a person's addictions and amenable life. Sandy and I would also have a weekly meeting with Pat. She provided many answers and solutions to the problem of alcoholism when we asked.

I was also working on improving my business. How could I improve sales, production, and employee relationships now that I was no longer drinking? During the early 1980s, there was a book that was very popular in the business world called *The Book of Five Rings*, by Miyamoto Musashi, written in 1643 in Japan. At that time, Japan was divided into provinces or states ruled by shoguns. The book discusses the discipline of the Samurai, professional soldiers who were available for hire to the highest bidder, mostly the shoguns. Samurai were also employed by religious temples, individuals, or anyone who wished or needed protection. The title of samurai could only be bestowed on those individuals, male or female, who were born into a samurai family. When the samurai couldn't find work as soldiers, they sometimes became schoolteachers, physicians, or priests, though some became criminals. Musashi was not a samurai, but was a very successful swordsman and teacher. By 1868, Japan became unified under one emperor, and that was the end of the samurai. *The Book of Five Rings* is a story of how to become the best at your chosen profession. It is about the discipline, dedication, and training required to reach ultimate success. People who come to mind that fit this model and level of success might be Peyton Manning, NFL quarterback; Tiger Woods, the golfer; Michael Jordan, the basketball player; or General George S, Patton Jr., a World War II general.

For those of you who have become bored with the simple problems in life, let me give you something to think about. Earlier in the prologue, I mentioned the Void. In the last chapter of *The Book of Five*

Rings is Musashi's explanation of the Void. Thirty-five years ago, I was totally confused with Musashi's explanation of the Void, and it has taken me many years to begin to understand what he was talking about. After all, Musashi is one of the most respected old teachers in Japan. Musashi said of the Void:

Of course, emptiness doesn't exist. Knowing of nonexistence while knowing of existence is emptiness. Wrongly viewed among people of the world, not understanding anything is itself considered emptiness. This is not real emptiness; it is all delusion. Being confused, one may call a state of helplessness emptiness, but this is not real emptiness. The way that is practiced by warriors in not obscure in the least. Without any confusion in mind, without slacking off at any time, polishing the mind and attention sharpening the eye that observes and the eye that sees, one should know real emptiness as the state where there is no obscurity and the clouds of confusion have cleared away. As long as they don't know the real Way, whether in Buddhism or in worldly matters, everybody may think their path is sure and is a good thing, but from the point of view of the straightway of mind, seen in juxtaposition with overall social standards, they turn away from the true Way by the personal biases in their minds and individual warps in their vision. In emptiness there is good but no evil. Wisdom exists, logic exists, the Way exists, mind is empty.

Sandy and I read this and the rest of the book and knew that this program was not going to be easy. Totally confused, Sandy and I asked Pat what she thought.

Her answer was simple: "I don't know, but I do know someone who might know."

Returning a week later, Pat gave us each a book. The book was *Shambhala, The Sacred Path of the Warrior* by Chogyam Trungpa. We read *The Sacred Path* and realized that the book was about meditation and a guide to enlightened living from the founder of the Naropa Institute. We were also introduced to the vision of Shambhala, the magical and mythical city. The answers to Musashi's void were not forthcoming from the Shambhala book, but Sandy and I became very interested in meditation and the teachings of Shambhala, so we decided to take classes to learn more.

The classes consisted of eleven weekends, Friday evening and all day on Saturday and Sunday. The weekends consisted of sitting on a cushion meditating and attending lectures. Sandy and I had no idea what we were getting into.

Sandy said, "This is something way beyond the things we have been taught. This is a whole new world of information. I want to go," Sandy said.

I would not have expected anything less from her. She was a true exploring woman and had an insatiable desire to learn. On the other hand, I was skeptical. What kind of group was this, some radical religious organization? I soon found out that I was very wrong in my apprehensions and that the founder, Chogyam Trungpa, had a background in Buddhism and was a man who wanted to create Heaven on Earth.

In the first class, we learned that Shambhala was secular without gods or fanatical beliefs and was mostly meditation. The practice of meditation can be very simple or very complex. I am sure many people meditate by relaxing, sitting, lying down, sitting on a cushion, or simply walking through a forest or a beautiful place. Some of these practices may only be daydreaming, and that is OK. I don't profess to know the best way to meditate. I don't know how the mind works during meditation. But I was soon to find out that Shambhala meditation takes tremendous discipline.

At the end of the first class lecture I asked what exactly Shambhala was all about.

The answer was as follows: "The Shambhala teachings are founded on the premise that there is basic wisdom that can help to solve the world's problems. This wisdom does not belong to any one culture or religion, nor does it come only from the West or the East. Rather, it is a tradition of human warriorship that has existed in many cultures at many times throughout history."

"Warriorship" here does not mean making war or outward fighting. A warrior is one who is brave and willing to combat fear. Warriorship in Shambhala tradition is not being afraid of who you are, not being afraid of yourself, and striving to be the best version of yourself. It is the opposite of selfishness, for when we are afraid, we become selfish. In fear, we want to build our own little nest, our own cocoons, so we can live by ourselves in a secure way. Is this the world we are experiencing today? We might just need more true warriors, willing to take a stand against fear.

In our world today, I believe people are in more fear than at any other time. We order physical things, such as food, clothing, and necessities through the internet; we play video games to be distracted and not have to confront reality. What are we afraid of? Is fear real or a manifestation of what we have on the internet, television, or radio news? There is always going to be fear, but we must separate real fear from highly-unlikely-to-happen fear. Isolated cases are often reported as common occurrences. For example, we all know that at some time an airliner is going to crash, but most people accept the chance of a crash as very low.

Please read the book *Shambhala, the Sacred Path of the Warrior*. I know you won't regret it.

CHAPTER 26

We all have dreams. In order to make dreams come into reality, it takes an awful lot of determination, self-discipline, and effort.

—JESSE OWENS

September 1984

By asking for a definition of the Void, Sandy and I were given a book about Shambhala, which lead us to Shambhala meditation. Was it coincidental that this book was given to us at the very beginning of our recovery? At this point in our lives, we were beginning to turn our lives over to God and trust His instructions and guidance supplied to us through his spirits. We did not research or investigate any other meditation practices but accepted that God, and/or the spirits, or something, or someone had found the best path for us. Maybe it was just a coincidence or luck that brought us to Shambhala training, but regardless, we embraced a new path and a new learning experience. These two young, inexperienced, and untrained warriors were about to go to school again.

We had procrastinated for several weeks, wondering whether mediation was the right thing for us. One night in an AA meeting, Step 11 was chosen as the subject. Step 11 states, "Seek through prayer and meditation to improve our conscious contact with God, as we understand Him, praying only for knowledge of His will for us and the power to carry that out."

Both of us understood praying from our religious backgrounds, and we would often pray together. But meditation? We had asked God and the spirits for direction, and the path that was presented was becoming clear. One of our teachers once said, "Whatever you ask for, you will receive, just the way you want it, no better or worse, just the way you want it; so be very clear on what you ask for."

We desperately wanted a new life, and so off to meditation we went. The first day of training was a Friday evening in Boulder, Colorado, in late summer. There would be five more weekends during the winter and spring and five more the following year. Each weekend consisted of sitting and lectures. We were both skeptical, fearful, and scared to start something completely new, something neither of us knew anything about. I don't think that separately we would have agreed to the program, but because we were in it together, we were able to step forward. And here we were, about to walk into the meditation hall.

The meditation hall was arranged very simply. There was no alter or any religious paraphernalia, just five rows of cushions on pads. At the front of the room was a raised platform, about twelve inches high. Centered on the platform was a lovely bouquet of flowers, arranged Japanese style. (We later learned this style of flower arranging is called *ikebana*.) To the right of the platform was another single cushion and pad, and next to the cushion was a beautiful brass bowl. This is where the timekeeper would sit and signal the start and finish of sitting by tapping the bowl with a wood handle. To the left of the platform was a chair and a small table with a glass of water and a vase with a single flower for the facilitator.

Selecting a cushion was challenging. In the front, I would be exposed, but in the back, I might lose interest. So, after removing our shoes, we went to the middle, where I sat down cross-legged with Sandy on my right. The program was to start at seven o'clock. We sat and waited. Seven o'clock came and went. It wasn't until eight o'clock that the facilitator arrived. My mind was slightly rattled. Shouldn't we have started at seven?

The lecture was to be about Shambhala and its history and traditions. The facilitator began by reciting a quote from *The Sacred Path of the Warrior*, the book we had received by Chogyam Trungpa.

"For the warrior, letting go is connected with relaxing within discipline in order to experience freedom—letting yourself go so that you fully experience your existence as a human being."

That was something to think about. And it was exactly what I needed to hear.

We ended at nine o'clock and headed back to Denver, anticipating arriving again the next morning at nine o'clock. During the drive back to Denver, Sandy and I talked about the program. We both agreed that this program was totally foreign to anything we had ever done or heard of—another step into the unknown. We knew a great deal of trust would be required and time to overcome our fears.

Saturday morning at nine o'clock we were back, seated on a cushion. The facilitator started his lecture with instructions on proper sitting and breathing.

"Sit down on your cushion and assume a cross-legged position. You begin to feel that by simply being on the spot, your life can become workable and even wonderful. You are capable of sitting like a king or queen on a throne. The regality of that situation shows you the dignity that comes from being still and simple. The upright posture is extremely important. When you sit, you proclaim to yourself and the rest of the world that you are going to be a warrior, a full human being."

He went on to say, "Because your back is upright, you feel no trace of shyness or embarrassment. You complete your posture by placing your hands on your thighs, palms down, and you don't randomly look around the room. Your gaze is slightly downward with your eyes open, looking maybe six feet in front of you. You will have a sense of deliberateness and definiteness. You take pride in being a human being."

He also added that conscious breathing is extremely important.

"You go out with the out breath, which dissolves, and then the inbreath happens naturally. Go out with the outbreath, and then come back to your posture. As you breath in, you will get a thought, and you say to yourself, 'Thinking.' You don't say thinking out loud, you simply say it mentally. It doesn't matter what thoughts you have. Your thoughts may be monstrous or benevolent, all thoughts are regarded purely as thinking. They are neither virtuous nor sinful and should never be judged."

He reminded us that this practice was from the book *Shambhala, the Sacred Path of the Warrior* and we should refer to the book as needed.

I thought that meditation was going to be simple. During my first meditation, all of my thoughts about meditation went out the window. The first thought that came to me was, "How am I going to ever learn this practice?" and then I remembered, just label it "thinking." And I began to learn meditation practice. After about forty-five minutes, we were instructed to stand and walk around the room to practice meditation while we were walking, exactly as we learned sitting.

Finally, it was time for lunch. Sandy and I found a local restaurant and sat down and relaxed. We both agreed that it was going to be a real challenge to learn meditation. We wondered, "Was meditation for us?" We were stiff. This idea of a "natural sitting position" was not so natural to us. We talked about what we had been thinking and agreed that we needed to figure out how we could possibly get comfortable on a cushion.

After lunch, the afternoon consisted of more meditation on the cushion and walking, about three hours. We also met with a meditation instructor and talked about meditation and how we were feeling. I admitted that I was confused.

"What exactly are we trying to learn?" I asked.

"Awareness," she replied. "We are learning to see and feel all the things around us. The point is to realize that everything has a purpose and the world is full of life and basic goodness."

"So, how long will it take to become aware?"

"Awareness comes in little increments."

She explained that first I had to plot my life goals. I needed to decide what I wanted out of life. Then I needed to find the teachings and teachers who would assist me in obtaining my goals and bring my goals to fruition. I had heard this before. There were many tools I would have to acquire and use in my daily life. She said that Shambhala could teach me many things I did not know and how to use these things, tools, and teachings in my everyday life. Shambhala was going to help me accomplish my life goals, but it would take determination.

"Sitting practice is like making a cake," the meditations instructor said. "You add all the ingredients together, and then you mix them. Sitting practice is the mixing of ideas, thoughts, experiences, feelings, teachings, and new ideas together until one can see how all these things will affect life."

Again, I wanted to know: "How long will this take?"

Her answer was: "A lifetime."

As I walked back to the meditation room after the conversation, I had one big thought: Was I going to have to spend the rest of my life on a cushion? That answer came many years later when I learned that mediation was like learning to drive a car. I had to spend time with an instructor until I was ready to practice driving on my own. Driving would become a part of my life that I would eventually be able do without thinking about every move. Of course, there would be those times when I would realize I was driving in the wrong direction because I was not thinking. This is also common in meditation, except going the wrong direction usually involves overthinking.

Four o'clock was tea time, a welcome break. This was followed by a group gathering to discuss what we had learned and how we felt. Then we had another hour of meditation and a final lecture on Shambhala teaching before finally heading home. I was so glad that Sandy was there, as it was a wonderful feeling to talk to someone on the same path and to share it with another so dedicated to a new life.

Over the next several days, Sandy and I talked a lot about the weekend, meditation, and sitting practice. We talked about what we had learned and how meditation might improve our lives. Was it worth the time and effort? We decided to buy a couple of cushions and pads so we could sit at home and meditate. Meditating at home proved very difficult, and it felt like trying to swim with only one lessen. The next Shambala weekend was a month away, and we hadn't made up our minds whether or not to continue. We thought to "fake it until you make it" with home meditating, but this didn't work. Sandy and I finally came to the conclusion that maybe there was more to meditation than just sitting and labeling thoughts and that maybe we were missing something. This much was obvious. Maybe one more weekend would help clarify our thinking and give us a reason to continue. With much difficulty, some fear, uneasiness, and apprehension, we decided to give it one more try.

The second weekend was the same as the first: sitting, meetings, and talks. We both realized that sitting was becoming a little easier, if only slightly. The subject for this weekend was fear.

What is fear, and how do we handle it? General George Patton once said that we all have fear and we must inventory our fears and then go beyond them. Fear is our mind or Instinctive Spirit telling us that something bad could and/or will happen. I've heard that 40 percent of our fears will never happen, 30 percent are things you can't do anything about, 12 percent are related to health, 10 percent regard miscellaneous items, and only 8 percent are things that can be affected or changed. I don't think we can ever be void of fear. Fear can only be diminished by education, training, and experience. If I have an assignment or mission that may cause me harm, I am going to fear doing it. This is a message from the Instinctive Spirit for self-preservation. But I believe many people fear things that they can't control. I know in my own airplane, if I let a passenger ride next to me, up front where they can see the instruments, they experience less air sickness. Was this simply because the passenger could see what was going on? Or maybe because the person was placating the mind, thinking he/she could fly the airplane even if they couldn't?

I have learned that training, experience, and hands-on activity will minimize my fear. When I was learning instrument flying, my fear level was through the roof. However, as I trained and practiced, I became experienced, and I was able to convince myself that I could land in instrument weather without damage to the airplane or myself. The more I practiced, the better I got at landing without seeing the runway until the last moment. Experience builds courage, the opposite of fear.

Yet, knowledge without training can increase fears. When I learned to skydive, the first jump was not as fearful as the second. After the first jump, I learned that there were a lot more things that could go wrong than I realized. We would jump once or twice a day. The mornings that I was going to jump brought up a lot of fear. I would look out the window of my apartment and see if the wind was blowing or if the clouds were too low to jump. I remember during my first twenty-five jumps or so, if it was not a clear day, I would have to overcome my fears or not jump. The "why" and expected end result has to outweigh the initial apprehensions. It was also very helpful to have Sandy join me, and as we drove to the jump zone, she would build my confidence. I believe it is very difficult to live life without a wingman. It was somewhere around fifty jumps that I began to believe jumping was safe and I could handle most situations. And this was confirmed by most of my jumping friends. After seventy-five jumps, I realized I had accomplished my goal of enjoyable jumping. Once I successfully mitigated my fears, the real fun began. I did star work, where two or more jumpers would come together and hold hands. I did accuracy jumping, landing on a target on the ground. There was also a water jump, landing in a lake intentionally, and the show-off jumps, like landing at the local hamburger stand to get a free lunch.

The second weekend lecture on fear seemed to bring me closer to the Shambhala teachings. This topic was familiar to me, and something was awakening inside my head and my heart. Was God telling me to keep going? Something was telling me: "Don't quit now!"

Yet, I was still very skeptical and hadn't convinced myself that I really needed meditation. It was a big commitment without any real rewards in sight. I asked Sandy how she felt about meditation, and Shambhala, and continuing the practice. She said she had the same hesitant feelings. However, she wanted to go on, even if I didn't.

Driving home after the second weekend, we both agreed that we wanted more sitting and Shambhala teachings. We did not know where Shambhala was going to take us. We would have to trust God had a plan for us, and Shambhala was the training we would need to complete our goals. We agreed the program was vast and challenging. There was so much to learn. If we were going to change our lives, we would have to change our thinking. Changing our thinking could take months or even years to do, but we were committed. Today, I am sure I could not have accomplished all the growth and the rewards of a new life without Sandy. Together, we would soon find out how much Shambhala would change our lives forever. AA was the most important program that we were working and would keep us sober if we practiced the 12 Steps, knowing we could not drink alcohol every again. Shambhala teachings would be the foundation of our new life.

CHAPTER 27

Set a goal to achieve something which is so big, so exhilarating, it excites you and scares you at the same time.

—BOB PROCTOR

January 1985

L evel III began our third weekend at the Shambala Center and consisted of two weekends. The topic for this weekend was synchronizing mind and body. Sandy and I were now getting used to the discipline of the weekend. The ease and comfort of sitting would vary a lot. Sitting at home had taught me that if I was tired, tense, or angry about something, I had a harder time sitting. In these circumstances, I would experience a little more pain and discomfort. Sitting in the meditation hall forced me to be more vigilant and to be aware of my posture and breath than being at home.

One afternoon, during the last hour of the second day of sitting, the timekeeper had struck the bowl to begin the meditation, and I tried to focus on my breath and thoughts. But I soon realized that my breath and thoughts were not synchronized, and my body began to slump.

"So much for learning the lessons," I thought.

I was tired, and I was irritable. If I had been at home, I would have given up sitting. But I was in Boulder in the meditation hall, and I had to finish the day sitting.. I was with the group, and I knew Sandy would finish the day, so I needed to finish as well. So, I sat up straight, and then I noticed the woman in front of me was sitting perfectly straight and not moving. If she could sit without moving, I sure could. The ego can sure make people do things that they never thought they could do. Pride can be a powerful influence also. I finished the hour without moving, and every muscle in my body hurt as a result.

Driving home that night, Sandy and I talked about the weekend. I told her about my last hour of sitting, and she almost died laughing.

Her only comment was, "You boys are so funny, but I love you dearly."

Sandy said that meditation was beginning to sink in. She said that she had never realized how many thoughts she had and how different they all were. The practice of labeling thoughts as "just thinking" without judging them was very freeing for her. She said she had thoughts of her childhood, our marriage, and the days of wild parties and drinking. Sandy was so happy to be sitting and working on our new program, which was so liberating. So was I. I agreed with her and shared some of my thoughts. We realized that the days of drinking and hangovers had taken a terrible toll on our minds and bodies.

Where we were going, we did not know, but our path felt right. The thought of a new life was fearful, and at the same time exciting. Working together, failure was not an option.

In Shambhala, there are three contemplative arts relating to discipline. These are *kyudo* (Japanese archery), *ikebana* (Japanese flower arranging), and *ocha* (the Japanese tea ceremony). We wondered why they were important in our meditation practice. What would we learn from them, and would we have any interest in them? We soon found out that they were going to be a game changer.

The second weekend of Level III began as usual. But on this day, sitting was short, and an elderly Japanese woman came into the room. She was followed by two assistants carrying flowers, a bowl, and water. She was introduced as Sensei Kita. We were told she was going to give us a demonstration of *ikebana* (Japanese flower arranging). Flowers are a large part of Japanese living. As you enter a person's home, you may see a flower arrangement in the entryway. Flowers calm the mind and create an atmosphere of beauty and harmony. In Japan, flower arrangements are generally not randomly created. We learned that *ikebana* is the art of placing flowers in a precise, prearranged order. The angle of the flower, the height, and the location in the arrangement are all very important.

Each flower represents three principles: one, Heaven is represented by the tallest flower; second, Man, is the medium height flower; and third, Earth is represented by the lowest, or shortest, flower. All flower arrangements follow this simple and basic form. Sometimes, we add additional flowers to enhance the three basic flowers and add additional beauty.

As Sensei Kita was arranging the flowers, I thought, "This doesn't look hard to learn."

When she finished her arrangement, she said, "I have been doing *ikebana* for forty years." She added, "I have one more level to learn, and I will be a master."

"Wait a minute," I thought, "forty years to learn the simple form of flower arranging?"

She went on to say that *ikebana* was connected to meditation and all the lessons we were learning about meditation and sitting on a cushion were connected to the practice of *ikebana*.

I learned early on, that many of the things Japanese people practice are very complex. Most of these practices are not learned in a few days or even a year or two but over many years and sometimes a lifetime. Each practice or art is, in some ways, connected to the Spirit World. It is a way of connecting the spirit of the flowers to the spirit of our mind. The world of meditation and the discipline of following the rules are set down by hundreds of years of practice and tradition.

The Japanese live very disciplined and meticulous lives. They follow many rules, one of which is never enter your home with your street shoes on, a good idea that keeps your home clean and doesn't damage the floors. However, there is another more important reason, mostly only known by the Japanese. The Japanese believe there are good and Rogue Spirits and by taking your shoes off, the Rogue Spirits can't get into your house and cause problems. Another rule is do not step on the threshold of the door, as Rogue Spirits can jump through you and get inside.

The *ikebana* class ended, and it was time for lunch, which my stomach said was way overdue. Sandy and I walked to a small restaurant that served Japanese food.

"Stay in the moment," she said. We had just watched something so incredibly beautiful that we had no words to describe it.

"She was a teacher at the top of her class, but so humble, gentle, and kind," Sandy said. "Who are these Japanese people?"

"Do they live in another world?" I added.

"Yes, they do," Sandy said.

Sandy had become soft and gentle as she spoke.

"Gordon, we need to learn from these people. I believe they are some of the true warriors of the world, and we must follow their teachings."

There was something deep in my heart that was awakening, and I knew she was right. We agreed that we would explore and learn the teachings, no matter how long it would take.

As we walked back to the meditation hall, a profound sense of calm overcame us. We held hands, and I think it was the first time I felt a deep desire to learn what meditation was all about. We entered the meditation hall. Sandy stopped.

"I think this is going to take many years," she said nonchalantly

I totally agreed, and we sat down to await the second half the day. We sat for another hour. Then the timekeeper announced that we were going to partake in *ocha* (the Japanese tea ceremony).

We entered a room that had been set up with several cups on low tables and a teapot for heating water. We were introduced to another Japanese woman who informed us about *ocha*. *Ocha* in Japan dates back to the fourteenth century and is known as the Way of Tea. *Ocha* is not exclusively about drinking tea. Presentation and aesthetics are equally important. Tea ceremonies were generally served in a teahouse, a free-standing building usually the size of a home living room. The teahouse was considered safe, and all those who entered into the teahouse were considered equal. In ancient times, business leaders, politicians, samurai, and other important people would meet for meetings and social engagements and indulge in *ocha*. Samurai couldn't bring their weapons inside, and the door leading into the teahouse was only four feet high. Thus, everyone would enter at the same height. The purpose of the *ocha* was that the guests would connect on a spiritual level.

The person making the tea for the ceremony would study and practice tea making for many years. Like *ikebana*, *ocha* is extremely precise, and the presentation is always the same, according to ancient tradition.

Building the fire for heating the tea and preparing and serving the tea requires detailed, specific, and defined procedures, actions, and discipline. Also, the tea cups are usually a work of art and can cost many thousands of dollars each. It is important to admire the tea cup and hold it properly. The tea used is a green powdered tea called matcha. A small amount of tea is placed in the cup, and then hot water is added. The tea preparer will use a bamboo whisk to mix the tea. Along with the tea, small decorative cakes or cookies may be served. Tea ceremony can last from one to four hours, depending on the guests.

The tea room at the Shambala Center had been set up with cushions and pads. We all sat down and wondered what was going to happen next. A short lecture was given on how to handle the tea cups, and what the tea maker was going to do, and what our part was in the ceremony. The preparation and serving of the tea was so precise and so beautifully executed. I felt like a special guest or a king. I couldn't help feeling a connection with all the people in the room and especially the tea maker. We were all equal.

On the drive home, Sandy and I talked about the beautiful tea ceremony and how we both felt so special, and yet, so humble. The *ocha* and *ikebana* teachers, the staff from Shambhala, and all the students had made this an unforgettable experience. The world is beautiful if you know where to look. The subject of *kyudo* (Japanese archery) came up, and I asked Sandy how shooting arrows could be spiritual.

"Let's wait until tomorrow," she said, "and I am sure we will find out."

Sunday morning, we arrived at the meditation hall and were informed that there would not be any mediation today and that we were to drive to North Boulder for a *kyudo* demonstration at a *dojo* there. "Do" in Japanese means "the Way," or "the Path," or "the practice of an Art." "Jo" refers to a place. So "*dojo*" means "a place to practice an art." *Kyo* is the Japanese word for "bow," so *kyudo* can mean "the practice of the art of the bow" or "the Way of the bow." Notice, there are no references here to sports or competition.

In the days of the samurai, the bow and arrow were considered the highest form of a martial art. Next highest was the horse—which was used as a weapon—while third was the sword, and the fourth highest was the spear. These were the only four weapons used by the samurai and the only martial arts practiced. The practice of judo and related practices were not considered martial arts. The samurai were also trained in other arts and became accomplished artists, mostly painters. They also had to learn to write calligraphy, the Japanese pictorial alphabet, in order to maintain communication.

What was the importance of art to the samurai? I learned that war and fighting created a lot of aggression and that painting would bring the mind back to a gentler and more peaceful place. With this, I realized that life is not simple and there is a lot to learn and practice, so we all must do our part to create Heaven on Earth. In the world today, we find a lot of aggression. We see sport events, politics, and business full of competition, realizing that aggression must be tempered by gentleness and love. I feel we are out of balance. There is a real need to create beauty: to let our minds rest and appreciate the sound of music, the beauty of nature and art, or to just sit and look at our inward beauty and appreciate how beautiful we are.

The *dojo* (shooting range) was divided into two segments. These were the training building and the archery range. The grounds were covered in trees, grass, shrubs, and a small creek meandering nearby. As I walked to the training building, I felt a sense of peacefulness, calmness, and serenity. No one spoke. The only conversation would be between teacher and student, no side talk.

Upon entering the training building, I was surprised by the simplicity of the furnishings, and there were several students waiting to greet us. They were all dressed in traditional *kyudo* practice uniforms, consisting of a wraparound blouse or shirt called a *gi*. The pants were a black split skirt, called a *hakama*. Along one wall were six straw bales on wooden frames wrapped in white sheets, used to practice indoor shooting. In the front of the room was a small shrine with two candles on a white silk cloth and a small bouquet of flowers. On the shrine was a picture of the current director and *sensei* (teacher) of *kyudo* and also a picture of Sensei's grandfather. The third wall was lined with bows and arrows and a bench for sitting. In one corner was a black wood stove for heating and a chair for the sensei.

In the center of the room were several rows of cushions and pads. We were directed to take a seat on one of the cushions. Sensei was sitting in the front of the room. He was fairly fluent in English and welcomed us to his *dojo*. He was average height, with coal black hair. He was slender but had a strong build and a very strong personality. On his right was his wife, Marsha, an American woman from Boulder. Sensei introduced his wife and said that she may at times help with his English translations, as she spoke Japanese very well. Sensei had married Marsha after his first wife died. Sensei Kanjro Shibata was born and raised in Japan and had married as a young man and fathered two daughters, now grown. In the early 1980s, Chogyam Trungpa, the founder and leader of Shambhala, asked Sensei to come to America and teach *kyudo*. Sensei accepted, spending half the year in Boulder and the other half of the year in Japan.

Sensei Shibata told us of the history of *kyudo*. It is believed that *kyudo* dates back to 600 BC. The first schools were founded in AD 600, he said. The bow used in *kyudo* is called a *yumi* and is about seven feet long, and the arrows are called *yaws*. The bow is constructed of an outer layer of bamboo and an inner layer of hardwood, which determines the strength of the *yumi*. The Samurai would often shoot while riding a horse, so the hand grip is one-third of the way up from the bottom of the *yumi*. The yaws were also made of bamboo.

Sensei explained that the room we were in, our teaching and practice room, was to be considered sacred. We were not to talk or chitchat, except when giving instructions and demonstrations. The training room was considered a meditation hall, and the teachings we had learned about meditation applied here. With my in breath, I would pull the string on the *yumi*, and a thought would come. I would label this thought "thinking" and then let the thought go on the out breath as I released the *yaw*. This is called "meditation in action." Some people say meditation should be a part of our daily life as we go about doing our daily chores. Sensei also told us that this practice would take many years.

"*Kyudo* is not just a practice of walking up and shooting an arrow," he said.

There are eight separate phases or segments the archer must do before each shot. Between each segment, the archer must pause about five seconds, allowing him or herself to breathe in and breathe out, always thinking and letting go. I was quickly beginning to understand why this practice would take many years.

"To better understand what I am talking about," Sensei continued, "I will briefly tell you about each segment as Mary performs it."

Mary was one of Sensei's oldest students who had perfected her shooting and meditation practice to a very high level. She picked up a *yumi* and a *yaw*.

"Remember, each segment is very precise and must be repeated the same each time," Sensei said. "The instructors will teach you the proper way," he added. "Learning the segment right the first time is easier than unlearning the wrong way and then learning the correct way."

Sensei explained Mary's movements as she performed. Mary walked to a hay bale along the west wall and positioned herself ninety degrees to the target. This is called *ashibumi* (positioning). Next, she took the correct posture, *dozukuri*, and readied the bow for shooting, *yugamae*. She then raised the bow to the proper height, *uchiokoshi*, and drew the bow, *hikiwake*. Completing the draw, she held the draw, *kai*, until it was time to release, *hanare*, and finally, lowered the bow, *zanshin*. Sensei paused for a moment while Mary put away her *yumi* and returned to her cushion.

"Thank you, Mary," he said, then continued his talk. "*Kyudo* is mainly practiced as a way of personal development," he said. "Mere technical skill and virtuosity is not prized. A humble approach is encouraged, and a quiet period after the release is necessary."

Sensei explained that there are no colored belts to depict rank. He went on to say that *kyudo* puts one's mind at ease by overriding conscious thought. Relating to the precision of the form, a natural process of development unfolds: hesitation, fear, and conflicting emotions subside, allowing serenity and strength to coexist.

"With each shot, the Way of the Bow unfolds, allowing one's natural dignity to shine through."

Sensei turned to Marsha and asked if she would like to add anything.

"Yes," she said. "Sensei's family is known throughout Japan as premier bow makers," Marsha said. "Sensei is the twentieth generation of bow makers for the emperor of Japan," she added. "Sensei has dedicated his entire life to maintaining and teaching the traditional *kyudo* practices. He was saddened when Japan began to turn *kyudo* into an archery sport."

I remembered reading abort General MacArthur, of the United States army, who became the sole leader of occupied Japan. MacArthur forbid any making of swords and bows, and he confiscated all the swords and bows he could find and destroyed them. I also remember reading somewhere that General Patton said, "Revenge is up to God, not man." I believe that General MacArthur thought he was God and he would punish the Japanese for the war. After the departure of the Americans from Japan, the making of bows and swords returned, with Sensei's family leading bow making. However, today, most of the bows made outside of Sensei's family are made of plastic.

After Sensei's talk, the students began practicing for the next hour. Sandy and I sat and watched, mesmerized by the beauty of the shooting. When class ended, Sandy began talking to several of the instructors, inquiring about joining and beginning the practice. I only watched. I was her wingman, but I knew what was coming.

CHAPTER 28

If you don't know where you are going, you might
wind up someplace else.

—YOGI BERRA

February 1985

Leaving the *dojo*, Sandy and I headed to lunch. I suggested the Boulderado Hotel, as they had a quiet restaurant and we could get an upscale lunch to celebrate our weekend. The owners of the hotel named it Boulderado, a combination of Boulder and Colorado, so that the guests would not forget where they had stayed. The Boulderado Hotel was designed with Italian Renaissance architecture and built in 1909. It was the centerpiece of Boulder when it opened on New Year's Eve, 1909, with a gala celebration. The hotel still retains its elegance and is a wonderful place to stay when in Boulder.

We were seated at a table for two next to a window. It was refreshing to see the table covered with a white table cloth, elegant silverware, plates, and long stem water glasses. We ordered, and I sat back and realized I had experienced the beginning of a new spiritual path that was beautiful, elegant, exciting, and educational. I reached across the table for Sandy's hands, and she responded by gently placing her hands into mine. We held hands for several seconds.

"I can't believe what we have seen and done the last several weeks," she said. "We have been given a choice, to move forward with this new spiritual path or choose our old ways while hoping AA will be adequate to get us through life."

I nodded in agreement.

Sandy continued, "I feel a desperate need to continue on this new path with the help of Shambhala, AA, our counseling, and a belief in God. I also want to add *kyudo* to our new path."

She smiled. "I know that is a lot to handle, but together I know we can handle everything that comes our way."

I was not surprised at what she had just told me. Sandy wanted the most out of life, and this was the way she could get what she wanted. I just listened as she continued.

"I believe *kyudo* is the crown jewel of this program and path. It will teach us how to connect with sitting and the outside world. It requires discipline and the unquestioning belief that there is more to life than what we have been taught. It is going to take a lot of time and several years to learn though. But I am willing to do whatever is necessary to learn these teachings."

Sandy would go on to become an accomplished *kyudo* archer. Her form and practice would become nearly flawless. She would flow, and I could see she was engrossed in total meditation. My practice would always be a bit rough, but shooting and meditation finally came together after twenty-three years.

My mind raced back to the day that Sandy told me she was pregnant and also to the day she went into treatment. I never questioned that I would always be there when she needed me. Today was no exception. I knew she could do *kyudo* on her own, but I also was aware that she would like me to come with her. I knew when I walked away from the *dojo* that morning that I felt the same as Sandy. I wanted, craved, and needed *kyudo*. I also could see a great teacher coming into my life. Sensei was a man of great knowledge and experience who had learned how to be a leader. He was also gentle and humble, all the attributes I needed.

Sandy was a great athlete, she loved tennis and later racquetball, but, Kyudo, Japanese archery, would become Sandy's favorite practice. She would rise to high level of accomplishment and proficiency.

I grasped Sandy's hands tighter and smiled.
"I am in," I said.

And I truly meant it. I wanted to share this experience with Sandy, and I wanted these teachings for myself as well. She grasped my hands.

"Thank you," she said.

We both knew that *kyudo* would teach us more lessons about life. And as time went on, Sandy and I developed a strong bond with Sensei. It was that bond that would take us to Japan several times and to his home there.

Sandy was right about the amount of time needed to work the program. We were attending AA nearly every day and living a life. *Kyudo* class was every Sunday morning from ten to noon, and we decided that was workable. Like all new students, we had a lot to learn.

Our first class of *kyudo* was just sitting and watching the other student's practice. We were given instruction on the care and handling of our equipment. The *yumis*, when not in use or when traveling to and from home, would be wrapped in a soft cloth. When we arrived at the *dojo*, we would unwrap the *yumi* and check to make sure it was not cracked or damaged. Next, we would string the *yumi* and place it on the storage rack.

"*Yumis* have a spirit," the instructor told us. "They are a living thing, and it is very important to pay homage to that spirit and always make sure it is cared for. The *yumi* will be your friend and help you with your practice. Or it will obstinate and make your practice difficult."

Later that afternoon, Sandy and I talked about the *yumi* and the spirits. To my surprise, she said she had felt something the first time she held her *yumi*. For me, it would be many months before I felt the spirit of the *yumi*.

One of the unusual aspects of *kyudo* is how we grasp the string. In most archery, we use our fingers. In *kyudo*, we wear a glove on our right hand and grasp the string where our thumb meets our hand. Twisting the hand locks the string into place. The advantage to this is that fingers can be weak, but the hand is very strong.

We walked onto the shooting platform, and we felt the energy from the other students shooting. Our instructor pointed to the targets.

"The targets have spirits too," he said. "Before we shoot, we must acknowledge the target and ask if it is OK to shoot at them. This is not done openly but by a gesture with the bow."

Standing on the platform and looking at the targets, my mind flashed back to a conversation with a Lakota Sioux Native American I'd had several weeks earlier. He told me that the Native Americans would ask the buffalo if they could shoot them. The buffalo spirits replied yes, but the Native Americans were only to shoot what they needed, nothing extra, and to use everything they took. This practice was an effort to pay homage to the buffalo they killed. The idea of spirits was coming at me from all directions.

It was becoming overwhelming, but something was guiding Sandy and me along our path, introducing new ideas and the best teachers. Of course, it could be just luck, coincidence, or God. But to Sandy and me, it was not about who was leading us. Our job was to do the work the way we were told. Chop wood and carry water. There is also a saying: "Rocks are hard, and water is wet; don't try to change things, accept them."

The following weekend, we finally began to practice shooting, and I soon understood what Sensei meant when he said, "To learn the practice of *kyudo* and shooting will take many years."

I had never undertaken anything so complex, but we two baby warriors were in the game head-on. We each had shooting gloves called *yugake* and our own uniforms: *hakama*, *gi*, and *obi* (a belt worn under the *hakama*). Sensei instructed us on how to fold and store our hakama, gi, and obi, and yes, this was also done in a precise and proper way.

He also said, "Keep your uniform neat and clean, and never look sloppy."

I began to realize that Sensei had high expectations from Sandy and me.

On the way home, Sandy said, "Sensei is watching us with added interest. He personally corrected my practice. I think he expects us to dress and look sharp also."

I agreed, and I remembered when I was in the Air Force. My sergeant insisted that I always wore a clean, starched uniform. To practice warriorship was more than just showing up. It demanded vigilance and discipline. We both wore a clean, starched *gi* every time we practiced. I think, but I am not sure, I saw a very slight smile from Sensei every time we came to class.

Sandy and I finished the last two weekends of Shambhala during the winter and spring. The year had been very demanding, difficult, challenging, frustrating, and rewarding. After reviewing what we had accomplished, we were very proud of each other. We felt good, and we both had a big feeling of accomplishment. We had taken the challenge, overcome the obstacles, and accomplished our goals. I told Sandy that I couldn't have done this on my own. She smiled and gave me a big hug and kiss.

"We are a team, honey," she said, "determined to change our lives. We have only begun, but there is no stopping us now."

What could I say; she had said it all.

CHAPTER 29

Great achievement is usually born of great sacrifice
and is never the result of selfishness.

—NAPOLEON HILL

July 1986

S andy had grown up in a home full of hardship and very little love. She was well taken care of by her father and stepmother, but she had to compete with her two brothers and sister for the little love that was available. On the other hand, Sandy had a lot of love to give. Is it possible that a person who gives love is motivated by hope for love in return? In her nursing career, she believed that her patients would recover from their sickness quicker by her giving love and attention. Yes, medications were used to help the healing, but could someone become sick just to go to a hospital to find love and caring? Sandy told me that early in her nursing career, women would check into the hospital for rest and relaxation, even though they were not sick. Were these women looking for someone to give them love, affection, and attention, if only for a few moments or days?

How strong is our need for love? I am not a therapist and have no formal psychological training, but I think the need for love is huge. I also believe this need is equal for both men and women and even exists in our pets and other animals. I believe women work hard to attract love. They sometimes sacrifice their own needs to attract love. This shouldn't be happening! Women should be unconditionally loved and cherished when they work to achieve their goals, desires, and dreams. However, in life, we must balance our needs with the needs of others. Sometimes I think it may be possible to do everything I want, but experience proves that I can't do everything and do it all well. Take sports, for instance. I can never be number one unless I devote nearly all my time and energy into practicing, and even then, it is not guaranteed. What is the balance between helping satisfy the needs of others and focusing on my own goals?

When considering accomplishing my own goals, I first must determine how much time and energy I should spend. I need to know what resources and teachers I will need or if I can accomplish my goals on my own. I have watched many people in AA try and work the AA program on their own. It can be done, but it takes a lot longer, sometimes years longer; a good teacher could have made the journey much shorter and enjoyable. I must also look into my feelings and emotions and understand how they affect my behavior.

Ruth Bader Ginsberg said, "Don't be distracted by emotions like anger, envy, resentment. These just zap energy and waste time."

The second thing I must do is to determine what time and energy my wingman will need from me in order to accomplish his or her goals.

What will be my contribution to their reaching their goals? Or do I need to stay away from their goals and let them achieve their goals on their own? Going back to *Top Gun*, I realize that each pilot must generally have equal skills to survive. However, one pilot may have a skill that the other pilot doesn't have, allowing him or her to take the lead. We are always relinquishing the lead as the need to survive surfaces. This requires true self honesty. This practice also requires each person to work toward proficiency in their chosen goals. It is not good for one person to always be in the lead. No person has the skills, time, and energy to do that.

However, I believe that life should not always be focused on a mission. We must take time to fly on our own sometimes. Time must be allocated to perusing my own personal and individual needs and doing the things that my partner has no interest in. For example, I have always been interested in railroad trains. I love to ride them, study them, and model them. As a little boy, I always was involved in model train layouts. Recall that when I lived at home with my parents, I built a train layout in the basement of my parents' home, with the help of my dad. In my adult life, I was a member of a train club at Denver Union Station. Sandy, on the other hand, loved to ride trains, but she did not have any interest beyond that. Her hobbies were tennis, racquetball, reading, and sunbathing. We always allowed each other personal time to participate in these hobbies.

During the summer after Shambhala training, Sandy and I added more personal growth programs. One program was suggested by my sister, Sharon. It was called the Institute for Self-Actualization (ISA) out of Chicago. Sandy and I participated in their weekend programs, and we learned more about ourselves and the behavior of other people. The program opened our eyes to personal behavior and gave us more tools to use in our own programs. We learned first about ourselves, how we look and act in the real world. On the second day of the seminar, the facilitator asked us to pick out a person who irritates us and ask him/her to lunch. I, being cocky and a bit arrogant, thought no one would invite me out. I was a good guy, well liked. Well, four women invited me to lunch. It was like a tribunal. They said I was arrogant, self-centered, and looked down on women. Needless to say, I had a lot to work on, and I tried hard to overcome these shortcomings. We learned about human behavior, how men and women think, and the differences between men and women.

Another, and one of the most interesting programs we participated in, was in Tucson, Arizona. We flew *Bonnie* to Tuscan for a few days of rest and another weekend program. The facilitator of the program labeled herself a *swami*, or a Hindu religious teacher, literally meaning "he who is one with himself." Her name was Mary. I had no idea what a *swami* was, so I asked Sandy if she knew. She thought they were teachers who could predict future events or developments from looking into a glass or crystal globe.

"Well," I said, "this should be an enlightening weekend."

Our flight was uneventful, and late on Friday afternoon, we checked into the lodge where the program was to be held. Saturday morning, we learned about *swamis*, and we found out that Sandy was right on. The only difference was that our *swami* instructor used crystals to see into the future. Mary was tall, maybe five foot ten inches, and was slender with black hair. At the morning break, she instructed us to search the property and find a rock. We were also told to remember where we found the rock and return it after the program was over.

"The rock you will pick is part of a rock community," she said. "It won't be happy about leaving its community."

We returned to the meeting room, and Mary said to carry the rock we had picked out for the next two days.

"Make friends with it," she instructed. "The closer the relationship you have with it, the better the rock can communicate with you."

So I thought, "If I really connect to this rock, will it talk to me?"

I had made friends with some really strange people but never a rock.

I did what I was told. I talked to the rock when no one was looking, and strangely, I began to feel a connection. If you, the reader, choose to work a spiritual program, you will find things happen to you that make no logical sense. I thought I was in the twilight zone, and Sandy later agreed with me. The afternoon was spent learning about the Hindu religion, and Mary told stories that related to Hinduism and meditation. I have to admit; I learned a lot of interesting new beliefs. One belief was we are on a path and what happens today will predict what will happen in the future. When we set a goal today, it is possible to see what will happen by looking into the rock for what the future will bring if I stay on my current path. Thus, if I don't like the future, I can change my path today and, thus, change the future.

The following morning after breakfast, we all met in the meeting hall. We sat and meditated with our rocks, and I silently reconnected with mine. After an hour or so, Mary said that we were going to break up and reconvene in a location about half a mile from the lodge.

"Please be there in half an hour," she said.

"Be where?" I wondered.

The lodge was surrounded by trees, rocks, and dry riverbeds, and I did not know any meeting places. The room was silent until someone asked, "Where is the meeting place?"

Mary replied, "Ask your rock."

"Ask my rock? Now there is a novel idea," I thought.

Then I heard my Guardian Spirit say, "Do as she asks."

I looked into my rock and quietly said, "Show me the way."

Almost instantly, in my mind's eye, I saw a dry riverbed that was wide, sandy, and quite walkable. I remembered that the day before I had walked near a dry riverbed that fit this description. Looking around the room, I could see other participant's looking into their rocks. I silently exited the room and headed to the spot that I remembered. To my surprise, the riverbed was exactly like the rock had shown me.

"Well, so far so good," I said. But why this spot? I had seen many other spots or locations.

I then asked the rock for further directions and maybe a confirmation I was on the right path. In my mind's eye, again there appeared a picture of the riverbed bending to the right and along the left side of the riverbed was a picture of a small sandstone cliff, maybe thirty feet high. On the cliff wall was a series of pictographs.

Pictographs were common among ancient people, but there are also people today who want to leave their mark on nature, which could be called graffiti. I suddenly realize that it was immaterial to know who put the pictographs on the wall.

"Wait a minute," I thought, "this is Arizona, not New Mexico or Colorado where ancient Native American tribes roamed." Pictographs? With some hesitation, I thought, "Well, the picture shows the riverbed. I'll continue."

Without any other choices, I looked to my right and could see many rocks and boulders in the riverbed. My rock picture guidance did not show any rocks, so I turned left and proceeded down the path. The path was wide, maybe eight feet and very sandy. I walked slowly, looking at the beauty of the surroundings. There were pine trees, scrub oak, and a variety of other plants, all characteristic of the southwest. As I turned another corner on the path, to my total amazement, there on the wall surface were scratched pictographs. Someone had scratched crude stick figures of people and animals.

"This rock thing is getting out of hand!" I wondered, "Do rock spirits talk to each other?"

I remembered that Einstein talked about energy within elements, like uranium. Could there be energy within these rocks, and I had connected with it?

I was totally mystified by what was happening. I had asked for confirmation, and I had been given it. I walked on and sure enough, around the next bend sat Mary and a couple of other students.

"Where have you been?" Mary asked me with a smile on her face.

I sat down, and to my surprise, the other students had a similar experience with their rocks. Mary said it was time to find the rest of the students, so she dispatched a young woman to find them. Shortly thereafter, we were all together. We talked about our experiences with the rocks, and there were many different stories. Some people saw a trail but did not relate the picture to a riverbed, some saw a narrow open meadow and became confused trying to find it, and some people saw nothing. If we don't have a clear picture of our goals, the rock can't help us.

The last class of the afternoon was focused around rock questions. Each person was to ask his or her rock a question about the future. After a half hour of meditation, Mary began asking students what their questions were and what answers they had received. The questions ranged from "Will I be rich, marry, divorce, take a trip?" and so on. The answers were varied, as you might expect.

I silently asked my rock, "Will Sandy and I have a good flight home?"

The answer was simply, "Sun."

Strangely, Sandy sat quietly, which was not common for her. What she asked her rock, she did not tell me. At that moment, a cold feeling came over me. I felt uncomfortable, but the feeling soon passed, and

I never thought about it again. A few final comments by Mary, and the class ended.

Sandy and I returned our rocks to their homes, checked out of the lodge, and headed to a Marriott Hotel to enjoy the next two days of relaxation. Sandy wanted to spend some more time in the sun, her favorite pastime. Our room was large with a king size bed, and we had a view overlooking the swimming pool. The weather had been warm, and from our vantage point, we could see several people relaxing around the pool. We unpacked, rested, and talked about the weekend. Sandy was happy that we had attended, and she said she really enjoyed Mary. I often wondered what her rock had told her, pertaining to the future. I would never find out.

That night, Sandy and I went to dinner at the local steakhouse. We were ready for a good steak and trimmings after the vegetarian-based meals we'd had at the seminar. The next morning after breakfast, Sandy and I headed to the pool. The weather was clear and warm. Surrounding the pool were many chairs and recliners, and since we were early, we had our choice. We spent the day reading and relaxing. Sandy was unusually quiet, which I assumed was because of the busy weekend and that she must be tired.

The next day, Sandy said she was going to spend another day at the pool and in the sun.

"The sun is my source of energy and regeneration," she told me. "If you have something else that you would like to do, I will be OK by myself."

I had heard that there was a large air museum in Tucson called the Pima Air and Space Museum, and I thought I might go and see it. I asked Sandy if she may want to go, and she said that she would rather lie in the sun. Airplanes were not on her list of things to see. Of course, that was not a surprise.

"I will be back around three o'clock," I said.

Along with my love for trains, I also have a fascination with airplanes, especially World War II airplanes. My father loved airplanes, and in 1927, he began his flying career. He obtained his pilot's license in 1928, and like many young men during this time period, he hoped to make a career out of flying. He was so infatuated with flying that he began building his own airplane, a Heath Parasol, a simple single engine, single pilot airplane. All his flying and airplane-building came to an end with the 1929 market crash and the Depression. My father sold his little airplane to another young pilot, who would someday become the president of Northwest Airlines.

Dad flew a little during the 1930s, and when the war started, he hoped to fly with the Army Air Forces but was rejected from military service because of a heart problem. After the war, my dad continued flying and bought his first airplane in 1948, a Cessna. In 1952, he traded the Cessna for the Beach Bonanza, *Bonnie*, that Sandy and I flew. Dad and I spent hours flying together. It is no secret that he, in fact, loved trains too. As I have heard it said, "Like father, like son." Flying and trains were part of my life for as long as I can remember.

So, since Sandy was doing her favorite hobby, sunbathing, I jumped at the opportunity to indulge in my favorite hobby too. The Pima Museum is very large, with all kinds and types of airplanes and related exhibits. I was ecstatic when I arrived and spent the next few hours joyfully looking at old airplanes from all periods of time. As an added bonus, I was able to take a side trip to the Davis Monthan Air Force Base to see the mothballed and stored Air Force planes. Davis Monthan was built in 1925, and served as an Air Force base during World War II, and is still active today. When an airplane has served its useful life, it is sent to Davis Monthan, where it is stored for possible future use or disposed of. The dry desert air makes for a good storage facility.

Driving back to the hotel, I thought about how the day had gone. Realizing that on my own I couldn't have planned such a fun day, I thanked the spirits for another job well done. I returned to find Sandy resting in our room. We talked about our day and how we each were able to partake in our favorite hobby. We agreed that we were ready to return home.

The next morning was a clear, sunny day as my rock had predicted. After breakfast, Sandy and I drove to the airport where we found a happy *Bonnie*.

"*Bonnie* looks happy to see us, and like a puppy, she is ready to go," Sandy said.

We filed our flight plan and headed home, two happy people, still in love after twenty-five years.

CHAPTER 30

Thousands of candles can be lighted from a single candle,
and the life of the candle will not be shortened.
Happiness never decreases by being shared.

—BUDDHA

August 1986

It had been a year and half since Gordon and Sandy began training for their new life. They had completed Shambhala levels
one through ten. When the student completes a level, he or she
can return and assist the staff, helping to support the weekend, by
keeping the meditation hall neat, keeping time, cleaning, and doing
any other chore that might need attention. It is also an opportunity
for more sitting. The next level of training for Gordon and Sandy
would be Warriors Assembly. Warriors Assembly is a two-week

program at the Shambhala Center northwest of Fort Collins, Colorado. Sandy and Gordon were signed up and ready to begin the program midsummer.

The *kyudo* practice was also moving along, but slowly. Sensei used to compare *kyudo* practice to a baby learning to sit up, crawl, and then walk. Each of the eight steps, or stages, of *kyudo* has to be learned individually, which is a slow and tedious process. There is so much to learn and then so much practicing over and over. The student learns how each stage is correctly executed and then practices each stage until it becomes routine and unchanging. There is always an instructor who offers advice and corrections. The secret to successful shooting is practice, practice, and more practice. It takes many years before the student can execute each of the positions correctly and shoot without thinking.

Hitting the target is a combination of the mind and the body working together in perfect harmony. In the beginning, the conscious mind is always thinking and trying to perform correctly. The conscious mind is trying to direct the student to shoot correctly in order to hit the target repeatedly, which is not possible. The object is to train the mind to think from the subconscious and not the conscious, thereby reacting from memory only—thus, the need for practice. In addition, the body must be physically conditioned and the muscles strengthened to handle the stress of shooting.

Think about driving a car. We don't think consciously to add gas when we want to go or break when we want to stop; it just happens. The practice is imbedded in our subconscious. With practice, we can stop exactly where we want to, time after time, never giving it a thought. To illustrate further, have you ever found yourself driving home only to realize you wanted to go to the drug store? Sometimes the conscious mind has to intervene and remind the subconscious that we are not going home, we are going to the drug store first.

In Shambhala, in *kyudo* practice, and in life, we are constantly reminded of the importance of balance.

In *kyudo*, Sensei would say, "Draw the string and arrow back about six inches past your nose, level with your mouth. With the left hand and arm, push forward until you are about two inches from full extension. When you release the string and arrow, the right arm swings open and the left hand and arm push the bow forward the last two inches. When this is done correctly, the archer will achieve full openness and perfect balance."

It is said that when a student in ready to learn, a teacher will appear. Sandy was more than willing and thus Sensei and Sandy created a very special bond.

By pushing the left arm the additional two inches, the arrow enjoys a little extra push.

Balance is also important in sitting practice. It is important to sit upright with a good alignment between the head and shoulders. All parts of the body are in perfect balance. This way, the mind is not occupied with correcting an out-of-balance body. Balance is natural, comfortable, and relaxing. Learning correct balance takes time. Learning correct balance in life means living a centered life, not having one extreme or another.

Today, we see people living far right or far left. Democrats versus Republicans, religion versus nonreligion, democracy versus socialism, women versus men, men versus women, and on and on. People tend to identify either one way or the other, sometimes simply for the comfort of belonging or fitting in. Yet, it is important to understand that we can't live all one way or another. We must balance our behaviors, beliefs, and ideals. We must find a center point where everyone enjoys what they want and we take the best of the right and left.

Shibata Sensei said it best, "How can we enjoy life if we don't have night and day, mountains and valleys, cold and hot, sweet and sour, sunsets and sunrises, hard and soft, love and anger, and so on?"

Love, I believe, is based on balance, being centered, accepting other points of view, and seeing that I must compromise or else live a life of anger, hate, frustration, lying, and maybe loneliness. We must give time to others, maybe half our time.

I have heard people say, "Giving half my time to help others is too much. I need most of my time to develop my own path."

My response is simple: I learn and focus on my path by helping others. In this way, you can give and receive at the same time. Watching others grow is a mirror of myself, my reactions and behaviors. Simply said, what I see in another person is myself. If I see anger in another person, I know I am angry. If I see love and happiness, then I know I am loving and happy.

Just for fun, I walk down a street, and look at other people, and acknowledge what I see and ask myself, "Is that me?"

These people are reflecting my feelings so I can understand my current state of mind.

The problem with balance is that one might think they have to divide life fifty/fifty on everything. For me, this isn't true. There are times when I will swing to one side or the other. But it is important to be able to see where I am and why I am on the far left or right. Once I understand where and why, then I can move back to the center. If I am strongly opinionated, I will probably alienate or frustrate other people. Yes, I can express my views, and sometimes, I might influence someone. Yet, the softer and more gentle way is to compromise and hope each person gets what he or she wants. A great deal of the time, our arguments, beliefs, and ideas change as time passes, and I must be continually aware that what I believed today may not work tomorrow. Change may take a few days, or weeks, or sometimes years, but in all cases, it is worth it.

Balance is a very complicated subject. It is interlaced with feelings and self-centeredness. I have tried to find an American example of balance, and to date, I have been unsuccessful. So, I turn to my Japanese teachings for a solution. It is very important to our personal and worldviews that we understand balance. In fact, it may mean our survival. I am going to reference two sources in relation to balance. First is the book: *An Offering of Light: Healing with Jyorei, Natural Agriculture, and Art* by Roy Gibbon and Atsushi Fujimaki with Gerard Rolfing. The second is an article from the *Shumei Journal* 2017 by the founder of Shumei, Mokichi Okada, referred to as Meishusama. (Mokichi Okada was a spiritual teacher who was active in Japan during the first half of the twentieth century. His life was dedicated to serving humanity through spiritual healing, the arts, and spiritual-based food cultivation.)

In this article, Meishusama says, "Generally, people believe that there can be no spiritual pursuit without a painful effort. I disagree with putting too much emphasis on severity. The purpose of spiritual practice is not harshness but to find a way to make life easier. It aims to improve one's spiritual condition. This is the essential thing I would like you to understand, and with this understanding, continue in your spiritual pursuits."

Meishusama went on to say that "The ultimate and the immediate are not separate but are actually one undivided whole," He explains that life has two overriding purposes: "the spiritual development of the soul and the simple enjoyment of the present moment. One appears distant and the other close, yet happiness and enjoyment depend, to varying degrees, upon both the sacred and the secular. Two things contribute to our sense of happiness: the soul's spiritual purity and the amount of peace and harmony in one's surrounding environment. In the joy that comes from experiencing beauty, both the inner and the outer come together because outer beauty can only be appreciated to the extent that one is inwardly capable of perceiving it. Thus, the higher our spiritual, the more we live in a world of beauty."

We must learn to love ourselves and others completely and unconditionally. We have two objectives: one, we must feel; and two, we must work toward higher values: truth, virtue, and beauty. This will help us grow spiritually and also help contribute to our overall enjoyment and happiness in our day-to-day lives. If the only purpose in life was enjoyment, then there would be no need for high principals. Kindness, loyalty, honesty, generosity, altruism, fairness, and many others human virtues would have only been used because they are pleasurable, not because they reflect something of higher value.

Meishusama says, "Eventually hedonism can become empty and meaningless, not to mention painful."

Our attraction to pleasure always coincides with an aversion to pain. They go hand and hand. And since no one can control everything, then none of us can avoid experiences that cause pain. Each of us will inevitably experience suffering in one form or another during our lifetime.

The objective of balance is to center ourselves. If I turn left, I must turn right or straight, or I will go in circles. When traveling down a road in my car, I sometimes go fast, other times slowly. I balance speed with road conditions and traffic. In our daily life, we need air to breathe, water, and food. Some people need more air, water, and food, depending on their lifestyle. High-energy people: athletes, construction workers, military personnel, and similar others may need more food and water than a person who works in an office. Here we see balance in our food intake, to maintain the body weight we want or desire for the lifestyle we are living.

I relate balance or equilibrium to flying. As the pilot, I am making constant changes in the direction of the airplane to stay on course and altitude. Sometimes only small changes are required, but other times, large changes are needed. It is absolutely necessary to determine the path or course I want to fly. I could trim the airplane, let it fly on its own, and just sit back and watch. However, at some point, I will need to land or I could just crash. As I sit in AA meetings, I hear people talk about their lives and realize some people are just sitting back and letting the airplane fly itself and are oblivious to what is going to happen next. However, others have found sponsors and are working on a clear path to recovery.

At this point in their lives, Sandy and Gordon are slowly beginning to understand balance. Pulling the bow string until it reaches balance improves the flight of the arrow so it hits the target. Sitting on a cushion, upright and straight, not leaning left, right, forward, or backwards improves the flow of thoughts and minimizes pain. But how can we organize our thoughts into something useful and applicable to life? Meishusama, the founder of Shumei, organized human thoughts, beliefs, habits, opinions, ideas, views, and assessments into two straight lines.

The first straight line is called *shojo*, the principal of inwardness. The second straight line is *daijo*, the principal of outwardness. *Shojo* is fire, which burns upward; *daijo* is water, which flows laterally. *Shojo* is the inclination toward spiritual growth; *daijo* is the inclination toward service to others. *Shojo* unites individuals with God; *daijo* unites people with people. The former is driven by the desire for truth and freedom; the latter is motivated by generosity and love. Freedom without love is joyless and uncaring; love without freedom is deluded and emotionally binding. On a mundane level, *shojo* represents conservatism and *daijo* represents liberalism. *Shojo* is analytical and detail-oriented, whereas *daijo* is holistic and focuses on pattern recognition. *Shojo* looks at the trees, whereas *daijo* sees the forest.

Gordon looked at Sandy and asked, "Do you understand any of this?"

"A little," Sandy said, "but I think together, and with the help of our teachers, we will be able to implement this into our lives." She continued, "It will be a challenge, and I see a lot of compromise. We will have to go beyond our self-centeredness. I also believe we will need to be patient, take our time, and understand this could take months or even years."

"If I understand this principle," I responded, "we need to find the point where *daijo*, the horizontal cross, and *shojo*, the vertical cross, intersect. I think they call this *izunome*. I can see balance or equality, or I can see a destructive balance if we don't compromise. I believe all living things require an agreeable balance in order to enjoy a safe and contented life, never one extreme or the other."

"I believe this is a balance between wisdom and compassion," Sandy said. "You, Gordon, lean toward wisdom and facts, and I, on the other hand, lean toward compassion. This will require both of us to understand and accept each viewpoints. We both must comprehend each other's perspectives, which are connected, yet separate. I must understand how a tree lives and functions so I can see the tree in its relationship to the forest."

"I agree with you completely, I said. However, I know the solutions may swing to one side or the other, depending on what needs to be accomplished. I will always be technical, and you will always be compassionate. As changes arise, we use what is appropriate. We each have our own talents."

"Yes, I agree. I think I see Eastern civilization as *daijo* and Western civilization as *shojo*," Sandy added. "Meishusama did say that the very idea that you have to be *daijo* automatically makes you *shojo*."

Sandy and I agreed to make a game out of this. We would look at each situation and try to find the balance by first relating it to *daijo* and then to *shojo*, and then we would seek a compromise. I think we both knew that all our needs and desires would not always be met. We also knew that sometimes we would be out of balance and that some needs and desires would not be equally met. The needs of one person may be more than the needs and desires required by the other person. These choices would require a complete understanding of truth, virtue, and beauty to work out a compromise.

CHAPTER 31

How we think shows through in how we act.
Attitudes are mirrors of the mind.

—DAVID JOSEPH SCHWARTZ

August 1990

The time for Warrior Assembly had finally arrived, and Sandy and I were on our way. The Warrior Assembly is a two-week program of intense meditation and teaching so that we may enjoy a better and more fulfilling life. Most of the time is spent meditating, with breaks for chores and personal time. Free time is very limited. We left Denver late in the morning for Fort Collins, Colorado. We had planned to eat lunch in Fort Collins, as we knew it would be the last chance to eat a real meat-and-potatoes lunch for two weeks. The food at the Rocky Mountain Dharma Center (RMDC) was guaranteed to be lean and healthy. After lunch, we continued our drive. It was a wonderfully clear and warm day with just a hint of wind. As we drove deeper into the mountains, I noticed that our silence for the past twenty minutes had been tense. Finally, Sandy broke the silence.

"You know, dear, this will be at the top of our list of uncommon things we have done. I know we both love doing new things and journeying into the unknown, but committing to sitting meditation for two weeks may be too much. Do you think we can do this?"

I paused in contemplation for a few seconds. "I have had the same thought for the past month. As you know, I like to know what I am getting into and have some control over the situation or program. But I'm at a total loss as to what is going to happen and how I'm going to react. I'm anxious and fearful, but I know we can do this."

"I agree with that," Sandy replied, "It also brings up a lot of fear in me."

"We are going in blind. But we have come this far with our meditation practice, so we can't stop now. I am sure glad we are doing this together."

I smiled at her.

"You and I do well together," I said. "Supporting each other has made our life a wonderful, joyous, and happy adventure. This is going to be an exciting learning experience for the next two weeks. Do you think we can use that balance thing we learned?"

"It sure is going to be challenging, and I think the time at RMDC will provide us with many chances to use balance," Sandy said. "Something tells me we are going to be pushed in all directions."

"I agree with that," I replied.

We returned to silence, but this time, it held an air of comfortable contemplation.

The drive to RMDC was through the rolling Colorado mountains covered with evergreen trees accompanied by otherwise sparse vegetation, due to the dry climate. We passed several ranches and private homes; many were very old. We finally arrived at RMDC and were surprised to see several small houses and trailers and one main lodge building. There was a sign over one of the doors that said Office. We were not alone. There were several other people with the same idea as we'd had: time to get signed in.

Sandy looked at me. "Not what I had expected," she said. "Looks a little primitive."

"Our adventure just got a lot more exciting and preternatural," I replied. "Let's check in."

We entered a room that was very basic. There were tables and chairs, and we had a feeling we had just stepped back in time. A single black leather couch, which had seen better days, sat along one wall. On two walls hung landscape paintings and behind what appeared to be a registration table was the Shambhala flag.

I heard someone ask: "Are you checking in for Warriors Assembly?"

Sandy nodded, and the lady beckoned us to a table with a sign that said Registration.

We gave the woman at the table our names, and with a big smile, she said, "Welcome."

We were told that we would be staying in separate tents with a roommate. Sandy and I looked at each other with looks of confusion and puzzlement.

"In tents?" Sandy asked.

"Yes," she said. "The weather is mild, and it will give you a feeling of being with nature."

"Shambhala is an ongoing adventure; let's do it," Sandy said.

We were given instructions on where to park our car and how to get to our tents. After parking the car, we walked to the center of the compound. On our left was the volunteer workers' quarters and kitchen, an older wooden one-story building. On our right was a white tent that would be our dining room. In front of us there were six twenty-foot-high poles with Shambhala flags and banners. Beyond the flag poles was a very large white tent that, we would learn later, was our meditation room.

"This is not what I expected," Sandy said, "but I think we are going to learn a lot about meditation in a more primitive form—or more about how it is related to nature."

I agreed that it was sure going to be different.

We located the trail to our tents just south of the meditation tent. The trail was single file; Sandy led off. The center was located in the middle of the forest with many large pine trees, typical of a Colorado forest. There were mountains on all sides, and the location couldn't have been more beautiful. The trail sloped down to a small streambed with green grass and small plants. We crossed and ascended up to the tent area. We had walked for about a half mile when the trail separated.

"I think my tent is to the right; is yours to the left?" I inquired.

"Yes," Sandy replied, then looked back to the main center. "I think we have found Shangri-La, but it needs a bit of work."

We both laughed.

The Shambhala Center would evolve into a more modern facility over the next few years and provide many more Shambhala, Buddhist, and meditation programs. Sandy and I did not know it at the time, but we would return many times to this center.

"Well, I guess this is where we part," Sandy said.

We kissed and hugged like we were not going to see each other for several months.

"See you at dinner," Sandy said.

My tent was not far from where Sandy and I had parted, nestled among the pine trees. There was a wooden floor, and the tent was about twelve feet by twelve feet with a seven-foot high ceiling. Entering through a door flap, I saw two beds and two tiny dressers. There was a horizontal pole to hang clothes on and two small plastic windows that allowed a small amount of light to enter. My roommate had not yet arrived.

As I looked around the room, my mind flashed back to twenty-eight years ago. I was sixteen, and my father had a very close friend, Bob, who was an underground water pipeline contractor. It was summer, and Bob had a water pipeline contract in Jackson Hole, Wyoming. Bob offered me and my friend Brian a job on the survey crew. It was my very first job away from home, and yes, we lived in a tent just like the one I was standing in. The following summer, Brian and I would be in San Antonio, Texas, together for nine weeks of Air Force basic training. Brian and I went from boys to men in a very short time.

The sound of someone coming into the tent rattled me back to the present. It was Jack, my roommate. Jack was from Denver, about thirty-five years old, tall, and had dark brown hair. We introduced ourselves and chatted about our past and why we here at Warriors Assembly. He was a likeable guy, and we would spend the next two weeks as good old friends. Jack and I settled in, and soon it was time for dinner. As we walked the trail back to the dining hall, I again marveled at the beautiful surroundings and thanked God for His handywork.

Sandy was already in the dining hall with her roommate, Helen. The four of us enjoyed a healthy dinner consisting of a salad, chicken, rice, vegetables, and a light dessert, which was all quite tasty. We all commented that steak and potatoes would have to wait until we returned to Denver. Near the end of dinner, the facilitators arrived, a man and a woman. We were given the basic daily routine. We would rise and shine at seven in the morning, eat breakfast at eight, and meditation would start at nine. At noon, we would eat in the meditation hall and would be taught *oryoki*, an eating practice using bowls and chopsticks. An *oryoki* set consists of five bowls, small to large, all stacked into one another, chopsticks, a cleaning spatula, and a napkin, which would be wrapped around the bowls and tied at the top when not in use.

At noon each day, we would pick up our *oryoki* set from a rack in the meditation room along with a small table and return to our cushion. We would then unwrap our bowls, place them onto the table, and wait to be served. Picking up our *oryoki* sets, placing the bowls on the table, eating, and cleanup had to be done without making a sound, including no talking. Once we had finished eating lunch, which meant eating every last morsel of food, the server would fill our smallest bowl with hot water. Using a small clean spatula with a cloth on the end of a stick, we would clean our bowls, pouring the water from one bowl to the other. Once washed, we would drink the water, which tasted like hot broth. Using the napkin, we would dry the bowls and then wrap and tie the napkin around the bowls and return the set to the rack in the meditation room, ready for our next meal.

This form of eating was taught to the Sangha people in India by the Buddha some 2,500 hundred years ago. If you were Buddhist, you would meditate for thirty days and would eat all meals *oryoki* style in the meditation room. But Shambhalaians are not that disciplined, so our practice was only two weeks long. After lunch each day, there was a work session. Each participant was assigned a job: kitchen duty, restroom duty, general cleanup, or any job that had to be done. There were also a few minutes for personal chores. Meditation would resume at three o'clock and last until dinner at six. After dinner, it was back to the meditation hall for another hour of sitting, usually accompanied by a lecture. Some days, however, study class would supersede sitting.

The lectures included living in a warrior world, how to live our lives, how to treat people, and how to respect ourselves and others. We also learned how to dress with beauty and respect, how to take care of and respect our homes, and how to serve others. One day, I was taught how to set a table and properly serve a formal lunch or meal. There was so much to learn, and I thought that I must have missed many classes growing up. I was so thankful for the Shambhala teachings and would say a little prayer each night thanking God for my good fortune. Yes, there were also times when the sitting and discipline became overwhelming, and it required everything I had to keep going, and there were several times I simply wanted to give up, but I didn't.

We all finished the two weeks with a celebration dinner. It was a moment of sheer joy and happiness. Sandy and I sat together and couldn't remember when we both had been so happy. We knew this was only the beginning of a very demanding path and practice. As we looked into each other's eyes and held hands, there was nothing to say; we had survived the two weeks in a world that was totally unfamiliar but would become routine in the Shambhala world.

The next morning, we packed and headed home. As you might believe, the drive home was light and happy. The tension, fear, and anxiety were gone. We both felt proud of ourselves for what we had accomplished. Sandy said that there were times when she thought she would give up and not finish, but she gathered strength and remembered what we had been taught about balance. We could have quit, or we could go on and finish. Both require a commitment.

Quitting would have left us disappointed, dejected, and I am sure angry. Finishing, we enjoyed the feeling of winning over failure. The two weeks were full of frustration, confusion, and hard work. On the other hand, it was balanced with joy, happiness, companionship, and that great feeling of "I did it." What we learned from Warrior Assembly will stay with us forever. Sandy and I were slowly learning to trust our Guiding Spirits and their ability to lead us through any situation. Could we have lived through and finished the program without the spirits? Yes. Would it have been the same experience? I don't know.

CHAPTER 32

Learn from the past, set vivid, detailed goals for the future, and live in the only moment of time over which you have any control: now.

—DENIS WAITLEY

September 1990

Sandy and I were so glad to get back to the comfort of our home, especially our own bed. The routine of AA meetings, Sandy working at the hospital, and me back to my construction business was so welcome. The following Sunday, we two new young warriors headed to *kyudo* class. After the Warriors Assembly, we both had a new appreciation and better understanding as to the goal of *kyudo*. The idea of shooting and meditation was coming slowly together. We were both anxious to tell Sensei the news about Warriors Assembly. After class, we cornered Sensei and told him how wonderful Warriors Assembly had been. His only reaction was a sensei smile that said, "I am proud of you." No words needed to be spoken.

The summer was coming to an end, and there was a feeling of fall in the air. Sandy and I hadn't planned much for the upcoming winter except to continue to work on our programs. We had volunteered several times to work at the Shambhala weekend meditation programs. Sandy had said that the two-day weekends were a wonderful way to get away and focus on only meditation and to help others through the program.

It was late September when George called and said he and Kathy were going to take the boat to the Mississippi River, near St. Louis, and head downriver to the Arkansas River. He wondered if we would be interested in joining them. I thought, "Leave it to George to find something new and adventurous to do." I told him that I would check with Sandy.

I picked up Sandy after work, and we headed to Olive Garden for a quick dinner. We caught up on our latest activities and how work had been.

I then asked, "George and Kathy are heading out for a boat trip; you interested in joining them?"

"Where?"

"Old Mississippi River," I responded.

Sandy hesitated for just a moment and asked, "When and how long?"

"In about three weeks, and if we want, we could stay two weeks or so."

Sandy looked around the restaurant, and I could tell she was thinking.

"Yes, but for only a week or so," she said. "I think I can get that off work."

I agreed and said I would call George and get the exact dates. We finished dinner and headed home. The next day, we were committed. We would meet George and Kathy in Memphis, Tennessee, on September 13, a Thursday. We would all travel down the Mississippi to the confluence of the Arkansas River and up the Arkansas for about three days. If all went well, that would put us at Fort Smith, Arkansas.

Sandy and I had made many changes in our lives: AA, Shambhala, and *kyudo*. True friends learn to adapt to change. George and Kathy had accepted our changes and knew that sex and drinking for Sandy and me had to stop, and they were OK with that.

Over the next few days, we talked about the trip. Like our hobo train ride, this was going to be a real adventure. I told Sandy that there was an old and fancy hotel in Memphis that my father and I had stayed at with a very unusual history. I went on to suggest that we could leave a day early and spend the night there. Sandy agreed. Before she could ask about the hotel, I changed the subject and asked about dinner. This diverted out attention, and the hotel was forgotten. I was glad because the story of the hotel was going to be a real surprise.

September 12 finally arrived, and Sandy and I were off to Jeffco Airport. The day before, I had fueled and completed a preflight check so that *Bonnie* would be ready to go. The weather was clear, and we had a nice tailwind out of the west, which would be appreciated. We opened the hanger door, and there was *Bonnie* in her blue and white dress outfit.

I truly think she was smiling and asking, "Where to this time?"

"Hi, *Bonnie*, ready to go the Memphis?" I asked.

"You sure look clean and pretty," Sandy added.

What a way to start a trip.

Our plan was to stop in Oklahoma City for lunch and then go on to Memphis, arriving around three in the afternoon. The plan worked, and we arrived just after three thirty local Memphis time. We found a hanger, and after cleaning the bugs off *Bonnie* and applying a little polish (the ladies like a little makeup), we bid *Bonnie* farewell. We told her that we would be back in a week or so, and she was good with that.

We arrived at the Peabody Hotel around four-thirty p.m. Sandy was impressed with the grandeur and elegance of the hotel. The Peabody was built in 1869 with an addition added in 1933. When the hotel opened in 1869, a room and meals would cost you four dollars. As we entered the lobby, Sandy was surprised and baffled to see five North American Mallard ducks, one drake, and four hens in the hotel lobby water fountain.

"What is that?" she asked.

"Wait, there is more," I said with a grin.

We checked in and returned to the fountain and the ducks. At precisely five o'clock, a bell man rolled a red carpet from the fountain to the main elevator. The elevator doors opened, and the ducks hopped out of the fountain and went directly to the elevator. Sandy turned and looked at me.

"That was unbelievable!" she exclaimed. "Tell me the story about the ducks."

I smiled. In 1933, as a joke, one of the owners of the hotel thought the fountain should have ducks in it. He found a couple of fake ducks, which were soon replaced with real ducks. The hotel guests loved the ducks and wanted them to stay. The owners, wanting to cater to the guests, decided to keep the ducks, but they couldn't stay in the fountain all day and night. A decision was made by the owners to build a house on the roof of the hotel for the ducks.

A simple wooden box home would not do for these fancy ducks. So, a large glass enclosure with a natural grass yard and marble replica of the hotel was made for their home at a cost of $200,000 dollars. The ducks come from a nearby farm, where they are raised. They only stay at the hotel for three months and then are released back into the wild. They have been trained to come down the elevator at exactly eleven a.m. and return at five p.m. every day since 1933.

Sandy was so impressed and couldn't believe what she had seen. At dinner that night, all she could talk about was the ducks, the beautiful hotel, and the lovely flight from Denver. It was a wonderful start for our next adventure. Early the next morning, we were off to the marina to meet George and Kathy. They had arrived late the day before and were busy preparing the boat, loading fuel and food. We were met with a rousing welcome. George and Kathy had become very close friends, and we always enjoyed the time spent together.

After loading our gear and finishing the last-minute chores, George and I sat down and planned out our strategy for the trip. It was one hundred or so miles down the Mississippi to the confluence of the Arkansas River and then up the Arkansas to Fort Smith, another three hundred miles. George and I looked at each other.

"Where do you suppose we can find fuel on the Mississippi?" I asked.

"Good question," George answered.

The river maps did not show any marinas on the Mississippi, so we began asking the locals if they knew of any marinas.

The stock answer was: "Nobody goes downriver."

The range on the boat was about one hundred miles. It hadn't occurred to George or me that there would not be a marina on the Mississippi River. The Mississippi was an industrial river, not a recreational river, so there was no need for marinas between the large cities like St. Louis or Memphis. We had the advantage of the river flow, but we still could come up short on fuel. The girls, who had been listing in, asked if we would be able to go.

"If we are going to make it, we are going to need more fuel," George said.

"Let's buy four five-gallon cans, fill them with fuel, and tie them to the swim platform," I suggested. "If we still need more fuel, we can walk to one of the towns that dot the riverbank behind the levy and fill the cans."

George agreed. We bought the cans, filled them with fuel, and secured them to the swim platform. By the time we finished, it was about noon, so we walked to the marina restaurant and had a wonderful fish lunch.

After lunch, we cast off and headed to the main channel. The marina crew wished us well. Once on the river, we learned very quickly that the Mississippi is not your typical river. It was like we had entered a lost world. The riverbanks were mostly green grass with occasional trees and scrub bushes. It was beautiful in a way, untouched and wild. We did not see a house, town, or indication of civilization the whole time we were on ole Miss. As this was an industrial river, we quickly learned that the only inhabitants were the towboats and their barges.

Cruising down the river was relaxing and calm. The river was generally wide and the current was gentle and increased our speed. It wasn't long before we met our first river inhabitant. There was a gentle bend in the river and slowly approaching around the corner, we could see the lead barges, four wide, brown and rusted. Soon there were many more, attached to a large towboat. It was pushing and working hard against the current and the river, diesel engines rumbling like some giant monster. It was understood that the towboat would not alter course or direction to accommodate us. We slowed our speed and drifted to the right-hand side of the river, allowing a clear path for our friend. As we watched the monster pass, several crew men came out on deck. We must have been an oddity to them. We waved our hands in a gesture of "How are you? Are you having a good day?" To our surprise, we got no response. We guessed that maybe we were not welcome on their river.

The day had been perfect with very little wind, mostly clear, and just warm enough to be comfortable. The girls had migrated to the rear deck where they could sunbathe, read, and relax. George and I had been looking downriver when we realized two beautiful and lovely women were standing behind us.

"We would like some dinner," Kathy said. "Are you two sailors ready to find a campsite and call it a day?"

"You must have been reading my mind," George said. "I was thinking the same thing."

Moments later, we spotted a cove off the river with a sandy beach at the end. The water was deep, so we slowly cruised up to the beach and tied off, just enough to be secure but not enough to become grounded. We could still see the river off our back deck. As we ate dinner, we commented on how alone we were, with no idea of what lie beyond the trees surrounding us. We were, again, in paradise. These were the times we talked about all the wonderful things we had done together and how we had become close friends. We all agreed that there would be many more trips ahead.

We ate dinner and had just cleaned up when we realized the sun was setting. This sunset was one to remember, orange and red, with a few clouds to accent the color. We were so relaxed that we did not move as night closed in around us. I think we were all half asleep when the flash of a big searchlight could be seen searching the river. Startled, we sat up.

"What is that light?" Sandy asked.

Before anyone could answer, the sound of a several thousand horsepower engine could be heard. We knew it was a towboat working up river, searching for any debris in the water and/or other towboats. We watched as the towboat slowly passed by, its running lights gleaming and the lights from the wheelhouse outlining the crew. Soon, there was complete silence again, and we all headed to our cabins, a very tired crew.

The next morning, we were up early and headed downriver. Sometime around two in the afternoon, we came upon the confluence of the Arkansas River, and there we turned west. The summer had been fairly dry, and the Arkansas was running low. Shortly up the river, we encountered a large, impressive Corp of Engineer dredge working to deepen the channel, which is maintained at a nine-foot minimum. Half a mile further, we came to our first lock and dam on the Arkansas.

Shipping by barge is the cheapest form of transportation, and on June 5, 1971, the Arkansas opened to barge traffic. From the Mississippi River junction to Tulsa, Oklahoma, is 445 miles and rises 420 feet through eighteen locks. Each lock is 110 feet wide and 600 feet long. George and I reasoned that the locks would be adequate for our eight-by-twenty-eight-foot boat. The locks range in height. The tallest is fifty-four feet, as tall as a five-story building. Each lock we entered would give us a strange feeling, like being locked in a big box. The gates would close and water would rush in, lifting us up to the next lake. At one of the locks, we were raised up to find a man standing next to the lock. He was the lock master responsible for controlling the flow of boats in and out of the locks, He was a talkative old fellow and wanted to know where we were from and where we were going. Finally, after a half hour of conversation, he opened the upper gates, and we were off.

The Arkansas attracts fishing and recreation, and as we traveled up river, we saw many homes and marinas. We stopped in Little Rock for dinner, and we thought we would try Little Rock Mexican food. The cook obviously had never been to the southwest, as the food tasted like old southern food, mixed with what spices the cook thought were Mexican. I had never tasted anything like it before and never since; however, it was tasty. We spent the night tied to the dock. The next morning, we had breakfast at the dock restaurant before finishing the last leg of our trip, which went beautifully.

We arrived at Fort Smith late in the afternoon. This time, we picked a recommended seafood restaurant for our last dinner; it was wonderful. Early the next morning, Sandy and I caught a commercial flight back to Memphis. We arrived in Memphis around noon. As usual, *Bonnie* was glad to see us and ready to get home, as were her two passengers. It had been a wonderful week: very relaxing and full of fun and a closeness that I had not experienced before. We all felt connected to each other and wanted to go inside each other and look for those feelings we had never felt before. It was like eating a fine dinner; we didn't want to leave any food on the plate for fear we might never taste the same thing again. Maybe the spirits could see into the future, and so they made this trip special. Sandy and I were ready to get back to work and prepare for winter. We had never felt so close to each other.

CHAPTER 33

The size of your dreams must always exceed your current capacity to achieve them. If your dreams do not scare you, they are not big enough.

—ELLEN JOHNSON SIRLEAF

March 1991

At the age of fifty, Sandy and I began to inventory our lives. We had each lived twenty years as children. Then the next twenty-five or so years had been spent together raising two boys and living a life of addiction to alcohol. And now, we were enjoying life and looking forward to winding down in what we call old age. Years back, I heard about a study conducted in Japan that questioned people when they were around forty-five years old. This study was meant to determine two things: at this age will a person 1) continue to grow (meaning learning new things, experiencing new adventures, exploring new ideas, and expanding their life or 2) decide to slow down and finish life in, let's say, the slow lane, by living the rest of life simply enjoying what had been learned, adding very few new things. The survey generally validated that, yes, there are those few people who continue to grow, but the majority merge into the slow lane where life is predictable and manageable for them. This decision happens subconsciously between age forty-five and fifty years of age, about the time many of us begin planning for retirement.

After eight years of AA, personal growth programs, meditation, and counseling, Sandy and I were finally enjoying a life without alcohol and extreme behaviors. We had made new friends and were settling down to a more peaceful life. We also knew that age would slow a person down; however, many of our old drinking friends were still going strong. Sandy and I were well aware that old behaviors would return if we did not maintain involvement in our new programs. We had seen many of our AA friends relapse back to drinking. As I mentioned, only 25 percent of AA members will stay sober the rest of their lives.

The world of recovery is very complex and complicated. We are constantly confronted with new ideas and programs, many of which are untested or unproven. There are many programs that people create, thinking to change their lives for the better, but in the end, they only create chaos and disappointment. As of this writing the AA 12-Step Program has been around for eighty-five plus years without change. It required many years to perfect but has proven the most successful addiction recovery program there is, if followed and worked. Over the years, there have been people who thought they had better ideas and would often modify the 12-Step Program, only to end up in failure. To change one's behavior requires constant practice and a 12-Step Program is a good place to practice.

The 12-Step Program allows people to tell their stories, what their lives were like, and how they were able to change and live a new, healthier life. Each person can tell his or her story about working the steps. It is a place to find help from people who have experienced the same destructive life addictions and to learn solutions through the stories of others. Even though there are no fees or dues, the 12-Step Program will reliably always be there when one needs it, and it will always be there in the future. It endures because it gets results, and people support the AA program by making contributions at each meeting.

For Sandy and me, the idea of sitting back, relaxing, and working a regular program with the tools we had learned was enticing. We could attend meetings, interact with other members, and occasionally attend workshops. We had also planned to work for the next few years or until work became unrewarding. For some reason, this plan did not fully appeal to us. We had learned many new useful behaviors and tools, and our lives were becoming happy, joyous, free, and loving—without alcohol. Somehow, merging into the slow lane did not feel comfortable, and we felt there was still more to learn, and we felt a need to help other AA members work their program.

Sandy and I had been working with our therapist, Pat, for about eight years. Recall that she was a believer in women's rights and a strong supporter of the women's liberation movement of the 1980s.

Pat claimed: "Women were suppressed by men, forced to work in the home, support the man, and raise the children." She supported the idea that women should have the opportunity to create their own identity, to become equal to men, to have equal rights and pay. Women should find a means to support themselves in case they were forced to live on their own. This would give a woman a feeling of independence and personal satisfaction.

There are people who would say that Sandy was riding on my

coattails. Although she had her own career and could be self-supporting, was she following my shadow? That could be true, but is that bad? If she were to go out on her own, would life be better for her? She had a career. She raised two wonderful children and was always there for them. She enjoyed the luxury of not having to plan every moment of her life. She was able to fulfill most of her dreams and enjoy the journey with someone she loved and someone who loved her. We enjoyed the journey together. Sandy, at this time, was flying wingman. She enjoyed not having to always make decisions. She could relax and create, work on her goals, or simply live out her dreams, knowing she would always be safe.

However, I was in total agreement with Pat and the women's movement. It made sense to me that women should enjoy the feeling of independence. If a woman was doing the same work as a man, she should be paid the same wage. If a woman wanted to climb the corporate ladder and was qualified, she should be given the opportunity to do so. I could, however, see a lot of backlash coming from men. A woman would be invading territory long held by men, and she might have to fight her way up the ladder without help from the men. She would also face men who never wanted a woman in his workplace world, which was dominated by men.

Sandy and I talked a lot about how she might work into management and a higher paying job. Pat had worked with her for nearly eight years, and Sandy began to feel more at ease in the role of an independent woman. She had tried taking more responsibility at the hospital and asked what she could do to work into management. She had worked nineteen years at the hospital and over thirty years as a registered nurse. During her time as a nurse, Sandy said there had been a lot of changes.

"When I started nursing, a hospital was a place where people went for treatment and to recover from an illness. The nurses would nurture a patient back to health, and the patient would stay as long as necessary to recover. The nurses connected with the patient. However, today, patients are admitted, medicated, and sent home with no time for a nurse to connect and nurture a patient back to good health."

Sandy once said, "I feel like a pill pusher."

She had less than three years to retire but felt that she wanted to work longer, as she loved nursing despite the changes taking place in the healthcare industry. And the idea of the independent woman was very appealing to her. She had succeeded in everything she ever tried, except the skydiving. We all reach our limits. I, on the other hand, did not quite understand the idea of the independent woman. Yes, I had the basics, but I didn't know how to help a woman become an independent woman. I was learning right along with Sandy. I helped where I could and offered encouragement as often as I could.

As humans, I believe we all want the best for those around us, especially our spouse and family. But does this mean I should put pressure on someone to change and force them to accept my ideas to improve their life as I see it? Let's consider what might be true for parenting our children. Parents want their children to enter adulthood with all the information and training they can give so the children will become successful and prosperous. If my child succeeds, society will give me a gold star for being a good parent, and I can impress all my friends with stories of my child's success. The question is, did I ever ask my children who they want to be? Maybe I pushed them into who I wanted them to be?

As a parent, which of the following feels better to say to your friends: "My daughter graduated from college and is now working for a name-brand company" or "My son is an electrician or plumber?" But which child is happier? There are also groups of people who believe they know what is best for other people's children, for example, some schoolteachers and counselors. But I also wonder if children are being pushed into college just to support the college professors and personnel. Working for a corporation can be glamorous. It may even pay well with many benefits. But that can come with stress and demands on a person's time beyond normal working hours. A trade job is often more limiting. What if a person works only to support his hobbies and family and doesn't want glory or fame? We must lead and create an environment that allows everyone to succeed and attain their dreams.

Should your child go to college? I understand that 40 percent of college graduates are working in a job that does not require a college degree. I know some students will make a lot of money with a college degree. But how many will spend the rest of their lives paying off student loans and find themselves in a job they hate? Would a trade school have been a better choice? I was told by the Jefferson County School District in Colorado that, proportionally, more technical school graduates become millionaires than the average college student. It is my hope that as a parent, schoolteacher, counselor, or a trusted advisor, we provide all job opportunities to our children and let them make their own choice for their future and then support them. If they actively choose their own career, they have a vested interest in succeeding and are not working to make their parents or someone else happy.

But not only are we pressured by the expectations of others, we are also constantly pressured to accept the ideas of society that will make us happy and joyful and enjoy a better life. I believe that the women's liberation movement put pressure on women to master two lives or careers. Is that possible? And where does this leave men? What is the role of men in the women's lib movement? Are men supposed to take on two careers as well? One, work to provide for the family and two, be a co-househusband? What do most men know about nurturing and child care? From what I see, most women often take on nurturing both her children and her husband.

The women's liberation group has given us the impression that a woman working for a corporation will be happier than a housewife. The corporate woman gets a gold watch at retirement. However, a mother acquires a lifetime of memories and achievement she created with her children. Who is happier, a woman who had a chance to direct her own life or the woman who was always serving the corporation? Yes, I know a woman can be both a mother and a corporate employee. My question is, can someone be completely successful and happy leading two lives? Is there enough time in a day to do both well? Can the corporate success replace the missed football game, back-to-school night, or family outing because the company needed her presence? I know a man faces the same standards, but are we or should we be held to the same standards? Men do well in the workplace and generally leave raising the children to the mother. Is this good? Is man genetically designed to raise children? Can we prove they can do child raising, or do we just think they can? I would like to know facts and just not a simple belief. I believe there are ingrained animal behaviors characteristic to men and women. Why do most children go to their mother when they are hurt?

The women's liberation movement is evolving still as we are learning what makes a woman feel accomplished and which marriage partnerships truly work and endure. From what I see, there are a lot of women who plotted their own life path, married or not, only to end up in divorce and alone. I will be the first to say, I don't know what works best, and I am sure there are a lot of happy marriages entering their golden years. But are there a lot of marriages where damage was done by competition, each partner on a different path? Or are there marriages in which responsibilities are shared equally only to find that one partner was never able to accomplish his/her full potential because of a lack of time? Instead of forcing a woman into a career, maybe it would be better to teach a woman to find self-esteem, independence, and leadership in being a mother. Why does our society downplay the importance of running a household? A woman could be a mother, CEO of the Home Corporation, and its stockholder. The father would then be the employee to the Home Corporation, providing income that would be used to run the company. The final product would be children nurtured, given plenty of love, and prepared for the real world after graduation. Sandy worked only four days a week and spent mornings with the children. I only had to feed or put the children to bed at night. My time was short. Sandy had off time to organize and manage the household. For us, the routine was workable. Unless some major problem occurred, Sandy could always get time off.

As we were lured by the promises of the women's movement, Sandy was full of hope that she could make a difference in the world, and I was in full support of her. Pat and I were helping in all ways possible. Sandy felt confident and decided that she wanted to help the nurses she worked with who were alcoholics. Many professional people don't want the general public to know they have a problem with alcohol. Through AA, there are many closed meetings that allow a person to participate in secrecy. Sandy worked in a hospital in Denver that had over 500 employees, and several of those employees were Sandy's friends and fellow program people. She knew that there was a need for closed AA meetings to be available to the hospital employees.

She asked me if I would help her organize an AA meeting of hospital nurses, in program, that might be held at the hospital. Many corporations supported and encouraged such meetings to improve the welfare of their employees. Sandy and I decided to approach the director of her hospital for help. Sandy did a great job of presenting her idea to the director, and I thought we might get his support.

However, the meeting turned into tragedy when the director looked straight at Sandy and said, "To my knowledge, you are the only alcoholic in the hospital."

We couldn't believe a man of his stature could be so naïve. Or maybe he saw her as a problem or threat. Sandy and I left devastated. She had tried so hard and thought she had followed all the rules of the liberation movement.

The story did not end there. Everyone who has ever worked knows that at some time or another he or she will make a mistake in their job. In most cases, mistakes are minor. Sandy had been a nurse for over thirty years and was one of the best, but we all know that when management wants an employee fired, it will happen. Three months later, Sandy was asked to resign from the hospital. Only losing a child or spouse can be more devastating.

She couldn't understand why this happened, and all I could say was, "The director saw you as threat to his hospital."

What could we do? The director had due cause, even if it was petty.

Sandy knew her career as a nurse in a hospital was over. Maybe the spirits were telling her that it was time for a change, but for Sandy, she couldn't see any future. Her attempt at power and independence had failed. This was not what she had been promised. Something had gone drastically wrong, and it was going to take a long time to figure out what.

Please, reader, I would like to know how, as a woman, your involvement in the woman's movement helped or hurt your life.

CHAPTER 34

*Life is inherently risky. There is only one big risk you avoid at
all costs, and it is the risk of doing nothing.*

—DENIS WAITLEY

September 26th, 1993

Driving home from the air show and dinner with Ben and Ann, I
was so happy. The day had been a lot of fun. I wondered how Sandy's
day had been. Had her dinner with her friends been fun? For some
reason, I began thinking about the last few months. Sandy had been
in therapy, and I wondered how she was holding up.

I know I was feeling sad and disappointed that I couldn't help her
more. I kept asking myself, "What more can I do to help her?"

Had I done everything I could to help Sandy get through this
time of disappointment and failure? I could not stop thinking about

our life when I realized there were only a few blocks left and I would be home. Suddenly I realized I was in extreme fear, and I was scared. I sensed something bad had happened.

Had Sandy been hurt or become sick? Maybe something had happened to the boys? Could there have been an accident? I made the last turn onto our street and could see some kind of activity going on. One block to go, and I realized there were several cars in front of our house, which I soon realized were police cars. I knew now that something dreadful was happening. As I pulled to the curb next to our house, I saw an ambulance parked in the driveway. All I knew now was something terrible was happening.

I jumped from my car and ran to the house. The garage door was open, and all the lights were on around and inside the house. As I approached the garage, a large Lakewood police officer stepped in my path.

"Hold on, son. Who are you?" he asked.

"I'm Gordon Calahan, and I live here," I answered. "What is happening?"

"We received a call that someone at this address might be in trouble," he replied.

At that moment, I saw Sandy sitting in her car in the garage. Her hands were holding onto the steering wheel, and her forehead rested at the top of the steering wheel.

"No, this can't be. What has happened?"

As I lunged toward the garage, the officer grabbed my arm.

"Hold on. I can't let you go into the garage."

He then called out to the coroner inside the house and asked if she could come outside.

A woman in her mid-fifties appeared at the door, dressed in a dark blue suit. She stopped a moment and then came over to me.

"Who are you?" she asked.

"Gordon Calahan, I live here."

She then asked for identification. My hands were shaking, but I was able to give her my driver's license. She examined the license and handed it back to me.

"Come with me," she said.

We had just started for the garage door when she stopped. She turned to me.

"Is that your wife?"

I cried out, and the tears began to flow. I wanted to stop a moment and just look, but she grabbed my arm and led me into the house to the living room.

"Please sit down," she said. "I have several questions to ask you. Where were you today and tonight?"

My mind was in total confusion, but I told her I had been with Ben and Ann since early that morning. She wrote down their names and telephone numbers. She asked about my relationship with Sandy: were we getting along, were we having relationship problems, and were we in therapy. I answered, and I provided her with names and numbers of our therapist and several friends. She made a comment that I was not to leave town until she contacted me. I asked why.

"You will be a suspect in Sandy's death until we can complete our investigation and determine how Sandy died," she said calmly. Didn't this woman see that Sandy had died of carbon monoxide poisoning?

It is funny how the mind works and where your thoughts go in the midst of tragedy. Was the coroner accusing me of killing my wife? Would I need an attorney? I then was lost in thought about which of my company attorneys could handle a criminal case. The coroner later explained that they have to investigate all possibilities. For example, I may have killed her and put her in the car to make it look like a suicide.

Finally, she stood, and we went back outside through the garage. Sandy was gone, as was the ambulance and most of the police cars. As the coroner drove off, the last police car departed with her. I turned back to the open garage and began crying like I had never done before. Life as I knew it was over, and the next few weeks were going to be very difficult and challenging. My wingman was down. The house was quiet. The policemen had opened all the doors and windows, and the carbon monoxide smell was mostly gone. I sat down to make the two hardest phone calls I would ever make: to my two sons. I told them what had happened as best I could, and Rich, my oldest son, told me to come to his house for the next few days.

It was then that I remembered our two birds and the cat. Were they OK? I rushed to check on them. Yes, they were fine.

There were two important and significant questions that loomed above all the other questions in my mind. The first was why Sandy would commit suicide, and the second was who called the Lakewood police to go to my house?

The answer to the second question came first. It was Pat, our therapist, who called the police. Sandy was to meet Pat, along with another therapist, and several of her friends for dinner the night she died.

When Pat arrived at the restaurant, she asked, "Where is Sandy?"

"She has not arrived," said Sandy's friend Sue.

From what I heard, Pat turned and said, "Sandy is in trouble; call the police and tell them to go to Sandy's house immediately."

The Lakewood Police arrived at our house about a half hour before I did, and I was grateful because it meant I did not have to come home to find her. I have asked many people if they would have called the police if they had been in Pat's shoes. All said no. What had motivated Pat to call?

Talking to Pat later, she told me she had felt Sandy's presence, and

Sandy had told her to call the Lakewood Police. I have tried to give you, the reader, a sense of how the Spirit World might work. Was it Sandy who came to my car on the way home that night? Was it her spirit who contacted Pat?

I have studied the Spirit World for many years. I have heard many stories about unusual events people have experienced. One story has stood out above most stories. I had a friend in program that worked as an RN in a leading hospital. One day, we were talking about spirits, and he told me in confidence that part of his job, while working in the ER, was to rush revival equipment to a patient's room when the patient had gone flatline or died. He said that every time, without exception, upon entering the patient's room, he would see a white shadow near the patient. If the doctor was able to revive the patient, the shadow would return to the body, but if the shadow left the room, the patient was not revivable.

To answer the first question that I had that night is very complicated. Humans want answers or solutions to all their problems. We make up answers that fit the situation to satisfy our need to know. The answers may be correct or they may be wrong, or they may be a personal belief that fits the situation. However, after twenty-five years of my personal research, I will give the reasons I think Sandy and other people commit suicide. Am I right? I don't know, but what I do know is simple answers won't always solve our big problems.

PART II

CHAPTER 35

*Everything on Earth has purpose, every disease an herb
to cure it, and every person a mission.*

—MOURNING DOVE

The world today is in a great deal of turmoil. Society has polarized into individual groups. Each group believes it has the solution to one or many of the world's problems. Each group is for or against something, and usually, compromise is out of the question. There are also people within these groups who use their power to manipulate or promise rewards that they can't deliver or have no intention of delivering. These people are simply using their power to gain more power. These individuals and groups can be well-meaning and believe that their cause is just, but they are people who reward themselves by external means. They live to be praised for the "good" they believe they are doing.

When we use external power, we are asking someone else to solve our problems. We look for outside validation to be safe, secure, happy, joyous, and perceivably free (but we are actually far from it). For thousands of years, many leaders and others who truly wanted to see a better world, would bend the truth or lie in order to get what they wanted and entice people to join their cause. To this day, some of these leaders have not studied or thought through the consequences of what they are teaching, suggesting, preaching, or what they believe. Their ignorance creates many problems in themselves and those following them, often inflaming anger and causing pain, agony, anguish, suffering, and torment. We must always be vigilant that ignorance can be passed on to his or her believers, thus creating more disastrous results.

I am well aware that there are many injustices in the world that must be corrected or eliminated, but this will never happen if we are lying to ourselves and others. I believe that together, with balance, we can solve all the problems the world is facing. But a solution will only come when people begin to tell the truth and instead of separating, come together so that we can contemplate and consider all the possible solutions to a problem. Indeed, as stated in the Bible, "The truth shall set you free."

In the book *Shambhala: The Sacred Path of the Warrior*, Chogyam Trungpa suggests that we should not be looking externally, but instead we should look internally for a solution to our problems, he said.

"A great deal of chaos in the world occurs because people don't appreciate themselves. Having never developed sympathy or gentleness toward themselves, they can't experience harmony or peace within themselves, and therefore, what they project to others is also inharmonious and confused. Instead of appreciating our lives, we often take our existence for granted, or we find it depressing and burdensome. People threaten to commit suicide because they aren't getting what they think they deserve out of life. They blackmail others with the threat of suicide, saying that they will kill themselves if certain things don't change. Certainly, we should take our lives seriously, but that doesn't mean driving ourselves to the brink of disaster by complaining about our problems or holding a grudge against the world. We have to accept personal responsibility for uplifting our lives."

When someone threatens to commit suicide, are they saying, "Things need to change the way I want them to—or else?" Is this a real solution to a problem? Does the person think punishing others or condemning themselves will change the world? The solution is to turn this outward focus inside. This can only be done by appreciation of the mind and body and realizing that humans do indeed have the power to change their lives, no matter what the circumstances. It is then that one can see that the key to changing the external world is to first change one's internal state. But if this is the answer to a threatened suicide, then the question I have is how do people get to the point of actually committing suicide and giving up completely?

All animals, including humans, must learn to provide for themselves. And for both animals and humans, survival is learned from our parents or whomever raised us. During our teenage years, we question and practice what we have learned and then venture into the world, ready or not. Living on our own, we find life is not easy. We must develop discipline, perfect our daily routine, and accept responsibility. Many of us enroll in higher education or a trade school, which may give us an advantage before entering the world. But what happens when these life skills are not complete? Often, we must search for the path of survival, which may lead to a world of drugs and unscrupulous people. There is also the possibility that we can go back to our parents for help, but they may not be available, or willing to help, or simply don't have the answers we need to survive and live happily, joyously, and freely. Our parents can only teach us the skills they live by. If those skills are lacking, then we may not learn what life can give and may only live a life of existence. Beware of the saying, "Do what I say, not what I do." If our parents lived a life of lying, addiction, or adultery, the time would come when they face the reality of failure.

As a child or student, we can't accept or understand a person who says, "I know what I am doing doesn't work, but it is the only way I know how to survive."

The student or child will say, "I need you to show me the way, not to tell me the way."

When I am left on my own, living alone, or living with someone who is not connected to me, I may struggle to survive. So, what do I need most to survive? I need a teacher who will connect with me and guide me, teach me, or redirect me. This person, I believe, must have the fundamentals of conformity, discipline, and responsibility. I need to know how to be accepted in society and work with others who believe as I do. Often, I need to know not to be different, to work with people, to carry my own weight, and to provide for myself and help the group. I was fortunate to participate in Air Force basic training, where I learned many of the skills my parents did not teach me. Once established and self-supporting, then I was able to plan my future. I can determine who I want to be and who I might want to live with. There are infinite opportunities and lifestyles, and one is not better than the other. I must decide what my mission is in this life. I would suggest choosing the path that makes you feel the way you want to. Life is your choice: to feel sad, victimized, and controlled or happy, joyous, and free. Some choices require a great deal more work than others.

As humans, the one thing we all want most is to be loved. That love should start with our parents or caregivers, but sometimes it doesn't. Later in life, when we fall in love with someone, our parents' love will become secondary but should never be forgotten. I also believe that we are all loved by God and that His love will never end. Even if we were deprived of love by our parents or those who raised us, the love God has for us is unfaltering and unconditional, we need only to realize its presence. Yet, to nurture the love in our lives, we need trust and the confidence that our partner or friend will always help us with support and guidance, if we ask. We also need to know if our partner will allow us to love him or her and to give support, if they ask. It may take me many years to know what a partner needs and wants from me and others and what I want from him or her. This is the beauty of life, learning every day and knowing there will always be changes happening. Awareness is the ability to see the change and adapt.

In the AA 12-Step Program, we recite the Serenity Prayer before each meeting: "God, grant me the serenity to accept the things I cannot change, the courage to change the things I can, and the wisdom to know the difference." This is total awareness.

I think we are all aware of the connection people create or experience when they come together; we call it love. I believe the key ingredient to love is giving; giving unconditionally for as long as your partner asks is a lifetime commitment. We buy or adopt an animal with the understanding that we must feed and care for it for the rest of the animal's life. The animal will also give love in return. Should human relationships be any different? We enter into relationships knowing that we are making a commitment to ourselves and our partner. This commitment may require sacrifices and unconditional giving.

Giving is not supporting; it is assisting your partner to obtain their needs and helping to accomplish their goals. In a partnership, we need to discuss what each partner enjoys most in life and what he or she will provide to the partnership. Businesses are structured around departments or individuals with special talents. The sales, accounting, manufacturing, and human resources departments each focus on what they do best and realize and accept when change is necessary for the company as a whole. So, to me, it is clear that my partner is here to live his or her own path and is here on Earth to learn and fulfill his or her own mission. The key to a successful partnership is balance between one's own mission and support of the partner's mission. Some days will take more giving than others. There is no mission that is more important than another. All missions have equal value.

Why is it that we can become so confused and frustrated with our mission or goals? The simple answer is that we become dissatisfied when we are looking to find happiness, success, pleasure, and contentment from external means. Nothing is ever enough when we let the outside world judge, control, and reward our actions.

I believe we should look inside ourselves and ask, "Am I doing the right thing, or am I simply doing things right?"

If we create truth, virtue, and beauty within ourselves, then it will also be created externally. Then the other people in our lives will notice this and will be inspired to create love and virtue within themselves also.

When we tell the truth without deception and in full honesty, we are creating love. When we are virtuous or giving, wanting the best for another without any conditions, we are expressing love. Love can also be accessed when we are fully present in the now moment, appreciating beauty. We may see a beautiful sunset, a painting, a home or building, a garden, music, a baby or child, or anything that we can see, touch, smell, hear, or taste can make us feel love, happiness, and joyfulness. This satisfies our internal longings.

When there is no love in our world and life, what happens? The human self-centeredness raises its ugly head. The focus turns to me and what can I take from another and, obviously, I won't give anything back because I need everything for me. I need love, but I can't share my love because you may use it against me. I can't buy your love, but maybe I can buy your companionship and maybe your friendship. Why create beauty unless it is for me? I need beautiful things to feel good, and external thinking ensues.

In the world I believe in, where there are spirits in everything, we connect to these individual spirits by creating, expressing, and giving love. All of these spirits are internally within people and things but are only accessed through love. To connect to the spirits, we must create a beautiful place for them to dwell that is harmonious, peaceful, and full of love. Would you enter a room full of smoke, drugs, dirtiness, unsafe conditions, and no beauty? Some people do and enjoy the atmosphere, but what is it that they are actually fulfilling for themselves? Others don't feel good entering these rooms, but do it anyway because they don't know any better. Create a beautiful home, which doesn't have to be expensive and large but well-kept and cared for. Keep your car and personal things clean and neat. And most of all, present yourself to others looking neat, clean, and beautiful.

Then ask yourself, "How do I feel when truth, virtue, and beauty enter my life?"

I would ask you to remember, please, do your part to create love in this world.

CHAPTER 36

Shine your light and make a positive impact on the world; there is nothing so honorable as helping improve the lives of others.

—ROY T BENNETT

Why does a person commit suicide? First, I believe that someone who is on the verge of suicide has lost the awareness of the world around them. This person has lost all love and trust and can't see a path that will make them happy, joyous, and free again—that is, if they were ever happy, joyous, and free in the first place. This person has lost connection with those they love and has become immersed in a world of fear. This is a perceived failure in the ability to survive. All options are seen as exhausted, and loneliness sets in. If there is an option, the desire or energy required to change is beyond the person's ability to accomplish. I believe this is what Sandy thought. Even if this person sees other options, they are discounted as unacceptable.

I strongly believe that when a person reaches that end, he or she has but one thought: "I have lived my life on Earth and have accomplished the mission I came for."

This person wants to return to where he or she came from, which may be Heaven, the Spirit World, or nothingness, but they desperately want to be any place but where they are.

After Sandy resigned from the hospital, she became very lost and wanted to know what to do and where she should go. Nursing had been Sandy's anchor in the sand, and she was adrift. The anchor was gone, never to be recovered. Pat and I suggested that she could work in a rehab center or nursing home. Rehab was out, as she said she was not a teacher or counselor. About that time, a volunteer nursing position opened up in one of the nursing homes, and Sandy thought this might meet her needs. She did not need the money, and volunteering would give her flexibility.

I don't think she put her whole heart fully into that nursing home job. She said that the people in the nursing home were not into starting a new life and that they only wanted to be taken care of.

She said, "I feel more like a nursemaid."

Sandy's mission in life was to help people to heal, and the nursing home was where people went to finish their lives. At one point, Sandy was asked to expand her role as a nurse and help in the management of the business. She agreed, knowing that it would be doing something new and it might be exciting. She worked hard to learn new management skills and felt she was making good progress. However, after about six months, she was informed that the nursing home would be hiring a full-time manager and that she would no longer be needed.

Sandy was becoming introverted and liked to spend time alone; she was a lost child who didn't want to fit in or be with a group. She was looking for a place to be by herself. The Ranch was one of those places, and she was looking forward to spending more time there.

Shortly after, three more major changes hit Sandy. During that summer, Sandy lost her stepmother, to whom she was not really close but was someone Sandy could always go to for motherly advice. She considered her stepmother's advice sound. Sandy and I talked about her family and whether her stepmother had treated Sandy and her brother equally to her own birth children. I'm sure Sandy believed she had, and I'm sure Sandy's stepmother tried to treat all the children equally. In most families, parents do not always treat each child equally. Most often, the firstborn gets more attention. Sandy's stepmother died just a few months before Sandy died, and Sandy was given the answer.

Her stepfather had died and left Sandy's stepmother very well off: millions of dollars. When her stepmother's will was read, Sandy and her brother received only $70,000. Her stepbrother and sister received over a million dollars. Sandy realized that the money and love were never equal. I think she thought or hoped that she would be treated equally, but then she realized that she was not equal in her stepmother's eyes. This had to have been a crushing realization. I hope she did not think that she was not good enough, for she had done more than all of the family combined to help other people. She lost her birth mother shortly after her stepmother. Maybe she was hoping her stepmother would take the place of a real mother, but that didn't happen.

The second loss occurred later that summer; Brian's wife found out that the three of us were more involved than she realized and told Brian to end his relationship with us. I have said Sandy loved both of us, and Brian and I loved her. Was Sandy so much in need of love that she looked to Brian as a backup in case she lost me? Was this possible?

The third disappointment came in late fall. Sandy loved to go to Mountain Air Ranch to relax and recharge. Several of the members had campers on site, and Sandy wanted her own camper where she could hang out, rest, or stay overnight. When she asked for permission to bring her own camper, the camp manager told her that all spaces were full and additional sites were not planned in the future. It broke her heart again. Where would she go?

I think we live in a world that doesn't understand love and may not know how to give love to others.

What if the hospital director had said, "Sandy, your idea of an AA meeting here in the hospital is a great idea, and I think I can make it work"?

What if the nursing home director had said, "Sandy, you are a real asset to our facility, and I think we can work you into management?"

Or what if the Ranch manager might have said, "I will do all I can to find you a spot, you have been a great member."

In love and life, if you can't give someone what they want, you should at least try to help them find other solutions. Yet, there was not any help or hope for Sandy. All three managers were looking out for themselves or using an easy way out. To bring people's dreams to reality takes a lot of work, but the rewards are infinite. There is also the possibility that the managers couldn't help Sandy because of outside influences. However, I always try to remember that if there is a will, there will always be a way.

Sandy was becoming very disappointed in life at that point. She had given so much. We talked about other jobs but could not see any other jobs that would be in her field of nursing or activities that she was interested in. Sandy had enjoyed life to the fullest. She and I had lived an exciting life and experienced so many things. In her eyes, her bucket list was nearly empty. Oh, there was retirement, but what would that bring? Sitting at home and watching Judge Judy on TV? Sandy also told me that drinking and drugs we no longer an option to improve her life or mend a broken heart.

At this point in Sandy's life, I realized the Rogue Spirit was strongly trying to influence Sandy into old behavior. Old behavior would keep her alive, but old behavior was what we wanted to change. Sandy may have looked back and seen that the path she had been on the last few years was not working as she had planned—too many disappointments. For the new path to work we needed goals, and Sandy couldn't see or find a goal that would fulfill her life. But as hard as the Rogue Spirit tired, Sandy would not go back to those drinking days.

I believe that when a person completes his or her mission on Earth and can't see any reason to stay on Earth any longer, that person will leave their life on Earth. Is it possible to influence someone to find another mission or goal? I would like to hope so, but this is not a decision an outsider can make. Completing our journey to enlightenment will take many lifetimes and many trips to Earth, if you believe in reincarnation. In our daily lives we choose goals that will assist us in accomplishing our mission on Earth. We train, practice, and do what is necessary to accomplish the mission we have committed to. When we have accomplished our primary goal or mission, we can choose another goal or mission while living out our time on Earth or we could bask in the glory of our accomplishments, but we must remember that all glory is fleeting and when the glory is gone, we may come face-to-face with the Rogue Spirit. At that point, we must make a choice.

When Sandy died, I realized I had lost the most precious thing in my life. We had been partners and companions, always helping each other accomplish our goals and making each other happy, joyous, and free. Most importantly, we were always there for each other. When times were tough or life became difficult, we could always depend on each other for encouragement, support, and love. One person may have difficulty conquering an obstacle alone, but two people can accomplish almost anything. When one person cannot reach the top of the obstacle, the second person can push the first up and over any obstruction. In life, almost anything we do requires team effort and leadership; it's what helps us accomplish our goals and help other people.

The question I kept asking myself was: Where had I gone wrong? What could I have done to help Sandy through the days, weeks, and months after she was forced to resign from the hospital? Sandy and I had always had goals and dreams we wanted to accomplish, individually or together. Together, all our dreams and goals had come to fruition. This time Sandy could not find a goal or dream she wanted to accomplish that was worth the time and effort she would need to put into it. Dreams and goal must include joy, happiness, pleasure, purpose, and a path to a greater life that will benefit other people and ourselves.

Failure may happen, but the things we learn along our path to failure will only make us stronger and provide the wisdom to accomplish future goals and dreams. The secret lies within ourselves to find the strength to go on. Sometimes failure and the lack of vision will destroy our ability to go forward. This is exaggerated when those people around us are not able to or do not understand what we need. How could they if I don't know what I need?

After Sandy left the hospital, I think she knew her life was over, but she did not want to leave me and our children, and so she began looking for other things to do with her life. When you are at the top of your game, it is hard when you begin to lose. I have heard it said that when a man retires, his life can be over. His life had been his job, and when he no longer has his job and has provided for his family, he dies from some illness. Could this be a form of suicide?

Sandy tried so hard, but there was one thing she began to lose, and that was love. She pulled away from her friends, family, and me. As I believe, Sandy never grew up with the love she needed as a child, and she was always looking to fill that void her whole life. Love is not something you give to someone one time or now and then. It must be given every day.

By the time Sandy died, many of the people who had provided love to Sandy were out of her life. Sandy had lost interest in many of our friends, and so it came down to me and the boys. I was the last person Sandy could depend on to love her. The boys would be around, but they were then on their own, living their own lives.

The world Sandy was living in was totally unknown to me, and I am sure I was losing faith in Sandy and could not understand why she could not move on with life. Pat, our therapist, our friends, and I all tried to help Sandy, but she could or would not listen. I guess it is hard to believe there is a safe harbor when you are in the worst storm of your life and the boat you are on is breaking up.

I think Sandy saw the last of those who loved her, which included me, were slowly leaving her, and without our love, she could not go on. She was becoming more and more lost. She had distanced herself from me to the point that we discussed divorce. I now see that I had put a condition on our future and our love. I broke the rule of unconditional love. I was scared, desperate, and also totally lost. What were the rules in a time like this?

I asked her, "What does our future look like?"

She could not or would not answer that because I believe she did not know the answer. Maybe she knew the only answer was we were going to leave each other.

She had been working with Pat, our therapist, up to the time of her death. Pat had made the comment that Sandy's death surprised her as well. Sandy kept many secrets to herself, but I think Sandy's most important secret was, I am leaving. Did she believe that her birth mother, who was waiting for her in the Spirit World, would give her the unconditional love she desperately needed and was deprived of as a child?

Sandy loved people and realized she was not going to be happy on the path she was on. She did not want to burden or create unhappiness with her family and friends. She knew that if a patient did not want to get well, there was nothing she could do to help them. I think I began to understand this. Maybe Sandy wanted the family to move on and find a new life that would be happy and joyful. I know I will never know the full truth while on Earth, and I will have to wait until I return to the Spirit World. I know I miss her a lot; she had been my soul mate.

Sandy had been volunteering at the Shambhala Center on weekends and had enjoyed a couple of retreats at the Shambhala Retreat Center (RMDC) where we had done Warriors Assembly. Spring was just around the corner, and Sandy had been offered the job of camp nurse at RMDC. She came home the happiest I had seen her in months—a nursing job that would be fun and leave plenty of time for meditation. I was so happy for her. She left home early in June. During the summer, I made several trips to the center and would spend the weekends with her. She appeared to be happy, but I felt there was still something missing. I think she knew that this was only temporary.

During the summer, Sandy meditated and journaled her thoughts; the following is what she wrote.

Here we see Sandy partaking in oreoki, while meditating. After years of practicing meditation a person will see meditation in everything we do, such things as cleaning, cooking, playing, working and yes eating.

REFLECTIONS OF SANDY, 1993

June 15, 1993

Day of Silence

The flowers growing wild are brilliant.

They are all colors of the rainbow.

Dotted here and there throughout the land.

What a joy to smell them and to see them

Swaying in the breeze.

I thought I had the gong timing perfect.

I was sure there would be a gong for tea at four thirty.

Not to be—A walking meditation instead.

Fifteen minutes later was our tea.

Trungpa Rinpoche's picture looked down at me and laughed.

June 17, 1993

I sit on my cushion; the day is hot.

I smell the outhouse, fragrant odors.

I hear someone crunching along the path to the outhouse.

The smell is neither good nor bad.

I remember "thinking" out with the out breath and dissolve.

The lightning strikes

The thunder crashes

The hail pelts down

The rain comes fast.

The night is full of power and brilliance

I feel so insignificant as Nature displays it's magnificent

Music and lights.

June 18 1993

I put two blankets upon my cushion.

I sat down on lumps, bumps, tilting and rocking.

OH—NOT SO GOOD

My back's shooting pains

I can't stay still

I know now, sit firmly on my seat.

Day 6

Donna Soft Hear

The alter in the shrine hall at RMDC was very elaborate.
However, Shambhala is always secular.

Always moving and changing just when we think we are organized. Negotiating weather-Hot-Cold-Rain-Thunder stuff taking up my mind. If we could only stay in one spot for a certain length of time. If the person in front would just stop juggling, we could do what we came to do.

It is really hard here; we moved from one meditation hall to another. Tents are cold, leaky roof.

"We would like to offer you better accommodations in future so you can be more comfortable," they said.

That's the future. This is what we have now, along with that, we have life's problems. Relationships that don't work. Job problems, etc. Something is never right. As the viewpoint of the drama, we can look at this as reminders, but they are not the whole picture, and it is not who we really are. Reminder—Level 1: basic goodness: Despite all the problems in each of us, there is fundamental goodness. That includes who we really are. It is not good as opposed to bad. It is good because it exists.

Rain—helps the flower blooming—good.

Rain—also drips on floor—bad.

Bucket—to keep floor dry—good.

Bucket—makes noise (catching rain)—bad?

Food served on an *orioke* set.

If we look around, we actually have everything we need right now.

In order to touch that goodness in ourselves, we have to soften. We have plenty of opportunity to soften with all the problems.

Start in on habitual behaviors—oh God, someone is on my cushion. I have to have my cushion. See that line as it happens, and open up to it. See what happens. In that moment, we have a choice to get our own way or see what we are doing that opens to other possibilities.

The great thing about it is, when we do the Blah Blah Blah—

If we wait a few days later, we will naturally have a Gap.

We just have to be open to those gaps—when they happen, be willing to acknowledge them and go from there.

Our situations are very generous. Let those open moments touch us.

When we take our posture, we are more willing to be aware of the little gaps that happen; our mind settles also.

Our teacher says that it is possible to do this at any moment. With the first breath we dissolve Gap—notice a wild flower when walking to the outhouse.

Why do we want to open this way? When we feel our heart that way, we know that it is real; there is no doubt about it. That's actually the path that we are on. When we are brave enough to feel our Heart, "The Genuine Heart of Sadness."

It takes quite a lot of exertion to be gentle with ourselves.

It takes a good amount of discipline to look at our thoughts and dissolve out with the breath, to be aware of ourselves. The act of seeing our thoughts and allowing them to dissolve. It allows gaps and light coming through to bring up our cocoon and habitual habits. The world is seen directly.

June 24, 1993

An owl hoots near my tent.

The coyotes are howling. Their chorus is eerie and beautiful.

The wind howls and shakes the tent furiously.

Night time is wonderful at RMDC.

Meditation Hall

The candle flames dances in the brisk breeze.

Bare footprints on the shrine, pollen everywhere.

A cough—many coughs.

A bird calls its mate.

The shifting of bodies from restlessness and pain.

A dog barks.

Boy scouts yell and sing and shoot rifles.

Cathy clears her throat to get someone's attention.

The motor nearby turns off.

A daddy long-legs walks across my path.

A bee buzzes around the room.

July 9, 1993

Sitting Practice

A sound of shifting bodies.

Of water containers and tinkling tops being removed—a glug, glug.

A cough—lots of coughs.

Target shooting at the Boy Scout range.

Laughter—bugle blowing and songs and shouts from down yonder.

The gong and bell going off at unpredicted times.

The sound of feet on the gravel heading for the outhouse.

A dog barks.

The timer's gong, time to sit again.

The blue and white truck heads up the hill, shifting gears.

My mouth waters, my stomach growls, time for *orioki* again.

A sneeze—someone is crying. Blowing one's nose. Deep heavy breathing from behind me.

I sit and sit: In breath, checking my posture. Out breath, thinking—whoosh, no judgment. Basic goodness all around me.

I see the incense curling around.

The bright colors of the shrine—the proud banners blowing in the breeze. Occasionally they're banging hard against the tent when the wind becomes gusty.

The beauty of the sun going in and out of the clouds. Suddenly it is dark, and next minute, the tent is brilliant with light.

The clanging of dishes, dropping and aluminum foil rustling. The smell of food drifting in from PMS room.

Dust everywhere—bare footprints on the shrine.

Beautiful flower arrangements, ever-changing.

The stroke brush leaning to one side.

Tasting the *Orioki*

Food. Pineapple, peanut butter, peppers, onions, chicken, tofu, carrots, broccoli, spinach, picante sauce. Brown sugar, breads of all types, pork, beef strips, rice of many types, pancakes, scrambled eggs, French toast, and many salads. Some like it well, some think—not so good.

A titter of laughter as someone spaces out in *orioki* practice.

Gap—come back.

A gentle breeze on my face. The candles dancing in the wind.

Walking meditation. Perky, the snow lion, sees everything.

Swing-push-press.

Swing-push-press.

My sore back, the numbness in my legs, a gap—a shift. No longer hurting, out with the breath.

Sit with my pain and anger, happiness and joy. Basic goodness everywhere.

Thank you RMDC and staff for the unique opportunity to be here on this powerful—unpredictable gentle land.

Many of use like to create a special place where we can go to study, relax, play or meditate. In such a place we may want to create a shrine that reflects who we are. This was Sandy's shrine at RMDC.

Sandy would return home and then two weeks later be gone forever. We will never know what Sandy was thinking in those last few days. She did not leave any notes.

Sandy's suicide was a total surprise to everyone who know her. She didn't leave a note and what ever was tormenting her, she did show or talk about it.

CHAPTER 37

Never forget the three powerful resources you always
have to you: love, prayer, and forgiveness.

—H. JACKSON BROWN

October 12, 1993

The memorial service for Sandy was delayed two weeks to wait for Sandy's younger brother, who had been on a safari in India. Finally, all of Sandy's and my family were together at the service. Since our son Don and I had both learned and practiced meditation at Shambhala and Don had also advanced through Warriors Assembly, we decided to meditate together before the service. Meditation can go in all directions and have many purposes and outcomes, but at times like these, it helps to bring focus and maybe even some understanding.

Don and I finished our meditation and proceeded to the main

sanctuary. The sanctuary was full, I guessed with over a hundred people. I saw people from AA, the Ranch, the hospital where Sandy worked, and many people from Shambhala, including the chancellor from Naropa Institute (a college in Boulder, Colorado, connected to Shambhala). In attendance were all our old friends and even friends of Sandy's that I did not know. I had decided to give the eulogy, which was a story of Sandy's life.

I approached the lectern with a feeling of extreme sadness. The room was quiet, and there was a sense of calm. I had arranged a small Shambhala shrine next to the lectern, a shrine Sandy had while she was in meditation. I truly believe Sandy's spirit was somewhere in the room. I finally gained my composure and began talking about Sandy's life. I talked about how Sandy loved people and had built her life around helping people. As I talked and looked around the room at all of the faces in attendance, I began to see that Sandy had become an anachronism. She was living in the past and hadn't changed or adapted to the present.

I just couldn't comprehend what had happened to Sandy that caused her to end her life so suddenly. My mind was looking for the answer as to why Sandy had committed suicide. The three years after she forcibly resigned from the hospital had been very difficult for her. She had finally decided to try home health care, but this would have required her to go back to school, and she was terrified of school. Could fear of the future have influenced her? Had her life changed, and she did not accept the changes? Was she angry at the world? Or maybe she was just tired?

I believe that Sandy was tired of the real world. I think she was through with plastic people living their lives from their heads, passing up the beauty of life and the world around them and always wanting something for themselves. I saw that in many ways, Sandy had become a lost child or was convinced that she had done all she could to help people or the world and slowly began pushing people away.

Sandy had spent fifty-three years living with her dysfunctional childhood. I think I understand how important love and support are and how they must be continually expressed every day, especially to those who have grown up with a childhood full of distrust, anger, confusion, and lack of true love. Friends, therapist, and programs, I feel, lack the deep knowledge and understanding of how love works and how important support and love is in our daily lives. This love must come from oneself and from one's partner and family. But the person to be loved must be willing to let love in and be understood. Understanding another person requires sharing our feelings, thoughts, and goals. The leader and the wingman must both know what the mission is and how they will accomplish it together.

I asked my friends and family what they thought was the reason Sandy ended her life. There are a lot of answers, as I think we have to satisfy our mind or subconscious mind in order to find peace. The following are some of the thoughts people had. Sandy must have been depressed. Sandy had been on medication, and maybe she had stopped or changed the way she was taking her dosage. Was she afraid she had failed in our relationship and that we might separate? She did mention one time that she did not want to leave me. Maybe she was tired of helping people who did not appreciate her help. Was she finished with her mission on Earth and ready to go home to the Spirit World where she would find the love she needed? Her mother had died at age fifty-three, Sandy's age. Could there be a coincidence? The world was not to change in her lifetime, and she couldn't adapt to the world as she saw it. Maybe her mission on Earth was complete, and it was time to let her family go and return to the Spirit World. Her life on Earth, like all of ours, was only temporary. She had given all the love she had, and those around her may not have provided the love she needed to be happy. Was she selfish? I think not. She just wanted to go home to the Spirit World and God, who she knew could provide all the love she needed.

It is said that spirits sometimes stay on Earth after death to help or guide the living. When Sandy returned from RMDC, a few weeks before her death, she talked several times about her birth mother. She said she wished she could have known her and oftentimes missed her. A few days later, a dream came to me. I saw Sandy and her mother driving in the mountains together. Maybe the morning of her death, Sandy's mother came to visit her. She would have seen the turmoil Sandy was enduring and may have told Sandy it was time to go home. Her mother's spirit had been waiting for a time. Sandy would need her. Only a person's mother can provide the comfort we need to conquer our problems. I could imagine that Sandy wanted to take one last trip through the mountains she loved, and so with her mother, Sandy went to the garage, and they were off. There is a road pass out of Georgetown, near Denver, that is the most beautiful and spectacular place in the world. The road winds high into the Colorado mountains. Maybe they traveled over Guanella Pass, Sandy's favorite. They could have travelled to the Shambhala Center, where Sandy had last meditated. Maybe Sandy did her last *kyudo* shooting, and I am sure every arrow hit the target. When they returned home, Sandy and her mother would have returned together to the Spirit World, hand in hand.

After the eulogy, I asked for thoughts about Sandy. The stories I heard ranged from how Sandy had changed people's lives to how she was always there to help and give her love and generosity. It was very clear that Sandy had given all she had to give and that she loved all of us very much.

CHAPTER 38

*Happiness is letting go of what you think your life is supposed
to look like and celebrating it for everything it is.*

—MANDY HALE

February 1994–August 1995

The next few months were a time of grieving, sorting out our
lives, and trying to make sense of what had happened. I heard
many reasons why Sandy committed suicide, but all the reasons were
external, and none of them resonated as truth for me. It would be
many more years and endless study to finally see a possible answer
that I could accept.

I have mentioned several times that humans come to Earth to live
out a mission or assignment given to us by God in order to grow spiritually. To assist us in this assignment, God provides us with spirits who

know the plan or mission and can implement the plan, circumstances, states of affairs, and situations in order to bring the plan to fruition. These things are connected to our desire to get what we want now or what we need know for the future in order to accomplish our mission. But it is the desire to carry out this mission that drives us. We must remember, the spirits will give us just what we want, the way we want it, no better or worse than how we ask for it. Think about the things you have asked for in the past, and you will realize you most likely received them in some form or another. However, in many circumstances, we are very focused on what we don't want, and so this is what we get. But think about the things you may have asked for that were useful and appeared at the precise time you needed them in order to solve a problem. We have free will, so we can make any choice we want, but my suggestion is to listen to the spirits, who communicate to us through dreams, people, and situations.

Soon, I was not surprised that the opportunity to learn more about the women's liberation movement was given to me. These ideas still weighed heavily on my mind as I connected much of it to Sandy's lost hope and death. One day, I received a phone call from Sensei's wife, Marsha. She asked me if I would be interested in meeting a woman from Vermont who was in Denver for a few days. Not thinking much of it, I agreed. She gave me her name, Kathryn, and her phone number. I called, and we arranged to meet for dinner at the Olive Garden Restaurant in Boulder the next day.

The thought of dating had crossed my mind, but I was not sure how long I should grieve Sandy's death. In Nepal, it was thirteen days, and in some Native American Indian tribes, it is only seven days. The people in Japan will grieve for forty-nine days. Is there a rule set in stone? I could have asked Pat, my therapist, if four months was enough. But I decided I may not have liked her answer, so I didn't ask. Yet, something was telling me to move on. I figured I could work out the problems, if any, later. As I drove to Boulder, my mind was in overdrive. Who was this woman, and would I enjoy her company?

The Olive Garden was crowded, and I wondered if Kathryn had arrived. Yes, she had indeed, as I saw her sitting off to one side. My eyes were immediately drawn to this beautiful, blonde-haired woman. Deep inside, I felt a connection, and something told me this was going to be a romance and an adventure. She was twenty years younger than me. During dinner and later that evening, we talked about who we were and the things we had done. She already knew about Sandy, so we passed on that subject.

Kathryn was born in Vermont and had lived and grown up with two parents connected to the hippie movement of the sixties. Her father was a very controlling man and owned a very large Christmas tree farm in Vermont. Her family was heavily involved in the Buddhist community and Shambhala. Her childhood and youth were not easy. She had experienced many of the same problems Sandy had, including sexual abuse by her grandfather. She had been married and had a daughter, nine years old, who was living with her dad and his wife. Kathryn owned a landscape business specializing in perennial gardens and a company that made Christmas wreaths.

Kathryn and I connected from the very start, and we spent the next four days mostly together constantly. I remember taking her to the airport, and while watching her leave, a few tears ran down my check. Over the next few weeks, we called and talked often, and I was soon on an airplane to Vermont. We spent a week together and became more involved and attached. We were soon making plans for her to move to Denver, where she could start a new landscaping business.

Life with Kathryn was exciting and adventurous. She was classy, refined, cultured, erudite, and sophisticated, and I loved her a lot.

She was the epitome of the modern woman. She was focused on what she wanted and was determined to get it. Her goals, when she achieved them, would all be external. I believe Kathryn, like Sandy, never received the love she needed when she grew up and so she tried to fill the void by becoming a successful businesswoman, garnering praise and accolades. She wanted to be able to live and thrive on her own and do things her way. I was very proud of her and encouraged her when I could.

After Kathryn moved to Denver, she was about to encounter a moving experience. As I mentioned, spirits sometimes stay on Earth after death. Kathryn and I had gone to bed early, as we were very tired. It had only been an hour or so when Kathryn awakened me. She was scared and confused.

"Gordon," she said, "I just saw Sandy. She came to me, and I saw her at the bottom of the bed. She said that our future would be full of problems, that we would experience great turmoil."

Kathryn was very confused, and so was I. What exactly was Sandy warning us about? Whatever it was, she was right; our time together would be traumatic.

Even though I believed we loved each other very much, we slowly became competitive and controlling of each other, which soon became entrenched as habit. One of the greatest enemies to a happy and joyful life is addictions, of which there are many. Addictions can be physical substances, but they can also manifest as patterns of thought, behaviors, and certain feelings. Addictions play havoc with other feelings as well. They confuse, distort, and disguise feelings, which makes it difficult to understand what is really happening: this leads to fear. Fear is the feeling that something bad is going to happen. Fear is our alarm bell that sounds to warn us to do something, change course, or prepare for possible harm. To mitigate fear, some behaviors may have to change, training may be required, our daily routines may have to be altered, and our relationships will need to be strengthened. It is important to recognize fear and bring those involved together to work out solutions. This could also require the need for outside counseling. To minimize our fear, we use anger, hoping our partner will change.

When fear arises, we must quickly look for the problem or thing causing the fear. Hopefully, the person or persons experiencing the fear will see a solution to the problem causing the fear. The frustration is that the people involved and those around us, including therapists, may not see a solution. They may become paralyzed or frozen in place. There is also the possibility that two or more solutions may arise, and each person believes he or she has the correct solution. At this point, to force one or more solutions can push us to anger or frustration in order to win our point. It is of monumental importance that one or more people will have to change their thinking, behavior, or actions, or the problem will continue to recur. We are always going to be faced with people who refuse to change and say, "My way or the highway." When that happens, the people around this unchanging person may have to make sacrifices that are unhealthy or dissolve the relationship.

Kathryn and I also experienced much insecurity in our relationship, and we began to demand changes from each other. Insecurity undisputedly comes from fear, and although I recognized this, I did not know what changes I needed to make to remedy it. I also wondered if it was even possible to make the changes that would be needed to eliminate our fears. At the time, I was living on my own and was used to being the only one who would make all the decisions about my life choices. The choices were mine, and I had to live with the consequences. I often wondered if I would make the right choices. Inevitably, fear of failure became a big problem. Somewhere I was taught that one way to mitigate fear is to push back against it and use anger. With

Kathryn, I thought anger could be used to make her change, therefore minimizing my fear or eliminating it. This did not work.

Through this relationship, I also learned that trust is something that has to be learned and experienced. You have to show me that I can trust you, not simply tell me that I can trust you. In a relationship, we all have basic needs, and to be happy in a relationship, basic needs must be met. These needs vary a lot, depending on my ability to meet my own needs and then what I expect to be fulfilled by another. Kathryn and I were both generally independent, but a relationship creates needs that only a partner can fulfill. These can be such things as, "Can I trust you to be available when I need you, when I am sick, overloaded, or just plain tired and need a little help—and the big one—when I need love?"

Kathryn and I knew our relationship was in trouble, and so we entered therapy. The therapist we chose utilized dream therapy, and so my journey into the world of dreams began. Yet, I am not sure our therapist even understood how a relationship functions. If he did, he was not able to provide Kathryn and me with a path that solved our problems. There may be the possibility that our therapist did give us a plan, but we could not understand it or we did not trust that it would work, and so we did not implement it. When we grow up in a family where there is no trust, can we ever learn to trust? In a relationship where trust and love is lost, can it ever be regained? Is this why today we see more and more people living alone? I wish I knew the answer.

Yet, despite our fears and trust issues, there was yet another problem we had. Kathryn longed to be with her daughter in Vermont, and I did not see how difficult it was for a mother and daughter to be separated. After about a year and a half, Kathryn and I separated, and Kathryn returned to Vermont to be closer to her daughter. Today she is recognized as a very successful businesswoman there. The sad part is that she has lost all contact with her daughter.

The spirits had done well giving me a picture and experiences of how a modern, liberated woman might live. I am beginning to believe that the liberation movement is focused on self-centeredness, on one's ability to succeed in the world at whatever one wants to accomplish. This success could come at a cost to those we love—to our family. We can't go back and change our past or completely repair the damage we have done to others. Maybe there is a balance that we can have it all, but do we truly believe that is possible? Is it working? Yes and no. Through this relationship, I glimpsed many of the problems that exist in our world today with the liberation movement. Is it possible to balance a relationship so both parties can get their needs met? Is there enough time in a woman's day to be a successful businesswoman, a mother, and a companion to her partner? I know her partner can help with some chores and the children. Kathryn succeeded in building a successful business on her own, but she lost her child. I believe children hunger for the love that only a mother can give. Can we create trust so fear can be minimized? I knew that time, training, workshops, and more interaction would be necessary if I was to have a happy, joyous, and free life. Several things became clear, but many more questions had to be answered and many lessons needed to be learned. There was still a lot of work left for me to do.

CHAPTER 39

*Two most important days in your life are the day you
were born and the day you find out why.*

—MARK TWAIN

I had learned many lessons about the women's movement the hard
way—living it. After Kathryn had returned to Vermont, I felt a
need to take life easier. For the next four years, I worked in my business and continued to indulge in personal growth programs, primarily
Shambhala, *kyudo,* and AA. I was determined to take it slow and learn
all that I could about myself, relationships, and the duality that exists
between men and women.

Kathryn had created a beautiful perennial garden in the backyard
of my house. Since I had been obsessed with trains and train model
building for more than forty-five years, I decided that this was the
perfect place to build a miniature garden railroad. This would be a

large undertaking and require a lot of time. I needed help. About this time, I met a man who was down on his luck. Bob was out of work and needed a place to stay, so I offered him a job in my construction company and the apartment in my basement. He also helped manage the house and helped me build my backyard railroad. (We did such a top-notch job that the train in my backyard is still running today, twenty-five years later.)

I was not one who wanted to spend life alone, but I also knew the world relating to women was changing. I did not want to be in competition with a woman, and as a man, I wanted to be a leader and implement the dreams, desires, and needs of my partner. I wanted a partner to share common individual pleasures and hobbies with, not someone to compete with. There had to be a way for two people to live together and complement each other. I knew that each of us had to have freedom to explore and prosper in our individual working worlds and enjoy our personal endeavors, yet find common ground to be together.

Learning the differences between men and women was a slow process for me. I found that many of the differences were mystifying. I began by first striving to know the mind of a man, which I had direct experience with. In general, the mind of a man is linear; we can only think of one thing at a time and enjoy having a set direction or path. When a man has an idea, the idea will have purpose and is very important. Men tend to formulate their ideas, plans, strategies, and courses of action and then implement the plan until completion. In olden times, when a woman, wife, or partner asked a man to go hunt for dinner, he would snatch his coat, hat, and gun and head out into the wilderness. His focus would be on finding dinner, nothing else, and he would not return until he had found and killed some animal or had dinner for his family. The hunter would return home happy and proud. And if his wife or partner were smart, she would always compliment him for a job well done. This praise would contribute to his motivation, and then she could depend on him going out over and over again to provide for her and the family.

However, I have found that women tend to have a more cyclical way of thinking and taking action. They see the wider perspective and have the ability to multitask. In the old days, these skills served women by allowing them to care for children while also providing all of the other needs for the family. A woman's mind can handle several subjects, tasks, and ideas together. A woman can move from one thought to another and never lose continuity. I used to watch in wonder as a group of several women could talk about one subject, move to another subject without finishing the first subject, move to a third subject and back and forth between each subject and never become confused or disorganized. I truly praise any woman who can have the patience to talk to a man!

It is so beautiful how a woman can be cooking dinner, talking to a girlfriend, keeping an eye on a baby, and still keeping track of her partner. I know a man can sometimes do two things at once, but it is often difficult for us. I have also learned that women are collectors of information and have a tendency to work toward perfection. This is important to women when managing and implementing a plan. From what I have learned, women will research and collect information, confer with their peers, and then implement a plan. I heard the statistic that some 50 percent of women talk to their mothers every day, maybe for the purpose of making sure ideas and thoughts are well thought-out. As to perfection, the better and more complete we do something, the better the results. If you are a man reading this, think about improving your perfection; it will greatly improve your relationship with your partner.

For many years, while I struggled to understand women, it confused me to watch a woman shop. In one of the seminars I attended, the facilitator gave an example. A husband and wife were having breakfast at home one morning when the wife said she needed a new pair of shoes. They needed to be red with a black bow to match a new dress she bought. She asked her husband if he would go shopping with her. Her husband, thinking this would not take long, agreed. And so, they were off to the shopping center and into the mall. The husband, wanting to show off his hunting skills, headed to the first woman's shoe store. He saw and quickly found a pair of red shoes with black bows. He was happy, as they could surely buy the shoes and head home so he could work on his new fishing rod. However, this was not to be. His wife said that, yes, the shoes he had found were just what she was looking for, but she wanted to check another store. So off to the second store; same story, found shoes, but his wife thought maybe a third store was worth checking into. The third store also had the shoes, but to the husband's dismay, the wife didn't buy the shoes and instead suggested that they get some coffee.

The moral to this story is that women collect information, as much as they can get, and then often share it with their friends, family, or peers. Unlike men, they generally work together. Yes, the wife will buy the shoes, but she'll confer with her mother or girlfriends to make sure she gets the best deal, or the best brand, or the most comfortable pair (depending on her individual needs and values). Today, when I go shopping with a woman, I have a lot of fun. Yes, I have to be patient, but I look forward to the coffee.

Men tend to have more direct solutions to a problem or plan while utilizing knowledge they have learned from experience. If they don't have all the knowledge they need to complete a project or plan, they simply go out on their own, experimenting with trial and error, and as a last resort, read the instructions or seek help from another. I think it is a blow to a man's pride when a woman corrects or instructs him to do something. My suggestion for a woman is to sit back, be patient, and watch a man be stupid. He will figure it out eventually, and then he can be your hero.

So let's look at another theory about modern man. Our ancestors relied on their stress systems and adrenals to gear up for a fight or flight for survival. Today, modern men experience more psychological stress than physical danger. But our bodies don't know the difference. The three stress hormones responsible for the fight or flight response are cortisol, epinephrine (also known as adrenaline), and oxytocin. Cortisol and epinephrine raise blood pressure and heighten the senses. Oxytocin softens the effects of cortisol and epinephrine by relaxing the emotions.

Men release less oxytocin than women and therefore have a stronger reaction from both cortisol and epinephrine. This means that under stress, men are hard-wired to rev up and stay that way until hormonal spikes return to normal. Men tend to compartmentalize and repress their feelings, prioritizing instead the quickest route to resolution or safety. This biological fact can shed light on both the healthy and unhealthy coping strategies men deploy when under stress. Men will channel stress into strategic competitive productivity. On the other side of this response is escapism. When stress levels rise, men will just as often lose themselves in competitive diversions that burn off the excess cortisol and epinephrine. As a man, I can fully understand this principal and hope, if you are a woman, you will look at us men with a better understand of how we function.

Another way that men and women differ is how they experience feelings. I have learned that most women often make decisions based on feelings. Women want to know how people feel and especially the people close to them. Harmony, amity, peaceful connection, and cooperation are all very important. Sometimes sacrifices and compromises are made to maintain this environment. For a woman, it is often important not to offend someone or create feelings of anger, disappointment, insecurity, or unhappiness. We all tend to want a happy and joyful environment, but I believe it is common for a woman to sacrifice her own happiness to maintain this peaceful environment. Men, on the other hand, are often more logical, single-minded, and direct. I believe that in this way, women and men (or femininity and masculinity) were created, or have evolved, and exist to perfectly complement each other. A man's mind has less feelings and more directness and compliments a woman's concern for feelings, beauty, and harmony. Please understand, I talk in generalities, and I know a woman's mind and a man's mind can work together, each person doing what they know and feel best about. We should complement each other. If a situation requires directness, firmness, and power, the man can step in, but if the situation requires gentleness, compassion, nurturing, and feeling, the woman probably can do a better job. To cross boundaries can cause a lot of fear and anger. Trying to use a behavior we have little experience with can cause chaos.

I believe that a healthy relationship is based on balance. There must be a balance of ideas, behaviors, beliefs, and health, and we must address each of these individual items equally. Ideas, behaviors, beliefs, and proper health must not be etched in stone. My beliefs were learned from other people. Were these people always right? I think not, as they seem to change from time to time. I know that I must be willing to flow, listen to others, and recognize if I am being one-sided. I may even discover that I have only half the insight needed to make solid and good decisions. If we live only on top of a mountain, we will never know what life is like in the valley, and if we only live on a farm, we can't understand the city. Living in darkness deprives us from enjoying sunlight. It is important to keep in mind that the perspective of another, no matter how different, can only enhance your understanding and effectiveness in this world.

If we want to create change, whether it be in our personal lives, our relationships, or in the world, we must learn what it means to create truth, virtue, and beauty. Yet truth, virtue, and beauty must first be implemented in our personal lives before we are able to apply them to relationships or outward situations. In this process of bettering ourselves, it is important to remember that our old thoughts and beliefs will fight any change because they are imbedded in habit and subconscious tendencies. And even if defeated, old habits and beliefs will not die or disappear completely, they will wait in ambush and will rise up and defeat the new ideas whenever possible. Personal growth is a relentless and never-ending process that requires persistence and courage. Implement the changes you want to make and practice using them as much as possible. Once your new beliefs are solidly embedded in your own life, then you can go out and change the world because you have earned the tools and the training required to make changes and affect others.

Chapter 40

Every great dream begins with a dreamer. Always remember, you have
within you the strength, the patience, and the passion to
reach for the stars and to change the world.

—Harriet Tubman

Winter 1998

Over the next four years, I was in training. During this time, I dated
several women, and I learned something from each of them.
George had died, and I dated Kathy, but the chemistry was not there.
Dating seemed to be external, fun, and enjoyable, but I never had a feeling of internal connection. I knew I wanted a woman who would enjoy
what I liked, and I also wanted to have fun doing what she liked. I was
looking for balance and some commonality. The way I saw it, my spirits
were in a holding pattern, just waiting for me to make up my mind and

to let them know when I was ready for a new permanent partner who would fit my needs. It's as if they were saying, "Make up your mind and set a goal so we can help you fulfill your dreams."

Soon, dating became exhausting, and I was through playing the field. I was ready to settle down and begin a new life with someone special. With this decision, my spirts and soul now had a direction, and they were excited to jump into action. Once I made the decision, it happened easily. Once a month, the Denver Art Museum held a Friday evening dance. Generally, there were over a hundred people, mostly singles, who would attend. The January dance was no exception. Several of my friends and I were excited to start the year off with some fun. To my surprise, an old friend from the Ranch, Paunch, was there with his wife. We caught up with the latest news and made a date to attend the next dance together. The Wednesday before that dance, Paunch called me and said he was bringing a woman friend who I might be interested in—kind of a blind date.

As I headed to the dance, I wondered about this woman Paunch would introduce me to. I was excited but full of anticipation. When I entered the dance area, I saw Paunch, his wife, several people from the Ranch, and a beautiful auburn-haired woman sitting at a table. The auburn-haired woman was stunning, smiling, and all radiant. I knew the moment I saw her that something amazing and fun was in store for me.

I quickened my walk to get to the table faster.

"Hi, everybody," I said. Then I looked at my date. "I'm Gordon."

"Well hello. I'm Nancy. Please sit down," she said.

The moment I sat next to her, I had a consuming feeling of serendipity. My mind flashed back several years to the early days at the Ranch. I remembered a woman and her husband who I had briefly talked to, and Nancy sure looked like that woman. Had our paths been slowly aligning? Were my spirits having fun at my expense?

Nancy and I talked a bit, and I asked if she would like to dance. She agreed. We moved together harmoniously on the dance floor, and I had the growing suspicion that I already knew her. We walked back to the table.

"Paunch and I are old friends from the Ranch," I said. "Are you a member?"

"My ex-husband and I were members for many years. Are you a member?"

"Not for the last four years, but you sure look familiar," I said. She smiled.

From the moment we met, I knew this woman was something special. Deep within myself, I felt that feeling that told me we were going places together. We danced a few more dances, and I asked if she would join me for dinner. Without any hesitation, she said yes. Dinner was fun, and we talked and shared stories about our past and what we were doing now. I told her I owned a construction company, and she said she worked for a manufacturing company called Norgren in Littleton. She worked in human resources.

"Our company has been doing construction work at Norgren for several years!" I said.

Looking totally surprised, she said, "I have heard your name around the company, but to meet you here is a real coincidence."

"Not for the spirits," I thought.

When dinner was finished, I asked if we could meet again. She immediately agreed. We set a date for the following week. I couldn't wait: another dinner with a charming and pretty woman. Hot damn, those spirits.

Nancy said that I was a lot like her father. Her dad was a contractor, and he had owned an airplane just like mine. Nancy and I both had similar backgrounds, which included traveling. For some reason, I knew this woman was going to be in my life for several years to come. My father taught me that a real man practices chivalry. He said that I must always show my commitment, appreciation, and love for a woman by buying some form of a gift now and then. The day of our second dinner and date, I sent Nancy a bouquet of red roses. Later, Nancy told me that she had been dating another man, but with the roses, I had won the rivalry.

A year earlier, there had been an auction on PBS television, and one of the auction items was a ten-day trek in Nepal for two people. I think it was my connection with Shambhala, which has its roots in Tibet, that inspired me to buy the trip. I didn't have anyone in mind to go with, but I believed someone would turn up. That perfect person would turn up nearly a year later. Nancy and I had been going steady since we met, and we became closer each day. We were having dinner one night when I asked her if she would like to take a trip to Nepal.

"A trip to Nepal is the last place I would have chosen for a vacation," she replied. "What are you thinking?"

I told her about the auction and the trek. She was very curious and had a lot of questions, many of which I couldn't answer. To my surprise, she then said she thought the trip would be a real adventure and something she believed would be a lot of fun. She asked how long we would be gone, and I told her about three weeks. I also told her that after Nepal, we would spend a week in Japan and stay with my *kyudo* teacher.

"I am going to have to ask for a leave of absence from work," she said, "but I think a trip like this is a once in a lifetime adventure."

A couple of days later, Nancy called me. She sounded sad, and I knew she might have bad news.

"Gordon," she said, "I talked with my supervisor about a leave of absence and the trip, and she said I had two weeks' vacation and that was it. I was really looking forward to the trip, but at this time, I will have to decline."

"I'm sorry to hear you can't go," I said. "There will be other shorter trips we can take though," I reassured her.

I was disappointed with the news. I had done so much planning and preparation, and I wondered if my spirits had failed me. Was there another way we could go on this trip? I wondered if maybe Nancy could talk to a higher up boss and get permission to go. But I decided to let it go and let things cool off. I would change my direction and look at another path that did not lead to Nepal.

A week or so passed, and then life was tragically interrupted by the Columbine School shooting. Nancy's company Norgren was but a mile from Columbine, and many of the employees' children were in attendance there. When word reached Norgren, many of the employees called Human Resources and asked if they could leave and check on their children. Nancy received the first calls and quickly asked her boss how to respond to the calls. Her boss instructed Nancy to tell anyone who wanted to leave the plant that they could, but if they left, they would not be paid.

Nancy was shocked at this response. People were beginning to panic. Had one of their children been hurt? If they left to check on their children, they would lose money? Nancy did not accept this response and immediately sent an email to the president of the company. She felt pay was important and that under these circumstances, the employees should be paid. The president agreed and emailed Nancy's boss to pay the employees. Shortly after, Nancy's boss called Nancy into her office and informed her that one: she should not have gone to the president and two: she was fired.

Late in the afternoon, Nancy called me. She sounded happy and sad at the same time.

"Hello, Gordon," she said, "there has been a change in plans, and I can go to Nepal now."

She went on to tell me what had happened at the plant and how her actions had gotten her fired. I asked if she was going to be OK without a job, and she said yes, she had money saved. We both laughed.

"Do you have time for dinner?" I asked.

"Yes, I do," she said, "I have all the time in the world."

CHAPTER 41

*Though no one can go back and make a brand new start, anyone can
start from now and make a brand new ending.*

—CARL BARD

Spring 1999

Nancy and I began planning our trip to Nepal. I called the travel
agency to make arrangements and was told that the company
was out of business but that I should call a man named Narayan Shrestha. Mr. Shrestha was the founder of Helping Hands Health Education, a nonprofit charity providing health and education to the people
of Nepal. Narayan said that he was not in the travel business any more.
He was focusing on Helping Hands, but he would look into our trip.
A short time later, Narayan called back and said he would honor the
trip. Narayan was a native of Nepal and had come to America in the

1980s. He had graduated college and owned several businesses. Nancy and I were excited to meet Narayan and excited for the trip.

For those of you who have traveled to the Far East, you know the plane ride is very long. Nancy, Narayan, and I boarded an airplane in Denver on a Monday morning, flew to San Francisco, boarded a second plane Monday night, and flew to Osaka, Japan, arriving Tuesday morning. We boarded a third plane Tuesday morning and flew to Bangkok, Thailand, landing Tuesday night. We had six hours of sleep, and then we were back on a plane Wednesday morning to Kathmandu, the capital city of Nepal. Wednesday afternoon and evening we met many of Narayan's friends and enjoyed our first of many Nepalese dinners.

As you can imagine, Nancy and I were exhausted from the journey to Nepal. We were finally able to get to bed around eleven o'clock that evening. Shortly after one o'clock, we were awakened by a loud knock on our door. The hotel was on fire. Dressing quickly, grabbing our passports and our video camera, we headed to the end of a smoke-filled hall to what we thought was an exit. Little did we know that at the time, safety regulations in Nepal were generally nonexistent. We reached the door at the end of the hall, opened it, and to our disbelief, there were no stairs. We looked down from a third-floor drop. The hall was filled with more smoke, but so far, no fire. We turned and ran back down the hall to the main stairs to the lobby. Down the stairs, through the lobby and outside, we turned to see that the fire was on the fourth floor.

Our next concern was Narayan. To our relief, we saw him nearby, talking with several people. The fire truck arrived and to our amazement, the firemen, without any fire protective clothing, grabbed a hose on their truck and headed into the building. The fire chief was the only man wearing a fire helmet. We found out later there were no fire hydrants. The only water was on the truck. To our astonishment, everyone survived unhurt, and the fire was out in about an hour. By two thirty, we were able to recover our belongings and head to a new hotel. We were jet lagged, had had almost no sleep, and were pumped with adrenaline from the excitement. It was four o'clock the next afternoon when we finally got out of bed.

For the next three days, we played tourists, and Narayan showed us the ancient city of Kathmandu. We found out that Kathmandu is the home of all the worn-out cars from other countries. How those cars keep running is beyond my understanding. Throughout the city, there were wandering bull cows that fed off garbage dumped in the gutter by the local residences. The bulls are sacred and have free reign of the city. Kathmandu had a way of growing on me, something about its ancient heritage. However, after four days of pollution and obnoxious smells, Narayan said we would leave in the morning for his rural hometown of Khandbari.

Flying to Khandbari was a short flight, about an hour or so, and we arrived late in the afternoon. The airport was small and had only one short gravel runway and a very small terminal, painted brown and in disrepair. Narayan suggested we eat dinner, after which we would head up to his village, which was located on top of a nearby mountain. The countryside was green, and some areas were heavily wooded, a lot like Colorado. With dinner finished, we rounded up our gear, and to my surprise, several Sherpas showed up.

"Narayan," I said, "are we driving or walking to your home?"

"We are walking," he replied. "We can't drive because the road is under construction. All work on the road is being done by hand. It may take several months to finish if the weather doesn't wash the road away before then. Anyway, it's just up to the top of that hill." He pointed and added, "It is a short walk!"

It turns out a short walk in Nepal is two hours, or four hours if it is raining or at night.

We finally made the four-hour short walk up the hill to Khandbari. Just before we arrived at Khandbari, all of Narayan's family and many of the town's people came excitedly walking and running toward us. They wanted to be the first to see Narayan, meet us, and welcome us to the village. It was a real celebration and party to welcome Narayan home after several months. It was one o'clock in the morning.

Gordon and Nancy arrived in Khanbari to find a village that needed almost everything. Narayan Siesta had been working with Helping Hands Health and Education, a nonprofit charity to bring medical and educational support to the village, but Nancy and Gordon knew that their help was badly needed as well.

The next four days, Narayan showed us his home town and surrounding countryside. Khandbari is in a beautiful part of Nepal and is very green and lush with many small farms and cottage businesses. To make a living, local men became tailors and made clothes for local men and women. Nancy bought two beautiful dresses for around fifty dollars. I bought a beautiful three-piece suit for only sixty-five dollars and dress shirts for eight dollars each, all custom-made and fitted. All consumer goods are transported to the town by Sherpas, as there were not any roads. The daily wage was eight dollars in 1999.

Narayan, in conjunction with Helping Hands, started a medical clinic in Khandbari. Narayan would arrange for doctors and nurses from America to visit Khandbari and treat the local people, usually for a week at a time, twice a year. People would come from all the surrounding towns to be treated. Medical help was a godsend for them. Yes, there were local doctors, but they were limited in number, ability, and medical supplies. The local people were so appreciative, and the stories of healing were amazing, though one story was especially sad. A woman from one of the villages had a very sick child, and she had walked three days to get to the clinic. When she finally saw the doctor, the doctor told her that her baby had died. I couldn't imagine the pain and sadness this woman endured, knowing she would have a three-day walk home with her dead baby.

Narayan and Helping Hands had also started an elementary school in order to give the children in his village a better education. At the time, there were about fifty children enrolled in a rented classroom. Each child's tuition and school uniforms were paid for by an American sponsor at a cost of about $175 per year. Narayan had purchased land to build a new, bigger school but did not have the money yet to build the buildings.

As our stay in Khandbari was about to end, we were grateful for the hospitality of the people. The people had given all they could, and much more, so graciously. Our stay had been happy and occasionally sad, and Nancy and I promised Narayan we would do all we could to help the people of his village and Nepal. I kept that promise, and a year later, we built the first school in Khandbari. It was not practical for me to physically help out, so all I could do was provide the money for the construction of the school. It was a real joy. The school went from fifty students in 1999 to over 900 students in 2019. And in 2019, we even added a two-year college program.

The children and adults in Khanbari were very happy and welcomed Nancy and Gordon with open arms. This touched both of them and they pledged their support to build a new school building, which was built the following year.

What about the trek we had come for? Nancy, Narayan, and I went for one day and one night, and we decided trekking was not for us. Instead, we spent several more days sightseeing and learning the history and mystery of Kathmandu and Nepal, which is a story in itself.

From Nepal, Nancy and I backtracked to Bangkok and spent several days touring and resting. From Bangkok, we went to Japan to visit my *kyudo* teacher. I had visited Japan several times, but this was Nancy's first trip, though not her last. Nancy and I were able to immerse ourselves in the Japanese culture and spend time with Sensei's family. It was the beginning of a long friendship for us all. We had a wonderful time on the remainder of the trip, but Narayan had made a comment that hung with us as we traveled on.

As we were leaving Nepal, Narayan had said, "I believe any two American people who can survive Nepal for two weeks should get married."

A year later, we took his advice. It was my fifty-ninth birthday.

Nancy and Gordon worked to support Narayan and HHHE all they could. They also loved to travel together and one day would travel to Tibet. Nancy and Gordon would also travel to South Africa, Alaska, Japan and many other exciting places. Nancy loved golf and Gordon loved Kyudo and they worked to support each ones hobby.

Chapter 42

Challenges are what make life interesting,
and overcoming them is what makes life meaningful.

—Joshua J. Marine

May 2000

After all the trials and tribulations of the trip to Nepal, Nancy and I still had a strong fondness for each other. There had been some hard times: the fire, the long hours, sleeping in unfamiliar hotels, and choosing food that would not make us sick. And there was the time that Nancy, Narayan, and I decided to visit a shrine. We chose horses to ride, and at a stop, my horse bolted, and I fell off. Needless to say, I was sore for the next several days. We dated and spent a lot of time together. By the spring of 2000, we were planning a wedding. I came up with the idea that a wedding theme of the Old South would be fun. Maybe it was my heritage and my connections to the South. My father's family had migrated from Ireland to Mississippi in the 1840's. My great, great, great grandfather had been a soldier in the Confederate Army. He had been captured by the North and was released after the war. In fact, I still have his release papers.

We all have a connection to the past, which we cannot change nor did we have any influence in. I feel a connection to the past is very important and gives us a foundation to build on. However, what I know about the past came from my parents. No matter what culture we come from, there is always a dark side, somewhere in the past. These dark sides are generally forgotten, or at least ignored. We hear about the good things our family experienced and sometimes the hard times the family endured. My great, great grandfather lived in Ireland during the potato famine, where a million people starved to death. He made his way to America; he was a farmer and thus he chose the South, as he believed it was good farming country. Thus, 180 years later I am still connected to the South. My grandfather never owned slaves, but he defended his way of life, which changed after the war. He paid a huge price for his beliefs. He lost everything, left the south and came to Colorado to start a new life and died at age 25.

My father loved history and he researched the history of the South. He talked about the injustice of slavery and that no one should enslave another human being. But he also talked about the beauty of the South. The beautiful homes and cities. The romances that evolved and the men that influenced our country. He talked about the fear the people felt. The belief that the end of slavery would change the country and the South would suffer greatly, which proved to be true. I guess I saw a time where romance and beauty went hand in hand. The beautiful dresses and the chivalry the men practiced. A moment in Camelot and I thought it would be fun to share and experience the beauty of that period in time. I was not wrong, all the women who attend the wedding said it was a weekend they would never forget and even today we often talk about the fun we had. I feel sad that the good in history may becoming forgotten. My only hope is that change and the elimination of uncomfortable history will make people feel better. Deep down, I feel that changing the outside world to make me happy is not the solution. I must look inside myself to find the problems of unhappiness.

The wedding would be based on the time period after the Civil War ended. The war ended on April 9, 1865, and the country was trying to reunite. The wedding would be a celebration of two people getting married, and the end of a terrible war between the states and the abolishment of slavery. The date for the wedding would be May 20, 1990. To plan a Southern wedding was going to be a real project. Nancy and I rented the movies Gone With the Wind and North and South. We knew one thing: the dresses were beautiful and had full, wide skirts. The guest list totaled thirty-two couples, which meant thirty-two dresses. The early 1800s was a time of elegance, both in the North and the South, which sadly has been discarded in our modern times. After we determined what the costumes would look like, the next question was where should the wedding be?

Nancy and I decided to push things to the limit and suggested that we have the wedding in Glenwood Springs, a small town west of Denver, deep in the Rocky Mountains. Glenwood Springs is famous for its sulfur hot springs. It is also home to a turn of the century hotel, the Hotel Colorado, which is adjacent to one of the largest hot spring swimming pools and spas in Colorado. An added benefit of holding the wedding there was that Glenwood Springs is on the Amtrak route of the California Zephyr, the train that goes through Denver from Chicago to Oakland, California.

During the planning, we had to decide just how far we were willing to go with our 1865 reenactment. We decided to go almost all the way. This meant transportation would be by train and horse and buggy. I had a friend who owned a private railroad car, and he agreed to rent the car to us for the wedding. The car was in Chicago, so we decided that my sons and their wives would ride it from Chicago to Denver. The owner of the car, a cook, and a steward would also ride with them and assist with serving while we were on the train.

The protocol for a wedding in the 1860s was to celebrate for a week or two. The guests would arrive early, and everyone had the opportunity to catch up on all the latest news and goings on. It was a time of reconnecting and seeing your friends. In those days, to visit your neighbor was a real chore, and visits were infrequent. People were separated by great distances, and travel was difficult. The wedding was a big thing to celebrate and a perfect opportunity to connect and socialize. One Southern tradition was to put a pineapple in the guest room. The pineapple was not to be eaten, but when the guest returned to his or her room and found the pineapple cut in half, it was time to leave and their stay was over. It was a polite way to say, "Party's over."

Though we wanted to stay in the spirit of an 1865 wedding, we decided that our wedding would only last three days. Our wedding would begin on Friday morning at the train station, where everyone would meet and be dressed in period attire. There, the guests would board the train for the trip to Glenwood Springs, which would take about six hours. Breakfast was served on the train. Upon arriving in Glenwood, everyone would board horse and buggies for the trip to the Hotel Colorado. All travel around town would be by horse and buggies.

Our group sure attracted a lot of attention, and I am sure many of the bystanders thought we were making a movie or some kind of a TV commercial. On Friday night, everyone was on their own, settling in and getting ready for the wedding to be held the next day. Narayan, along with his friends from Nepal, had arranged a dinner for Nancy and me that night.

The Hotel Colorado, built in 1893, is beautiful and one could easily imagine the luxury of the old South. The interior is mostly wood paneling with hardwood floors and carpet. Outside is a veranda and a large, very elegantly landscaped courtyard. The guests began arriving on Saturday in the early afternoon, all decked out in their finest dresses and suits. The dresses were a rainbow of colors and silk lace, and the large hooped skirts added to the elegance, topped off with fancy hats. The ladies at the costume shop who made the dresses had created an unbelievable fantasyland for us. Nancy and I were delighted to revel in the ultimate beauty we had helped create, and everyone was so happy and jubilant. Several of the ladies commented on how elegant and beautiful they felt and wished that this could happen more often.

The wedding ceremony was set to begin at four o'clock. Around three thirty, everyone began migrating to the chapel room. The chapel had been decorated with a variety of flowers. Today, flowers are used to show elegance and beauty, but in 1865, flowers had a second purpose: to mask the odors of those who did not or were not able to bathe. The flowers worn by the men on their lapels and by the ladies on their dresses were very large and colorful.

Music is an important part of every wedding. The wedding needed a band, and so the word went out. I imagine that the spirits were becoming exhausted trying to bring the best people together to make this wedding an outstanding affair. I had remembered a Civil War military band that often played music during the summer in local parks. I was able to find them and asked them if they would be interested in performing at a Civil War themed wedding and dance. The answer was yes, they were very excited to come to Glenwood and be a part of the wedding and dance. The band consisted of six members and a portable organ about the size of a large suitcase. The wedding march had not been written in 1865, so we had to choose other southern music and marches for our celebration.

As the guests were escorted to their chairs, the diversity of people and dress at the wedding became apparent. Nancy's sons, Devin and Kurtis, dressed as riverboat gamblers. There were also two rancher cowboys and their wives. Sensei was dressed in his finest black kimono, and his valet was dressed to match. Narayan and his wife, Sreejana, were wearing formal Nepalese dress. The band was dressed in dark blue army uniforms, including hats. Together, all the beautiful wedding attendees created a fantasy land of a time long gone.

The band began to play, signaling the ceremony was about to begin. First, I made my appearance. I was dressed in a formal gray Confederate general's uniform with a sword, a gold sash, and lambskin gloves trimmed with gold lace. My two best men, Dave and Morrie, arrived next and stood next to me. Dave was wearing a Confederate colonel uniform with a red sash and sword. Morrie was dressed as a senator from Washington DC. The flower girl, my granddaughter Hannah, developed cold feet and had to be helped by her older sister, Cassie, down the aisle. They dropped flowers as they walked the aisle. Next, my grandson Jake delivered the rings. The maids of honor followed, each dressed in beautiful, wide skirts of silk and lace.

Nancy's and Gordon's wedding was based on the old South in 1865. It was a gala and elegant event, lasting three days in period dress. Gordon was dressed as a Confederate General and Nancy was a Southern Lady for the wedding.

The music stopped, and a new hymn began to play. Nancy, escorted by her two sons, slowly walked down the aisle. She was dressed in an auburn satin colored wedding dress trimmed with white lace and wore a large matching hat. She was carrying a large bouquet of flowers, which matched and complemented her dress. She was gorgeous: a page out of a fairy book. I was so happy and proud that we had come together and were planning a life together.

The wedding was followed by a Southern banquet buffet with all the trimmings. The table cloths were beige satin, and the chairs were covered with a matching material, which had been rented from a specialty shop in Atlanta, Georgia. Flowers were everywhere, and the setting was reminiscent of the Disney movie *Cinderella*. The dinner consisted of roast prime rib, fried chicken, mashed potatoes, black-eyed peas, collard greens with bacon, corn bread, and grits. Turns out that finding someone to bake a Southern wedding cake is a real challenge. We found a woman who had retired from the bakery business but agreed to make the cake. The cake was covered with flowers made from frosting and matched the wedding flowers. The servers were also dressed in Southern uniforms.

After dinner, it was time to dance. The band began playing all the southern dancing songs, including the Virginia Reel. The Virginia Real is a dance where partners walk in a circle, and it was intended to show off the suits and dresses that the couples were wearing. This was a gala time and also included speeches and toasts. The cake was cut using my sword and served to all the guests. The wedding came off flawlessly, and everyone had a happy, cheerful, and joyous time.

The following morning, breakfast was served, and the wedding guests prepared to leave. The train would arrive around two in the afternoon on its way back to Denver. Dinner would be served on the train, including Southern fried chicken. Nancy and I, along with another couple, continued on to Chicago in the private car for our honeymoon. It was a fitting way to celebrate our first day and night as newlyweds.

*The wedding started in Denver, where the wedding party
boarded a private rail car for the trip to Glenwood Springs.
Here we see Nancy and Gordon in their traveling attire.*

The wedding had been a great success, and we were so happy. We had created beauty, joy, and something most of our friends would long remember. It was a weekend in fantasy land, a land of make believe. Maybe it was also a chance to return to the feelings of our childhood days, when anything can happen and dreams always come true. The wedding was a moment of Heaven on Earth.

*Narayan and his wife, came to the
wedding in formal Nepalese dress.*

*Sensei was dressed in formal
Japanese attire and added a touch
of Japanese culture.*

CHAPTER 43

Remember the happiest people are not those
getting more, they are those giving more.

—H. JACKSON BROWN, JR.

2000–2004

My life had finally come to a crossroad. This thought came to me
during an AA meeting one day, and I was compelled to look
back at my life. I had lived an adventurous life. There had been good
times and bad times. Sandy and I had sure pushed life to the fullest,
engaging in all forms of activities. We had pushed to the edge of the
sound barrier and then pushed past and had gone supersonic.

Thinking about my relationship with Sandy, I realized that life is
all about learned behaviors. Some people call these learned behaviors "programs" or the things running our day-to-day experience.

Whatever the label, during childhood, we all learn to copy our parents' (or guardians') path and behaviors. As a child, we are taught a way of life, a program of survival, which is usually based on the life our parents were living. Having no other choice when young, our parents become our role models. We believe that our parents know best for us, and so we copy and perfect their lifestyle and skills. As a teenager, we are exposed to other behaviors and lifestyles. At this point in our lives, we often become confused and bewildered. We step outside our boundaries, challenging our parents' beliefs, which soon leads us to conflicts with our parents.

Our life skills and programs are well entrenched by our early twenties. I had been introduced to alcohol by my parents and grandfather, a little taste here and there. I learned that alcohol was a big part of life. A real man would have a drink now and then and sometimes several. By age eighteen, I could legally buy 3.2 percent beer in Colorado (not the case now). Alcohol was generally a part of my life for as long as I can remember. When I joined the Air National Guard, I found that alcohol was a way of life. Most everyone drank, and naturally, I joined in. Later, many of my drinking friends were my old drinking buddies from the Air Guard. Drinking became a part of everyday business and life.

It took me a while to understand that heavy drinking people, nondrinking people, and people who drink occasionally generally don't mix. When Sandy went to AA the first time, I continued to drink, and our friends drank also. This probably made it inevitable that Sandy would go back to drinking. When Sandy went to treatment, I began to realize that our old drinking friends had to go. It was not only the drinking, but it was the lifestyle they had been leading. Alcohol, itself, generally is not what creates problems in one's life. It is the lifestyle, or program, that creates addictions to alcohol. There are those who think alcohol addiction is a disease or may even be hereditary, but really, we don't know for sure. What I believe is that when alcohol becomes a problem, for whatever reason, one must find a way to stop drinking and eliminate the problem. Abstinence is generally the only solution to alcoholism or any other addiction.

After fifteen years of my AA program, I was beginning to change. New behaviors were becoming routine. I was ready for a new life, and Nancy was just the ticket. Life with Nancy was going to be different, and many of the things I had done in the past were going to change or go away. One of these things was flying.

Nancy and I had taken several trips in *Bonnie*, but Nancy was losing her interest, or desire, to fly in a small airplane. Nevertheless, Nancy and I had planned to travel to Phoenix, Arizona, for a flying convention. *Bonnie* was in top form, but the weather was not. On the way home, a storm front moved in front of us. The weather was clear, but severe winds were blowing, which made our trip extremely rough: not unsafe but very uncomfortable. By the time we reached Santa Fe, New Mexico, Nancy had had enough and wanted to land, which we did. I assured her that the winds should be less severe the next day. The upside was that we were able to stay in a beautiful Spanish hotel, the LaFonda, and enjoyed magnificent, true Mexican food.

The next morning brought the same weather as the day before, but Nancy thought she could endure the trip back to Denver. Crossing the Continental Divide near Alamosa, Colorado, we encountered the down slope winds east of the Rocky Mountains. Yes, it was rough, but I knew *Bonnie* was built to take rough turbulence. Nancy was not so sure. All she wanted was to get home, and quick. Reaching the outskirts of Denver, we determined travelers saw the beginning of an enormous snow storm. We called Jeffco Airport tower, and they informed us that we could beat the storm if we hurried. We pressed on. The light snow that we landed in only added to Nancy's anxiety. She said that she was finished with small plane flying forever.

Flying had been a large part of my life. I had been flying for over forty-five years, and during that time many changes had occurred. Many of my flying buddies had retired from flying, lost their flying licenses, or died in crashes. My son Rich had also flown *Bonnie* a lot, but ultimately, Rich and I decided to sell *Bonnie*. I was going to lose an old friend and companion. I took the loss hard. *Bonnie* had given me years of wonderful and dependable flying. I felt that *Bonnie* was also sad and unhappy to leave, but she understood. *Bonnie* was sold and resold several times. Rich was curious one day as to what had happened to *Bonnie* and who owned her currently. The search was very sad and disappointing. We found out that her owner had forgotten to lower the landing gear and landed wheels up. The damage to *Bonnie* was extensive, and repairs would have required a new engine and propeller, along with major structural work. The cost was too much, and so ended the life of *Bonnie*.

Though we gave up flying, Nancy and I would go on to live an enjoyable life for many years. Nancy loved trains and train riding just as much as I did, and we would ride trains around America, South Africa, and Alaska. Nancy also loved golf and played in several leagues. I had tried golf, but it was not a fit. Besides, I had archery, which required a lot of time. We had a condo in Phoenix, Arizona, and once a year, we would plan a golf trip there for Nancy. I found plenty of things to keep me entertained, and often our friends would join us as well.

Though our hobbies were different, we shared one common desire. This was a desire to grow spiritually in order to enhance our understanding of life and relationships. To this end, Nancy came upon the personal growth program (PSI) seminars. PSI is a well-known and established personal growth program. Nancy went to a three-day PSI weekend basic program and found a multitude of helpful information on relationships and individual personal awareness. I soon followed since a wingman never leaves his leader, and together we shared and enjoyed working on what we were learning.

We found that life is vast, intriguing, and interesting. There is so much to learn and what we know about life is only a small part of the total picture. I like to think that what we know about life is like a movie trailer: we see glimpses of the total movie, but we need to see the entire film to truly know the story. Thus, one way to further our understanding of life is through personal growth seminars like PSI. The PSI programs look into who we are as humans and how we react to the influences of everyday life. PSI makes us aware of how self-centered we are. We also learn new behaviors such as win/win and how win/win is misunderstood. PSI teaches us to recognize our feelings and how these feelings control our lives.

PSI offered a seven-day personal intersubjective program at their High Valley Ranch in California, and both Nancy and I attended. Still searching for knowledge, we later attended the PSI ten-day program on leadership, also held at the Ranch in California. To cement the beliefs and knowledge we had learned, we would often staff the PSI weekend program in Denver and attend other PSI programs.

Life was happy and enjoyable for us. I was also heavily involved in *kyudo*, my archery training, and it would often require traveling to the East Coast to help Sensei, my teacher, with teaching. Nancy would often tag along, and it gave her a chance to play golf at a new golf course.

In September 2004, Sensei was invited to the International Horse Archery Festival in Fort Dodge, Iowa. We decided that Sensei and I, along with Nancy, a Scottish *kyudo* student, and an old *kyudo* student, Carolyn, would be the ones to attend. Carolyn was maybe forty-five years younger than Sensei, but she had known him all her life. She was infatuated, or maybe I should say, she was in love with him. For the past five years, Carolyn had tried, without success, to create a relationship with Sensei even though Sesei's wife, Marsha, had left Sensei ten years earlier. Carolyn had been rejected by Sensei many times, but this did not deter her constant determination to have an intimate relationship with him.

For the trip, I had planned to take my son's house trailer and pickup to be used as a base of operation and a cooking/sleeping facility while in Fort Dodge. Sensei had asked, no, insisting that Carolyn attend with us. The trip to Fort Dodge was uneventful, although it was a bit crowded and uncomfortable in the pickup truck. Arrangements had been made for Sensei and the Scotsman to stay with a local doctor, who was also a *kyudo* student. The plan was that Carolyn would stay in the trailer with Nancy and me.

On the third day, Sensei informed us that Carolyn would stay with him at the doctor's house. The Scotsman, who had been sleeping in one of the two bedrooms, was told by Sensei that he would sleep on the couch and Carolyn would use his bedroom.

After five years of rejection, disappointment, and heartbreak, Sensei finally opened his life, love, and heart to Carolyn. And Carolyn joyfully gave her love to him in return. All of a sudden, they were like two teenagers, madly in love. It was then that I realized that love has no age boundaries. Carolyn would move into Sensei's house when we returned to Boulder, and they married shortly after. The marriage would last twelve years, until Sensei's death.

There are few men in this world who achieve greatness and become great leaders. Sensei was one of these men. He had grown up in Kyoto, Japan, and as I've mentioned was the twentieth generation in a line of bow makers for the emperor of Japan. His family, the Shibata family, had been making archery bows for over 400 years, serving the emperor, samurais, and later students of *kyudo*.

Sensei was firm, but gentle. He was passionate in his excellence to make bows and teach his students *kyudo*. He continued teaching until the day he died. He had been a commander of a horse-drawn artillery company during World War II and was an expert on horses. I am sure the allure of seeing archers shooting arrows from horseback brought back many memories. Sensei's son was training and studying to become the twenty-first generation bow maker and his grandson also would become the twenty-second. The skill traditionally passed to the males in the family, and one question I was often asked was how the family always had a son to carry on the linage. They did not. Sensei had two daughters, and one of the daughters married a man who changed his name to Shibata, and became Sensei's adopted son, and agreed to carry on the lineage of bow making.

At the Archery Festival, Carolyn sat next to Sensei as we all watched the program open. Sensei became very agitated, and I asked what was bothering him. He said the horses were not trained for horse archery, and he was afraid someone might get injured. He was right: several of the archers fell off their horses, but luckily, no one was hurt badly. There were, however, several very talented archers who came from Japan, Mongolia, and Europe to show off their talents. It was apparent that learning horse archery required many years of practice, well trained horses, and good teachers. I asked Sensei if he would teach me to do horse archery.

"Buy a horse," he said.

That ended that thought.

CHAPTER 44

A journey is part of the experience—
an expression of the seriousness of one's intent.

—ANTHONY BOURDAIN

Americans love and, in some cases, demand instant gratification. In general, Americans are impatient and are not willing to commit to the years of practice and training required to achieve greatness and/ or perfection. This pertains to our jobs, hobbies, and relationships. We are distracted by personal pleasures, TV, internet, texting, Facebook, or Twitter. To become accomplished in anything requires a lot of practice, study, and training with a skilled teacher. All great men and women have mentors.

When I began my practice of *kyudo*, I had no idea what would lie ahead of me.

"You can learn to shoot a bow and arrow in a few days," Sensei had said. "Developing the knowledge and skills to implement the different parts of Kyodo shooting will take five years, if you practice often. Understanding the principal of shooting and the connection to meditation will take at least twenty years. And even that will change over time as you mature."

For me, it required twenty-three years.

Sensei and I traveled a great deal. I remember one trip to the Shambhala Center in Vermont. Sensei was giving a lecture to a group of *kyudo* students about the practice and how important it was to execute each movement correctly. He then began talking about rapid shooting, called *koguchimi*.

"When practicing *koguchimi*," Sensei said, "the archer will shoot 100 arrows in ten minutes, one arrow every six seconds."

After eighteen years of practice, Sensei asked Gordon to learn rapid shooting. Gordon would learn to shoot 100 arrows in ten minutes, one every six seconds.

He then slowly turned and looked at me.

"It is my hope that Gordon Calahan will learn the practice of *koguchimi*."

Later, Sensei and I talked about *koguchimi*, and he said the practice would take a lot of work and commitment. He said that I had reached a point in my training where he knew I was ready to advance to a higher level. When a teacher takes on a student, he or she expects total commitment. Sensei said that my practice of *kyudo* was for me only. If I trained to impress, compete, or show off, he would not teach me. In the practice of *kyudo*, we would shoot two arrows, releasing two thoughts. In *koguchimi*, I would be releasing 100 arrows and 100 thoughts. In order to do this, I would have to learn to shoot without thinking in pure, focused meditation. What a challenge. I wondered if I could do it. Yes, I had to.

Sensei and I spent a lot of time together over the next several years. I had a lot to learn. I had to learn how to take care of the equipment and inspect it for defects. Koguchimi also required me to learn new techniques and shooting without thinking, all on automatic pilot. I rearranged my daily schedule and committed to three days a week, two hours each session. Sensei would give me instructions and correct my shooting as necessary. In the beginning, my arrows would go everywhere, rarely hitting the target. In rapid shooting, there is no time to aim the arrow, and the shooter must develop eye and body coordination. In other words, where the eye looks, the arrow will go without aiming. This requires a lot of practice, a year or two, maybe three, to become proficient. So, you may ask, why spend the time, energy, and money to learn this practice?

Sensei said that this practice would teach me discipline, commitment, and most importantly, meditation in action. This still did not answer the question for me. I wondered if it was all worth it.

"There are three important practices in life," Sensei said. "These are truth, virtue, or goodness and beauty. As for Truth, you can't fool the bow. The bow knows if I am truthful, clear in my intentions, and good in spirit. If I am in truth, the arrow will hit the target. If I am deceptive, misleading, dishonest, false, unreliable, or elusive in my thinking, the arrow will miss the target and the bow won't function properly. This is why you must sit on a cushion, meditate, and listen to what your mind is thinking. You will never reach perfection, but you can become aware."

"How long will this take?" I asked.

"For you, many years," he said. He paused for a moment and then went on to say, "Virtue or Goodness is the internal equality of kindness. I must be kind to myself first and then be kind to others. We can't be unbalanced in our giving. We give in kind, tangible items, first to ourselves and then to others. How much we are to give and how much we keep will become clear as time passes. The second part of virtue and goodness is giving of your time. I must be open to other people's needs, both physical and spiritual, and help make those needs come to fruition. I must give love to everyone, without exception, even the people I don't like. Choosing who to love and who not to love, for you, Gordon, will be very confusing."

"You have given me a lot to think about, Sensei," I replied. "But what about beauty?"

A few moments passed, then Sensei spoke.

"Beauty is to become one with the bow. Once your mind and spirit are clear, shooting will become natural, creating a form of beauty. Gordon, you must create beauty in everything you do. This includes in relationships with every person you come in contact with. The way you treat your *kyudo* equipment, your home, your car, and all things you come into contact with is a reflection of your understanding of beauty. But remember to reject that which is not beautiful, for it will only poison your soul and cause you pain and suffering. Also, remember that truth, virtue, and beauty must always be accompanied by wisdom. Use whatever wisdom you have to properly implement truth, virtue, and beauty into your life, and you will create a happy, joyful, and free life."

Sensei was a true special teacher for Gordon and Sandy. He would often times shoot Kyudo to show the students how years of practice would produce a form of ultimate beauty.

Koguchimi became a big part of my life, and I have reveled in the joy of shooting with Sensei. Sensei, Nancy, and I traveled all over the United States, giving demonstrations of Koguchimi. One notable experience included a demonstration at the Smithsonian Institute in Washington, DC.

CHAPTER 45

Human greatness does not lie in wealth or power;
it's in character and goodness.

—ANNE FRANK

Nancy and I shared a wonderful life together for seventeen years. The life I led with Nancy was full of adventures, but not some of the craziness that I had experienced with Sandy. We enjoyed traveling and participating in family affairs. There were trips to Albuquerque, New Mexico, to see Nancy's mother and shorter trips around the state. Nancy's oldest son would marry, and Nancy would be the proud grandmother of a grandson. She also filled the roll as grandmother to my grandchildren: one boy, Jake, and four girls, Maura, Makenna, Cassie, and Hannah. We also enjoyed the theater, symphony, traveling, and our respective families together. I enjoyed working in the backyard garden and operating my toy railroad, and Nancy would occasionally help.

However, sometimes there comes a time when two people realize that they have accomplished the goal or mission that they set out to do together. Their paths diverge in different directions. This was the case with Nancy and me. We had found a great deal of love together, and shared common experiences and adventures, but there came a time when I was going in one direction and Nancy in another. Life is like climbing a mountain. There comes a time when one person has had enough, but the other person is determined to reach the top.

Sensei sang a song about birds. He would sing that one bird, flying alone, would be joined by a second, a third, and so on. Some birds would leave, and others would join the flock. In time, all would leave, and the single bird would be left to fly alone again. The song referred to life. Friends, spouses, and children would come and go, eventually seeking out their own lives and paths. So it was with Nancy and me. When the time came, we agreed to a friendly and amicable separation. We shared the household furnishing, and we each had enough to furnish two separate houses. I provided Nancy with enough down payment money to buy her own condo. We also each had prenuptial agreements, so the separation went smoothly.

I would adjust to a single life and perfect a routine that I could live with. I had hoped that Nancy would be a part of my life as we both grew older, but this was not to be. Separating was a sad time, and I had a difficult time adjusting to life without her. Yet, I was busy with work, Shumei, AA, and other projects, and time heals all wounds.

Will there be another woman in my life? I think so, but only when I am ready. I know that all I have to do is ask the spirits, and like rubbing the magical lamp, the genie will appear with the perfect woman in hand. If you don't believe this, see the movie *Aladdin*.

CHAPTER 46

To get the full value of joy, you must have someone to divide it with.

—MARK TWAIN

So, where are we going? I was sitting on my meditation cushion, contemplating the future. What I wanted had not yet been determined, but when the time came, I would know. I would plunge into whatever I decided with enthusiasm and determination to have a great and wonderful time. A slight chuckle came to mind as I readjusted my seat on the cushion. All these years of sitting, and I still couldn't find a comfortable position. Spine straight, back to breath, breathe in and out, and I thought: What happens when I die? Where are we going? Who knows, but the thoughts would not leave.

My eyes began to close. I knew I had been able to sleep while sitting. I remembered a night at *kyudo* when I was extremely tired and had gone to sleep while sitting on the cushion, only to be awakened by Sandy who whispered, "You were snoring."

Meditation was turning into dreaming. "Back to breath," I said, but it was no use. I saw my three spirits in my dream, sitting on a log, laughing at me, when my Guardian Spirit said, "He is just a beginner."

"I am not," I replied.

"So why are you here?" the Instinctual Spirit asked.

"I am not sure," I said, "but I think I would like to know where I will be going after I die?"

"We can't tell you or show you that," the Divine Spirit answered. "Only God can authorize that."

I looked at the Divine Spirit.

"You have a direct connection to God. Is it possible you can ask God to allow me a small look into life after death?"

The Divine Spirit looked back at me sternly.

"You know," I urged, "it is part of the reason why I am writing this book! Where are we going?"

There was a long pause, and I could see that the request was causing the Divine Spirit a great deal of mystification. Was he afraid to ask God? Maybe the question had never been asked before.

"I will ask," the Divine Spirit replied in a small voice, "but don't be disappointed if God refuses you."

And with that, he was gone.

The air was heavy with anticipation. The Guardian Spirit was quietly talking to the Instinctive Spirit. They were speaking so softly that I couldn't hear what they were saying. My goal had been to learn something about death and what happens after. But maybe there is no life after death. Maybe the spirits knew this and did not want to tell me. Maybe I had pushed my spirits too far?

Knowing I was in a dream, I thought back to my dream therapy work. I struggled to remember what the therapist Carl Jung had said about what we can learn from our dreams. What could I learn from this interaction with the spirits?

Distracted by thinking about dreams, I hadn't noticed that my Divine Spirit was back. He had a small smile, and I sensed the answer I was looking for was yes.

"Did God grant my wish?" I asked excitedly.

There was a long pause, and finally my Divine Spirit answered.

"God has said yes, but there is one limitation. I will show you where you are going, but we will only be allowed to stay a little while."

"So, where are we going and when?" I asked.

"Hold my hand; we are going now," he said, "so you can finish your book."

I did not know what to expect: a big bang, a tornado wind, or the transporter used on *Star Trek*. But to my surprise, a beautiful white cloud appeared, and we slowly walked into it. On the other side, we were in a beautiful valley—where I did not know but quite reminiscent of Colorado. We were standing on a trail, and I could see tall rugged mountains in front of us. On our left was a shining blue-green lake being fed by a meandering small stream, cascading over rocks and under scattered fallen trees and logs. The hills around us were landscaped with pine trees, plants, and a patchwork of flowers, all radiating joy and happiness. The sun was rising over the rugged mountains, glistening off of everything around me, making the scenery warm and inviting. The rising sun, signifying life, is a symbol of beginning and growth.

I turned to my Divine Spirit, who was scanning the horizon.

"We are such a small part of this great universe, so insignificant," I said.

"We may be small," he replied quietly, "but in relation to the total, we can if we choose, make a big impact on humankind and the world."

He turned to me.

"Gordon, God is expecting you to spread the word and to be available to teach those who are interested in new ideas. From this point on, you are on your own. I will be here when you return. Use your time wisely."

"Thank you," I said. "You have been a trusted friend and mentor. I won't be long."

The trail was clear and easy to follow. I quickened my pace and headed up into the mountains ahead of me. My mind was asking me, "Where are you going? These mountains are impregnable."

I answered my internal voice, "I haven't come this far to be disappointed."

I knew this journey would not be easy. Onward I trekked, when the trail suddenly turned, and I could see a small crevice in the rocks. The walls of the rocks were rugged and sharp, but the opening was just wide enough to get through. I hesitated for a moment, wondering if I should go on.

Was I ready to embrace what was coming next? I suddenly realized that I was really scared; my fear was off the scale. There was still opportunity to turn back. Did I really need to know where I was going? Yes. Closing my eyes, I squirmed into and through the crevice. Slowly opening my eyes, I was confronted with a valley so beautiful that I can hardly describe it. Before me, the trail continued, and I didn't hesitate, leaping forward at a full run. The trail wandered forward, meandering through a forest of beautiful pine trees and lush vegetation. I was in an open valley, and I saw a sign on the side of the road that said, "Welcome to Shangri-La." Was this where I was destined to be?

Farms were in abundance, and there were many farmers tending to their crops, practicing natural agriculture. They were happy, and as I passed, they all waved and smiled at me, and I responded with a loving wave back. I could see the outline of a village, or maybe a small town, ahead. To my right, I saw a small airport and parked next to the runway, with several other airplanes, was *Bonnie*. I had to look closer so I walked up to the small Beech Bonanza. And sure enough, all shiny and clean, there she was.

I am sure I heard her say, "Are you ready to fly? I am."

"Yes," I said, "but not now, I don't have time now." I rubbed her nose and said, "Good to see you, old friend," and turned and headed toward town.

The trail had widened into a neatly manicured road. There was a feeling of serenity and peace. Each person I passed expressed joy and happiness, and I had the feeling that they had become enlightened. The farmland gave way to rows of meticulously cared for homes, their owners occupied with creating a small oasis of loveliness. My attention became focused on one single house; it was painted white with an inviting porch, and I could barely see two people sitting on the porch. I was drawn toward them, and I soon recognized them.

"Mom! Dad!" I called out. They immediately looked in my direction. They stood up, and descended the two steps from the porch to the sidewalk.

"Gordon," my mother cried out, "what are doing here; you are not on the list."

Ignoring her comment, I ran up the walk and embraced my mother with a big hug. Then I turned to my father and wrapped my arms around him. At that moment, I realized how happy I was to see my parents. It had been several years since we had been together. I explained that I could only stay a moment or two and then I asked if any of our family or my friends were here.

"Everyone on Earth will come here eventually," Dad said. "We all go through a debriefing when we arrive, reviewing what we had learned while on Earth, and then we begin planning for our next journey back to Earth."

"I have so many questions I would like to ask, but there is not time," I said. "I will be back in fifteen or so years, and we can spend more time together then."

"That will be wonderful," my mother said. "That will be only a moment in our time. Now it is time for you to get on your way."

We hugged again, and as I turned to go, I stopped and turned back.

"I love you both so much," I said. "What you taught me while we were together on Earth has made my life a real joy to live."

They both smiled.

"We never questioned your love, Son," Dad said.

"And we will always love you," Mom added.

I began a brisk walk and turned at the next corner and headed to town. Coming in my direction, I was startled to see George.

"George," I said, "what a surprise. Where are you headed in such a hurry?"

"Gordon," he said, "what are doing here? I did not see your name on the list."

"I am only here for a few moments. I will be back sometime in the future though," I said. "Are you going someplace?"

"Yes, I have to get back to Earth. There is a group of pilots, some thirty years from now, that will need my help," he answered matter-of-factly.

We hugged, and then we were both off in opposite directions.

I could feel the warm sun reenergizing me as I pushed on, and finally, there it was. It was the hospital that Don and Rich had been born in. I walked up the driveway while taking in the landscape. Flowers had been planted everywhere, and it was alive with a kaleidoscope of color. The grass was a deep green, and I could tell it had just been cut. There was a sign over the door that read: Shangri La Hospital. Something told me that this was why I was here.

I opened the door and entered. I was confronted by a lovely, spacious lobby. In the center, there was a reception desk, and behind it was a young woman, dressed in a light blue uniform. Several chairs lined the walls, and there was a painting of Christ behind the desk, hanging on the wall. I could swear he was looking at me with a large smile. To the right was a door with a sign that read "Waiting Room."

"Can I help you?" the woman from behind the desk asked.

"Yes," I said, but I didn't know for sure where I wanted to go. "I think I have been here before but in a different place."

"I understand," she said. "You are welcome to look around, and please let me know if there is anyone you would like to see."

"Thank you," I said. "I think I would like to sit in the waiting room for a moment or two. Is that OK?"

"Certainly," she said. "Would you like a cup of coffee?"

"No," I said. "I'm not sure I have time."

I walked to the waiting room door, opened it, entered, and looked around. There were several high back leather chairs and a table next to each one. In one corner was a small table with an instant coffee pot. The smell of coffee was mesmerizing and tempting, but there was not time. I sat down and closed my eyes. In my memory, I could see the moment when the doctor walked in and said, "Gordon, you have a baby boy, and Sandy is doing just fine." The tears began to flow. So much had happened since that day. I wiped my eyes and stood up, knowing it was time to go.

I walked back into the lobby and thanked the receptionist. I turned to go when I heard a familiar voice, "Gordon, is that you?"

I turned toward the voice. There in a white uniform with a nurse's hat, pure white shoes, and the figure of an angel, was Sandy.

"Yes," I said and ran to embrace her. "You can't imagine how much I missed you."

"I missed you too," she said.

We kissed and held each other for several minutes. Finally, she stepped back and looked at me.

"Do you have time for dinner?" she asked.

"Yes, just enough time," I said.

Epilogue

*Never give up because you never know what the
tide will bring in the next day.*

—Tom Hanks

It is my hope that after reading this book, you the reader may have found some interesting ideas and beliefs that you can use in your everyday life. What we don't know may cause us a lot of pain and hardship, or at the least, deprive us of a happy, joyful, and free life. The book is just a snapshot—exploring the Spirit World, suicide, relationships, and maybe enlightenment. Life doesn't have to be hard and filled with suffering; that is optional. Yes, there are a lot of things that we humans may not like to do, but generally, they must be done. The nice thing about life is that we have choices. If you don't like washing dishes, you can always eat your food from a can, heated on the stove, using plastic disposable spoons. Who likes washing clothes; is it really necessary?

I think we all live somewhere between a can dinner and a formal dinner, although I have done both, but the formal dinner provides me with a lot of joy. Having a formal dinner, a clean house, and dressing neatly will give a great deal of joy to others and myself, but it takes work on my part. Life in today's world has become very casual and lazy. Do you feel good about this? I don't. I believe casualness creates casualties. Today many of us live alone; so why does it matter? Today we can work at home, order food and necessities through the internet, and be entertained by TV or the computer. Does that create happiness, joy, and freedom? Some people have a cat or dog, which they can control and does not talk back and requires very little sacrifice. Is that the solution?

I live alone, and I don't like it. Of course I can say I am not ready for a new partner or that living with someone will require me to be more responsible. I may have to do things I don't like, so poor me. Life is responsibility, giving to others and fully receiving from others. Yes, I might have to sacrifice a little so my partner or others may enjoy what they like to do, or more importantly, need to do to accomplish their goals. This is what life is about, balancing each other's needs. One key ingredient is not always being a taker. If I can't provide what my partner needs, I must allow them to look elsewhere. This will only enrich your relations, if you and your partner are truly committed and love each other.

The key to a happy and rewarding life is 100 percent commitment and responsibility; anything less will lead to eventual failure. I have been asked by several people, did Sandy give up her life to make me happy or did I give up my life to make her happy. We each gave 75 percent of our time and energy to make each other happy. When she lost her job at the hospital, I was helpless. I believe that at some point in our lives, we finish our mission, goal, or job we came to Earth to do.

When that happens we all must ask the question: where to go from here. There are many choices: ending one's life is one.

I have also been asked where did the spirits come from and how do they know everything. I can only guess, but I think they are souls that have matured or become enlightened. I don't think they know everything; they have God to refer to, and they also communicate with other spirits. If, as humans, we had the network that the spirits have, we would not need them. Spirits work together to make dreams, goals, and needs happen. Humans are a little lax in that area.

My book and my story are a lifetime of experiences. I don't know if spirits or God exists, but I do know that what I have learned and practiced makes my life wonderful and adventurous. I have learned to love everyone in or out of my life, for I know every person on Earth is here on a mission.

All of my teachers have said, "Gordon, don't try to change or help people unless you understand their mission completely and they have asked for your help. Remember, you may find joy or you might suffer pain and sorrow helping others. Live your life wisely."

As we say in AA, "Take what you want and leave the rest."

I will happy to answer any question about my life and life in general. Please see my website for further updates and information: http://gordoncalahan.com.

Namaste.

Acknowledgments

Writing where *Where Did We Come From, and Where are We Going*, required a lot of help, especially from my spirit world. English, spelling, and grammar are not my best subjects and the spirits knew that. So my spirits had to find people who could help me write this book. The first person was Allicen Maier, who in the beginning spent many hours editing my first drafts and encouraging me on. She is a member of Shumei America and a close, truly personal friend.

Second was Tammy Star, also a member of Shumei and a trusted and sincere friend. She would read my story and encourage me on. When I would get writers' block, I would think of her and know she was waiting for the next segment of the book. She was always positive and there when I need her.

My friend Olga Colman, who I have known for many years, came towards the end of the book to help editing. Olga knew Sandy and Nancy and with her help, she added missing history and gave me ideas to improve my book. She is a close friend who I can always depend on and know she is looking out for my best interests.

I also want to thank my Publisher Andrea Costantine, My Word

Publishing; Jen Zelinger, Proofreading Services; and my Editor Bobby Haas, Write On, who have guided me through the writing of the book. Their help has made writing the book much more fun and their guidance has kept me organized.

I also want to thank my Spirits for a job well done, bringing all of us together to create, *Where Did We Come From, and Where Are We Going*. The Spirits would provide me with ideas and direction through my dreams, people, magazine articles, TV stories, movies and books. When I needed ideas or direction in writing the story, something would always appear in front of me that I could use or needed in the book, exactly when I needed it.

Lastly, I want to thank my High Power for choreographing the entire story and directing all those involved in bringing this book to fruition. It has taken a lot of time and effort from all those involved and I wish to thank every one of you.

Gordon

ABOUT THE AUTHOR

Gordon Calahan was born and raised in Denver, Colorado. He graduated from the University of Denver with a degree in building and real-estate. He married Sandy Williams and for the next twenty years, worked in the family construction business while Sandy worked as a nurse at a local hospital. Gordon and Sandy raised two boys, Richard and Donald. It was a time of partying, hard drinking, and living life to the fullest. They enjoyed adventure, which included flying their own Beach Bonanza airplane, named Bonnie, sky diving, scuba diving, sports, and traveling. In 1984, at the age of 44, their lives changed dramatically. Gordon and Sandy finally realized that they were alcoholics and that their lives had to change. The use of alcohol was out of the question. Their life style would have to change and extreme behavior would have to be brought under control and softened.

Thus, Gordon and Sandy joined AA (Alcoholic Anonymous), attended many personal growth programs, learned mediation, entered therapy, and found new friends who were working in similar recovery programs. To further his education, Gordon enrolled at

Colorado State University and graduated with a Master's Degree in Business Administration.

Life finally began to change for the better. They were happy and enjoyed the recovery work. Gordon became involved with a dear friend, Narayan Shrestha, and together they worked with a charity, Helping Hands Health and Education, to build schools and hospitals in Nepal and Bhutan. Gordon built a school in Narayan's home village in Nepal.

After 34 years of sobriety, Gordon still works in the family business, managed and run by his two sons. He works AA, enjoys attending personal growth programs, and assists people who are in recovery. He is also very active in the financial activities of the Jefferson County School system, second largest school district in Colorado. At age 80 he is still going strong and is in perfect health, no medications. He says he will continue working and giving of himself to helping others as long as he can.

To learn more about Gordon, visit http://gordoncalahan.com.

www.ingramcontent.com/pod-product-compliance
Lightning Source LLC
Chambersburg PA
CBHW051721040426
42447CB00008B/921